The POETRY of
THOMAS HARDY

The POETRY *of*
THOMAS
HARDY

By *James Granville Southworth*

New York

COLUMBIA UNIVERSITY PRESS

1947

TO HYDER E. ROLLINS

Surely one day the gods
Will bless you for your generous help to me—
If gods there are: if not what use our toil?

EURIPIDES: IPHIGENIA

PREFACE

THE PRESENT STUDY of the poetry of Thomas Hardy needs little explanation which a glance at the text itself will not provide. The task has engaged my attention over a longer period than I first intended, and the study has assumed greater proportions than I at first planned. The reason lies in the puzzle Hardy's poetry has provided. My own thinking has altered much since I began work on the book. At first I was in hearty accord with Hardy's views. I have steadily moved farther from them. In the light of this change in my own thinking, I have completely rewritten and expanded the first section of the book, have reworked most of the second, and have added to the last. Before, as well as during the reworking, I have re-read the poetry with great care.

Where I shall be found to differ with many who have preceded me is not only in the greater number of illustrations, but in the impression received from the poetry. Every critic must honestly express his own convictions regardless of their divergence from those commonly held. Each must judge the poet from the point of view of his own conditioning. I have been as independent as I could be, and yet my debt to other writers on Hardy is necessarily great. With much that has been written I agree; with much I differ. With almost no one have I been in full accord. I belong to a different age from those who have written largely about Hardy, and I cannot share their exuberance. Where they see victory, I sense defeat; where they see vision, I sense short-sightedness.

The reader should constantly remember that anything I report on love, woman, life, death, and so forth, and any conclusions I draw in the final chapter are based solely on the poetry. Had I drawn from the novels the book might have been richer, but the act would have defeated my purpose.

Many persons will perhaps wish that I had included a chapter on Hardy's humor. I have from time to time suggested in Part I the various aspects of humor found in Hardy. The qualities are the same as those found in the novels, although in the poems they are confined to a narrower range. I know of no subject more difficult to write about, because none is more dependent on the state of the reader's mind at the time of reading. Hardy's humor is frequently of such a borderline quality that what is successful at one reading misses fire at another. At other times it is so broad that no one could miss it. I have preferred that the reader furnish the details from his own observations to illustrate my general statements on the subject.

A word is perhaps necessary about the division of the material. Part I attempts to synthetize Hardy's poetic aesthetic as well as his poetic thought. My role has been essentially that of a reporter. I have not consciously edited what he has said, nor have I attempted a critical evaluation of his thought in relation to that of his age. Such an attempt would have turned out to be the tail that wagged the dog. I have aimed at completeness in representing his ideas. It becomes increasingly clear that Hardy formulated no philosophical system, nor did he intend to do so. Concerning God, for example, he shows a familiarity with the ontological, cosmological, and teleological arguments, but nowhere is he perfectly consistent. His subject matter is, as he said of it, a series of "impressions."

Part II, being an examination of Hardy's technical methods, is essentially critical in tone; critical, that is, from a prosodic point of view. It makes abundantly clear, I think, Hardy's consciousness as a poet. Critics may disagree, as to the legitimacy of some of his methods for securing his effects, but no one can any longer deny his possession of methods. I am not aware that Hardy's changes in his manuscript have previously been examined. The chapters on Diction, Imagery, and Prosody, as well as much of that on Architectonics, are essentially for the serious student of poetry, who, I assume will have a copy of the poetry close at hand for ready reference. The general reader will do well to pass over these chapters and return to them later.

Part III is an attempt at a general evaluation of Hardy's achievement as a poet, not as a thinker. The short space allotted to *The Dynasts* will strike some readers as being either too short or as not contributing sufficient new material to warrant its inclusion. I have made no attempt to do again what Mr. Chakravarty has already done well. I thought it necessary, however, to give my reaction to the work. I have several times read *The Dynasts,* and, although I can admire many things about it, I find it fragmentary as a work of art.

I have drawn heavily from Mrs. Hardy's *Early Life* and *Later Years,* particularly from those passages in which Hardy speaks in the first person and from letters to his numerous correspondents. I have preferred this procedure to that of borrowing the same material from other books in which the chief difference is the lack of acknowledgment of Mrs. Hardy's work as the source. Of recent books, Mr. Edmund Blunden's is the most useful to the scholar and to the general reader. Mr. Arthur McDowall is one of the best of Hardy's modern critics.

My indebtednesses are many, and I should like to acknowledge them. To the Macmillan Company for permission to quote "Weathers," "The Darkling Thrush," and shorter selections from the *Collected Poems;* to Harper and Brothers for the lines from *Wessex Poems;* and to the Oxford University Press and to Mr. A. Chakravarty for passages from the latter's *"The Dynasts" and the Post-War Age in Poetry.* To the staffs of Harvard College, the University of Toledo, and the Toledo Public Libraries, and particularly to Miss Dorothy M. Wells of the last-named, for their many courtesies and invaluable help. To Mrs. Ernst Mamlok for resolving the difficulties of the Swiss-German text of Littman's *Die Metapher in Merediths und Hardys Lyrik;* to Miss Stella M. Sayers for her accuracy in transcribing the holograph manuscript; to Mr. James McCrimmon and Miss Anna Kitchell for their careful reading of the manuscript and for their suggestions, many of which have been incorporated; to Mr. Martin Scholten for his help with the proofs; to the members of the staff of the Toledo Museum of Art with whom I have threshed out many ideas on aesthetics; and last, but not least, to Mr. Hyder Rollins, under whom it is impossible to work without becoming imbued with the desire for accurate scholarship.

James G. Southworth

Toledo, Ohio
November 20, 1946

CONTENTS

PART I

THE THING SAID

Those, however, who aspire not to guess and divine, but to discover and know; who propose not to devise mimic and fabulous worlds of their own, but to examine and dissect the nature of this very world itself; must go to facts themselves for everything. Nor can the place of this labor and search and world-wide perambulation be supplied by any genius or meditation or argument; no, not if all men's wits could meet in one.

FRANCIS BACON

⇶ I ⇷

INTRODUCTION

THOMAS HARDY'S POETRY has never lacked readers; but it still remains largely unknown to the reader familiar with his novels and is known only through anthologies to a more restricted group primarily interested in English literature. By this latter group he is often misunderstood; and for three reasons: the anomaly of his historical position, the lack of familiarity with his aesthetic, and an incomplete grasp of the scope of his subject matter.

As a novelist his position is reasonably secure in the Victorian world; but not his position as a poet. That he bridges two worlds and belongs wholly to neither partially explains the qualities of greatness or lack-of-greatness in his poetry. Because it was largely written after 1895 we tend to forget that it is the work of a man whose roots were in, his mature being of, and his sympathies essentially with an earlier age, although not with the poets of that age. His sympathies were with the scientists: Darwin, Huxley, Mill, and others who began in the 1850s to upset so-called Victorian complacency.

A thorough knowledge of the biographical data is not essential for an appreciation of Hardy's poetry, but a knowledge of the intellectual background and the social conditions of the period during which he grew to maturity is. Biographical data are important to the psychologist who would know why an author writes as he does. A knowledge of his age is important if we are to understand what the poet felt he could rightly assume on the part of his reader without the necessity of elaboration. What traditional beliefs were accepted or being questioned? What germinating forces were vitalizing the thoughts of those who were sensitive enough to apprehend them?

Hardy's poetry furnishes us with all the biographical data we need to know. No biographer can, in fact, neglect the poetry if he is to achieve a living portrait. It is a finer key to the man behind the work than are the novels. Hardy himself said that, speaking generally, a hundred lines of his poetry contained more autobiography than all of his novels, a statement which accords with Meredith's remark to a would-be interviewer: "Our books contain the best of us. I hold that the public has little to do with what is outside the printed matter beyond hearing that the writer is reputedly a good citizen."

Valuable and important as a knowledge of the background of ideas is, the present discussion of Hardy's poetry permits no more than a suggestion of this background. To give more than a suggestion would relegate the immediate purpose—a survey of his poetry—to a minor position. We must bear in mind, however, that from nineteen years of age to thirty he witnessed and reacted to an intellectual ferment at work in England of such far-reaching results that we still inadequately measure the strength of that ferment. Ideas which had sprung and flourished during unscientific centuries were sent reeling to their graves by the vigorous ideas of men who inductively sought the truth and faced it unflinchingly when they encountered it. The rapid social changes effected by the industrial revolution and the spirit of inquiry fostered by the French Revolution stimulated the young men of the Victorian Age to examine all phenomena with relentless diligence. Nothing, perhaps, can give a clearer thumbnail sketch of what was happening in the years from 1859 to 1881—Hardy's most impressionable years—than a glance at the titles of a few works published in that period.

Darwin rocked the foundations of man's universe with his *The Origin of Species* (1859).[1] In the same year John Stuart Mill published his essay on *Liberty,* the high point of his work and of English liberalism. He followed this with his *Essay on Utilitarianism* (1863), *On the Subjection of Women* (1869), and had written *Three Essays on Religion* (posthumously published in 1874), in

[1] See appendices for an account of the reception of *The Origin* and the *Revised Version.*

which he discussed his attitude toward religion, his concept of God, the problem of immortality, and other matters—ideas so similar to those found in Hardy that it is difficult not to think them the fecundating source of many of Hardy's ideas on the same subjects. Huxley, that great teacher, interpreter, and popularizer, published *Man's Place in Nature* (1863), *Lay Sermons* (1870), in addition to his essays in support of Darwin; Herbert Spencer, *A System of Synthetic Philosophy* (1862), *Principles of Biology* (1864), *Principles of Sociology* (1876), *Principles of Ethics* (1879); Bagehot, *Physics and Politics* (1872); Leslie Stephen, *Essays on Freethinking and Plain Speaking* (1873); George Lewes, *Foundations of a Creed* (1873); and finally appeared the *Revised Version of the New Testament* (1881).

It would be easy today to lose sight of the importance of the *Revised Version*. The partial effect of some of the ferment may be simply stated. It meant that Darwin and his defenders were not to be silenced by theological abuse, that man would find his place in nature among the animals as the appeal to the supernatural yielded to the rigorous methods of science, and it meant that human life would be shaken to its foundations. It meant freedom for speculation on matters hitherto avoided. As a reviewer in *The Literary World* (May 30, 1885) expressed it:

One signal benefit conferred by the Revision of the English Bible has been the silent, unperceived, but final and annihilating blow delivered thereby at the old dogma of verbal inspiration; a dogma which was long a stumbling-block in the way of Truth, and which, once out of the way, leaves access open to minds which Truth has not been able hitherto to enter.

The *Revision* encouraged action and progress in religious thinking; it expelled the danger of stagnation. It stressed the idea that "the true books of God are growths, ever developing and expanding by forces within to adjust themselves to the evolution going on without." More startling, and indicative of the far-reaching influence of Darwin was one item in the reviewer's credo: "We believe in evolution," he said, "and what will not evolve when its turn comes must be left behind as we go on."

In art it meant that in spite of Ruskin's diatribes against the tendencies of the illustrators, perhaps partially because of them, the subject matter explored all phases of life.[2] It appealed to a man of Hardy's temperament to see the beauty in ugliness. Ruskin objected to the depiction of "every species of distorted folly and vice—the idiot, the blackguard, the coxcomb, the paltry fool, the degraded woman," and condemned the tendency for "catching the last gleam in the glued eyes of the daily more bestial English mob—railroad born and bred, which drags itself about the black world it has withered under its breath."

The second reason for misunderstanding Hardy's poetry is the failure to understand his aesthetic—that is, the purity of his reaction to form as an object of emotion rather than as a means of suggesting emotion or conveying information. This failure prevents the full appreciation of his accomplishment. His aesthetic will not be an infallible guide, of course, to an understanding of his poetry; we must examine the poems themselves for that. To see his reactions to visual and auditory art, however, may well give us a clue to the refinement of perceptions we should expect to find carried to a much higher level in his poetry. A person's appreciation of a visual work of art may be impure and yet his appreciation for poetry pure. It is rare that a creative writer of Hardy's caliber, or anyone for that matter, is equally capable of experiencing a pure aesthetic emotion in literature, painting, and music.

Contrary to the tenets of some aestheticians, who exclude from a work of art anything that is any way representative of incidents in life, representation is not necessarily bad or to be deplored. Highly realistic forms may be extremely significant, as we can see in the

[2] The influence on the illustrator of the 1860's of the Pre-Raphaelite Brotherhood gave a new impetus to book and magazine illustration that through the genius of Sir John Everett Millais continued long after the dissolution of the Brotherhood. Hardy's own illustrations are in this tradition. Rarely has a movement like the Pre-Raphaelite Brotherhood, with so small a corpus of good work to commend it, exerted so wide an influence. Although Millais's characters lost much under the hands of his engravers, they still had dignity, even with their Dundreary whiskers, the crinoline, and peg-top trousers. In his work one is in the presence of actual human beings beautifully drawn. Later the German artist Menzel exerted a powerful influence on men like Fred Walker and Charles Keene. Few persons perhaps realize that the magazine *Once a Week,* first published on July 2, 1859, was the earliest attempt to provide a magazine with original illustrations by the chief artists of the time, among whom were Fred Walker, M. J. Lawless, John Leech, John Tenniel, Arthur Boyd Houghton, Sir John Everett Millais, Charles Keene, William M. Thackeray, Frederick Leighton, and others.

work of Rembrandt, Vermeer, and Breughel, and even in Hardy's own poetry, as I shall later point out.

In his *Hardy of Wessex* Mr. Weber has listed the painters mentioned by Hardy in his writings. Nothing in this list indicates particular acuteness in Hardy's taste. It is the list of painters that any cultured man of the late nineteenth century could be expected to know. He makes no mention, for example, of the work of Cézanne, Renoir, Degas, or those other painters whose work has only received popular acceptance in our age. The painters are those in vogue in Hardy's day and those whose work would be prominently hung in Victorian galleries. An obvious quality of these painters is the fact that the majority of them are what for want of a better term we might call descriptive or anecdotal painters.[3] The subject matter is of a psychological or historical value, of topographical interest; the pictures tell stories and suggest situations. The painters do not see the things they paint as ends in themselves but rather for their associations. In Ruysdael and Hobbema, for example, the interest for most persons is not in the sense of form that underlies their best work, but in the emotions of fear and terror that some of Ruysdael's deserted graveyards or overgrown ruins arouse, or the story and topographical interest innate in Hobbema's. I am not implying that this representative element is necessarily harmful, but from a purely aesthetic point of view it is irrelevant, even superfluous. We have no indication from any of Hardy's statements about visual art that he looked past this irrelevance to the significant form. The converse is nearer the truth, although a note made in 1877 indicates that subconsciously at least he was aware that nature in the raw frequently lacks the arrangement in forms necessary to evoke a pure aesthetic emotion.

I think, in fact, that we should not be far wrong if we said that Hardy went to nature for as much of his inspiration as he did because natural beauties are in themselves so often incomplete and fragmentary. It is, in other words, this richness of material in nature of a partial and incomplete beauty and form that inspired him to attempt to give completeness to what he saw. Frankly,

[3] It was probably the influence of the illustrators that created the vogue for these painters.

Hardy's own illustrations for his work are not such as to inspire a person with a conviction that his sensitivity to visual art was beyond the commonplace. His composition is often faulty and his execution amateurish. He believed that an object or mark raised or made by man on a scene was far more valuable than any such formed by unconscious Nature. Hence, he believed that clouds, mists, and mountains were unimportant "beside the wear on a threshold, or the print of a hand." This accords with his congeniality for the landscape methods of Boldini and Hobbema. Because they infused emotion into the boldest external objects by placing either a human figure or some mark of human connection with them, he liked them. He preferred, he said, a "beloved relative's old battered tankard to the finest Greek vase." But, as has been said, the nature of Hardy's reactions to visual art or music is not necessarily an indication of his attitude toward or practices in poetry.[4] The fact that his poems are, superficially at least, essentially descriptive or narrative must not blind us to the possibility that behind this surface quality the poet pays a strict attention to form as an end in itself rather than as a means to the emotions of life. Hardy knew that his aesthetic principles must have a referent. He knew that for an artist to achieve the beautiful or the sublime he had to do more than sit down to create something beautiful or sublime. He must know where to begin, where to end, why he follows the path he does. In other words, he must canalize his emotions and his energies on something more definite and easier to handle than that of creating an object that will arouse a pure aesthetic response.

In much of his earlier poetry, I think Hardy often lost sight of basic form. He reveals this in an attention to minute detail for the sake of verisimilitude and not for its integral part in the basic architectural design. Later, as his convictions on the craft of poetry crystallized with an increasing control of his technique, he used detail with greater economy and solely as a means for giving greater significance to the basic form; for achieving, in other words, an essential architectonic quality in his poetry. He believed, in fact, that

[4] See Appendix C, "A Footnote on Music." Hardy's strong sentimental qualities are most evident in his attitude toward the visual and auditory arts and animals.

a close analogy existed between poetry and architecture in that both arts had to carry a rational content inside their artistic form. His insistence on "rational content" will help us when we come to appraise his work. He knew that form gave stability and firmness to a poem; that it was the means of conserving and keeping alive the rational content. He knew it, recognized it in others, but often failed to achieve it in his own work. He also believed, however, that intense emotion could largely compensate for form, but did he not overlook the essential form that makes intense emotion possible?

The question naturally arises at this point as to the importance of Hardy's architectural training on his poetry. Did he achieve a stronger sense of the architectonics of poetry because of this study? The answer must remain a largely subjective one because of lack of confirmatory evidence. At best we can but examine his use of architecture in his poetry. Nowhere is his interest in architecture charged with significant expression. As the primary subject for poetry he employs it but a few times. That it is never far from his mind, however, is evident in his use of architectural terms, the images drawn from it, his sense of form derived from it, and his accuracy and solicitude in selecting significant details for the embellishment of his background. Even the statement "primary subject" needs defining. Hardy never employs architecture divorced from the emotions of life. His interest is man, and essentially the soul of man. Architecture as the primary subject means only that it plays an important role in commenting on these emotions of life. Nowhere does he dwell on architecture as the basis for a pure aesthetic response, and his overwhelming interest in Gothic does not indicate that his essential interest is in purity of form, particularly since it was the ogive work and tracery that most fascinated him.

His best poem dealing with the technical aspects of architecture is "The Abbey Mason." The wealth of technical details is sufficient to reveal his intimate knowledge of the subject. He loved the perpendicular style of Gothic, and the poem is an attempt to explain its origin. As with so many mythical explanations of Gothic he achieves only a sentimental account of the creation of a particular phase of that great imaginative style. The technical phraseology and the adroitness with which it is handled will afford little pleasure to the person unversed in the professional vocabulary of the architect. It reveals another quality, however, more interesting than the legend or the technical facility. It gives us a further glimpse into his aesthetic:

> "Nay; art can but transmute;
> Invention is not absolute;

> "Things fail to spring from nought at call,
> And art-beginnings most of all.

> "He did but what all artists do,
> Wait upon Nature for his cue."

He everywhere substantiates this general statement by his practice.

More typical of his treatment of architecture is his use of it as a commentary on life, his insistence on the impossibility of judging the souls of the occupants of a house from its architectural character. It is the human rather than the architectural equation that essentially interested him. He selected two examples—one an ivy-covered house with mullioned windows that gives the American visitor to England a sense of the gracious past; the other, one of the modern villas that deform the landscape. Ironically, the occupants of the former are sordid souls attracted by the lure of gold; those of the latter engaged in literature, art, and music "lead inner lives of dreams." This willingness to distrust appearances is a further clue to that insight that leads him to distrust other sense and non-sense phenomena; to avoid over-hasty judgments based on external appearances. He senses and crystallizes the associative value of objects in a poem about two houses. The old one is not "void as a drum," but is peopled by the ghosts of past residents in their activities of birth, life, and death.[5] He possessed, too, the sensitive person's awareness of the noises that make up silence; a silence without any noise, even that of a fly's hum, is significant and awful. Of many silences, that of a copse after the wind has died down, or of a belfry after the last reverberation of the tenor bell has died away, or of a lonely pond where a man was drowned and not even the croak of a frog is audible—none can be compared to the silence of an empty house:

[5] "Architectural Masks," "The Two Houses."

> But the rapt silence of an empty house
>   Where oneself was born,
>   Dwelt, held carouse
> With friends, is of all silences most forlorn!
>   —"Silences"

Clearly, it was not in the purity of form that Hardy found his interest in old churches and houses but in their associative value with human emotions.[6]

Hardy, wishing to write and to do a good job, naturally turned to subjects he knew best. Had he led a cloistered youth he might have inclined toward the art for art's sake school of thought. But he had rubbed shoulders with the world from an early age, had closely observed man as a social animal, and had not become embittered to the point of escaping from reality, and was therefore inclined to reject such a theory. He preferred to utilize the results of his knowledge and observation. He drew his subject matter from material with which he had close association and an intimate knowledge, although it may have been knowledge from observation rather than participation. He has attempted to justify his procedure by the formation of theories that fit his practice. This accounts, I think, for many of the aspects of his poetry that have puzzled his critics. Many of his poems appear to be a curious mixture of the formal and the casual. He has frequently sacrificed smoothness and polish, which in a person with less to say would be suicidal, but he has attempted to capture the vividness of the impression. Often no amount of carefully wrought expression can lift his poems into life.

He realized that a writer who found his interest in associative values must know "how to strike the balance between the uncommon and the ordinary so as on the one hand to give interest, on the other to give reality." He liked the contrast and comprehension of opposites, between the transient and the permanent, for example, and between the present, past, and future. He never made the mistake in his thinking of confusing photographic verisimilitude with art; he sometimes erred in his practice.

He was fully aware of many truisms: that any artist must not

---

[6] "Old Furniture," "To a Well-Named Dwelling," "The Church and the Wedding," "Drawing Details, etc.," "A Man," "The Young Glass-Stainer."

only see what all men have seen, but he must see it with a difference; that he must feel with fervor what he observes if he is to rescue it from the ephemeral; that he must not mimic the notes of his predecessors; that any copy, however slavish an imitation of the original, differs from the original in a subtle but positive way. The form of the original, significant because of some quality of the mind that has conceived it as an end in itself, has been altered. The copy will lack the quality of mind, the spirit, which invests the original. This, of course, does not mean that a poet, visual artist, or musician must discard tradition. He accepts and alters that tradition by translating the permanent qualities of his predecessors into his own language. What he needs, therefore, is not a deft mechanical skill by which he can achieve superficial resemblances, but to be able to feel as a poet, a painter, or a musician feels.

Now I think Hardy felt this way. He believed implicitly that in verse was concentrated the essence of all imaginative and emotional literature. And he was certainly not interested in achieving a facsimile of the life that moved before him. He preferred that a strong emotion should underlie every poem, and he instinctively knew that for him it came through the contemplation of the familiar objects of life. The little everyday happenings of his Wessex provided the material which he would shape into an artistic form that would "intensify the expression of things, as is done by Crivelli, Bellini, etc., so that the heart and inner meaning" could be made vividly visible.

The way of "uncommonness" is beset by pitfalls. Astute enough to realize that to achieve uncommonness in the reigning modes of expression was more apt to lead to empty and barren mannerisms than to anything significant, Hardy circumvented most of them. He knew that once the ultimate has been achieved in a medium it is dangerous to continue to work in that particular medium. He knew, too, that technical swagger is not enough. It is not Sebastiano del Piombo or Piazetta in painting, nor Bruckner in music, nor those continuing the empty grace of the Russian ballet tradition without attempting to revitalize it that we remember, but those who broke from the tradition of Michelangelo, Raphael, Wagner, and the traditional ballet.

Hardy, instinctively aware of this, particularly as it is found in literature, attempted to make a fresh and vital adaptation of technique for the expression of significant thought. In his case, however, the influences of the older technique are so apparent as partially to conceal his innovations. He realized, as the more popular of his contemporary poets did not, the revolution in human minds caused by science. With changed concepts of the world steadily gaining wider acceptance, he knew that in certain realms of thought man must broaden or alter his views if he is to continue to make a vital appeal to the vanguard rather than to the rear guard, who at least could do no more than delay the advance of the new elements. This ready acceptance on his part is one of the better reasons, I imagine, for the frequent comparisons made between him and Lucretius.

Hardy was one of the first to introduce into poetry concepts of nineteenth century science. Tennyson used a few metaphors and similes (and not always accurate ones) from science, but he did not make them an integral part of his thought. Hardy, on the other hand, found congeniality in the ideas of Darwin, Mill (particularly the description of justice in his *Essay on Liberty*), Huxley, and in the discoveries of the astronomers.

The great social changes of the nineteenth century find wholehearted acceptance in his poems: acceptance and impulsion. Impulsion, because we must not minimize the powerful although frequently unacknowledged influence that he has wielded. I doubt if many of the younger poets have wholly escaped his influence. (Auden, for example, has confessed his early indebtedness.) He has been as instrumental in affecting their way of viewing the world as have Hopkins and Eliot their way of expressing themselves. He has been concerned in achieving uncommonness less in the outward form than in the content. Squarely facing the problem of every creative artist of what he should write about that has not already been exhausted, he decided early (July 17, 1868) that perhaps the thing for him to do was a volume of poems consisting of the "other side of common emotions." To do so was not going against his inclinations. He believed implicitly in the personal element; that the artist should follow his own bent. It is the same, he says, as, in looking at a carpet, by following one colour a certain pattern is suggested, by following another colour, another; so in life the seer should watch that pattern among general things which his idiosyncrasy moves him to observe and describe that alone. This is, quite accurately a going to Nature; yet the result is no mere photograph, but purely the product of the writer's own mind.

Above all, he should feel the subject emotively.

He had earlier said that the function of art was to change "the actual proportions and order of things, so as to bring out more forcibly than might otherwise be done the feature in them which appeals most strongly to the idiosyncrasy of the artist" (August 5, 1890). The reader must constantly be alert to this disproportioning in Hardy's works if he is correctly to judge the poems. Every artist "filters" his subject; that is, brings into higher relief those details which enhance the emotional mood at which he aims and removes those which mar the unity of mood. Even in a painting which has photographic realism, the artist is likely to jam his shadows. Hardy does just that.

The volume dealing with the other side of human emotions was not immediately forthcoming, although he did write some poems at this time as an exercise in his theory. Because he also thought it "the essence of individuality" he strove for "a certain provincialism of feeling." He recognized, as did Whitman, that true genius must be rooted in the common ways of men and nature, although his approach was the opposite of Whitman's. Whitman wanted the youthful country where all was promise; Hardy preferred the old country where everything was "scored with prints of perished hands." After attending Tennyson's funeral in Westminster Abbey, for example, where he found the music "sweet and impressive," he added: "but as a funeral the scene was less penetrating than a plain country interment would have been." In this lies the clue to much of his subject matter. He liked the basic simplicity of the common man against the background of nature. He has written many fine pure nature poems, but his essential interest, like Wordsworth's, was in man. Hardy, in fact, more closely follows the dicta of Wordsworth's Preface to *Lyrical Ballads* than did Wordsworth himself. His characters are simple, unadorned creatures, undeterred by generations of Public School ideas of good form from exhibiting their elemental emotions.

Critics agree that as a chronicler of Wessex life Hardy has no peer. His feeling for that section of England was that of a country-man born and bred, and he recognized the advantage, from one point of view, of being thoroughly at home in one region, however narrow, although he envied the men who had been thoroughly at home in all. What many of them do not realize, however, is that the reason for his pre-eminence as a chronicler of Wessex life is that he approached his material as an artist. He is concerned with people, but never with the labels others apply to people. He is concerned with them chiefly as a means to an aesthetic emotion. In other words, he is not interested in branding them as bad, good, and so forth. He refrains from moralizing not only because he was not a moralist at heart, but because he looked at the people of Wessex as ends in themselves and not as a means to such practical ends as the improvement of the world. I think he had little use for didactic poetry. "Rake-Hell Muses" and "The Christening" are ex-cellent illustrations of this aspect of Hardy. He associates himself so completely with his characters, many of them open to censure by conventional standards, that we never know what his inmost feel-ings are. Does he approve of Rake-Hell or of the young man in "The Christening"? Although inclined to think so, we do not really know. He has given us only as much of the scene as the thinking of these young men warrant. We have only their points of view, short-sighted as they may be. The egocentricity of the man in "The Christening," for example, blinds him to his greater responsibility.

This attitude does not mean that his poetry could not be a tre-mendous power for good. A pure aesthetic emotion never leaves a person in the same state he was in before he has experienced it, be-cause any man who has glimpsed truth can never be quite the same as when he walked in darkness.

I like to think that by "the truth of poetry" Hardy understood that it lay beyond photographic representation and a too great con-cern with pointing out irrelevant minutiae. It was in essence an abstracting of the basic qualities of the life about him in which he had so profound an interest. He did not, of course, overlook the fact that some of the abstracting could be supplied by rhyme, meter, imagery, and other technical aids.

It is readily apparent that during those years when he was writing but not publishing his collected poems, his ideas on poetry were crystallizing along definite lines. He had long cherished the highest opinion of "the truth of poetry" and "of its supreme place in literature." With the years, however, he formulated a narrower idea of the function of the poet in the modern world. Hardy himself shows us the route by which he arrived at the narrower view. "Scenes in ordinary life that are insipid at 20," he wrote April 19, 1888, "become interesting at 30, and tragic at 40." And we, when reading his poetry, must remember that it is essentially the work of middle and late age, and that the earliest of the poems in the collected edition were written when he was past 25. When he writes that "the business of a poet and a novelist is to show the sorriness underlying the grandest things, and the grandeur underlying the sorriest things," I cannot believe that he would wish the statement to be taken dogmatically. He did not believe in overlooking the defects of nature, but in making those "defects the basis of hitherto unperceived beauty" (June, 1887). Or, as he later wrote (August 5, 1888), "To find beauty in ugliness is the province of the poet." He broadened his conception in a note of April 25, 1892: "Courage has been idealized, why not Fear?—which is a higher consciousness, and based on a deeper insight."

There is little doubt that economic pressure led Hardy to relegate poetry to a secondary place, just as freedom from economic pressure and his awareness of the futility of attempting to go against public opinion led him to reinstate poetry in its rightful place in his life. He simply would not prostitute his art to the insincerity which he considered the besetting sin of modern literature, in which he felt that half its utterances were "qualified, even contradicted, by an aside," and this particularly in morals and religion. Whether he made his decision too late is a matter we must consider in the final chapter. But that it was the rightful place is clear from a jotting made on Christmas Day, 1890: "While thinking of resuming 'the viewless wings of poesy' before dawn this morning, new horizons seemed to open and worrying pettiness to disappear."

Poetry was an exploration of reality which afforded him a medium for remaining honest with himself as an artist.

Perhaps I can express more fully in verse [he wrote on October 17, 1895], ideas and emotions which run counter to the inert crystallized opinion—hard as a rock—which the vast body of men have vested interests in supporting, to cry out in a passionate poem that (for instance) the Supreme Mover or Movers, the Prime Force or Forces, must be either limited in power, unknowing, or cruel—which is obvious enough, and has been for centuries—will cause them merely a shake of the head; but to put it in argumentative prose will make them sneer, or foam, or set all the literary contortionists jumping upon me, a harmless agnostic, as if I were a clamorous atheist, which in their crass illiteracy they seem to think is the same thing. . . . If Galileo had said in verse that the world moved, the Inquisition might have let him alone.[7]

We must not think that by the foregoing he meant that he wishes only to reason in verse. Those poems which have been universally acclaimed as outstanding amidst the great store of lesser poems are those in which he has combined his profound interest in life with a consummate mastery of technique, and in which we, through a pure aesthetic emotion, have glimpsed a portion of the truth. We can faintly comprehend the unconditioned and universal.

Hardy nurtured few illusions about the reception of his poetry, although bitterness sometimes overcame his accustomed tolerance, particularly bitterness toward "the unwilling mind," a state which has ever retarded the appreciation of new poetry. He became particularly annoyed at first, but finally resigned himself to certain clichés which critics persisted, and have continued to persist, in attaching to his poetry. I am inclined to think that the reason for the persistence of the clichés may be attributed to the general tendency of anthologists in making a selection from his work. Until very recently they have weighted the scales against an unbiased view, and consciously or unconsciously have lent a certain credence to the most persistent of all clichés—his pessimism, one largely responsible for the prevention of a fair appreciation of his achieve-

7 See Mill, *Three Essays on Religion,* for similar ideas.

ment. It has obscured the humor and graciousness so frequent in his verse; humor of that quality which enlivens *Under the Green-wood Tree,* and the graciousness of the opening scene of *Tess of the D'Urbervilles* with the girls dancing on the green or of those at the dairy-farm. The humor in Hardy's poetry is more apt to be Swiftian than Dickensian, and many of his verses have a satirical, dry, caustic, or farcical cast.

Hardy deplored this pigeonholing of a poet with a neat but limiting label, and objected, particularly, to the label of "pessimist." He rightly believed that the term "pessimism" applied less accurately to his own ideas than to some expressed (without this label) by Gray in his "Ode on a Distant Prospect of Eton College." He realized, too, that the cynical disbelief in human nature characteristic of Swift, and Job's cursing of the day he was born—examples of real pessimism—were absent from his own work. Only once—and then humorously in his "Epitaph on a Pessimist," an adaptation from the French—did he use the term in its literal sense:

> I'm Smith of Stoke, aged sixty-odd,
>   I've lived without a dame
> From youth-time on; and would to God
>   My dad had done the same.

I am not here concerned with the possible pessimism of the novels; say, for example, of *Jude.*

Galsworthy sympathized with Hardy's objection to being branded as a pessimist and satirized this critical tendency by affixing to a portrait of himself which he sent to Hardy his own earlier definition of the term as he had used it in "The Inn of Tranquility":

The optimist appears to be one who cannot bear the world as it is, and is forced by his nature to picture it as it ought to be; and the pessimist one who cannot only bear the world as it is, but loves it well enough to draw it faithfully.

Hardy, according to Vere Collins, was inclined slightly to modify this definition. "I shouldn't say 'love,' " he is quoted as saying. "He need not necessarily love it. It may be because he is indifferent enough." In what he once called a pessimist's apology, he wrote in his notebook in 1902 his own definition of what the term would have to mean if applied to him:

Pessimism (or rather what is called such) is in brief, playing a sure game. You cannot lose at it; you may gain. It is the only view of life in which you can never be disappointed. Having reckoned what to do in the worst possible circumstances, when better arise, as they may, life becomes a child's play.

As he told Archer, he preferred to think of his attitude as evolutionary meliorism:

My practical philosophy is distinctly meliorist. What are my books but one plea against "man's inhumanity to man"—to woman—and to the lower animals? [8] . . . Whatever may be the inherent good or evil of life, it is certain that men make it much worse than it need be. When we have got rid of a thousand remediable ills, it will be time enough to determine whether the ill that is irremediable outweighs the good.

He qualified this statement by another:

A good deal of robustious swaggering optimism of recent literature is at bottom cowardly and insincere. I do not see that we are likely to improve the world by asseverating, however loudly, that black is white, or at least that black is but a necessary contrast and foil, without which white would be white no longer. That is mere juggling with metaphor.

If to look at the world with clear, unblinded, and unflinching eyes, if to look at it with tolerance, kindness, sympathy, and understanding, if to ponder on the nature of God and not to find Him in his heaven and all right with the world, if to be one with eyes open who has lived through the last three decades with the stream of life flowing over, around, and through him and is unable longer to postulate a God who is a kind beneficent parent meting out equal justice to all—if to be one of these is to be classed as a pessimist, then the term has certainly changed its connotation since it was first used against Hardy, and is a term of praise rather than of abuse. This does not mean that Hardy's concept of God is more readily acceptable than that which he rejected.

Hardy's attitude toward life largely arises from the fact that he himself had not suffered what he saw others suffer. Had he done so he would not have felt as bitterly over the injustices about him as he did. I think Stevenson gives us a clue to Hardy that we cannot afford to overlook. Writing to William Archer he said:

[8] See Appendix D for a brief account of Hardy's poems on the lower animals and on his humanity.

That which we suffer ourselves has no longer the same air of monstrous injustice and wanton cruelty that suffering bears when we see it in the case of others. So we begin gradually to see that things are not black, but have their strange compensations; and when they draw towards their worst, the idea of death is like a bed to lie on. I should bear false witness if I did not declare life happy. And your wonderful statement that happiness tends to die out and misery to continue, which has put me on the track of your frame of mind, is diagnostic of the happy man raging over the misery of others; it could never be written by the man who had tried what unhappiness was like.—Stevenson: *Letters,* I, 370.

Hardy actually never rages over the misery of others; he broods. His brooding frequently lapses into the sentimental. But I cannot believe he had much personal knowledge of unhappiness. An older Shelley would never have written "I fall upon the thorns of life— I bleed." He would have transmuted his suffering into a lyric of boundless ecstasy.

We must be careful, too, when reading Hardy's poetry—as some of his champions have not been—not to treat certain of his momentary impressions or emotions as if they were his undeviating beliefs. Many of his poems are, true enough, of little intrinsic worth taken per se—and that is how they must finally be judged, but even these relatively insignificant poems furnish necessary details for a sound understanding of Hardy.

It is readily apparent that Hardy's consciousness as an artist was greater than is generally recognized: that is, in his poetry, where he believed most of his art to lie. Much of it lay, however, in the art of concealing his art. Readers ascribed many things in his poetry to ignorance instead of to full knowledge.

It is Hardy's sincerity as an artist that unconsciously or not his critics seem to have questioned. They have questioned it because they have misunderstood. I think that in his poetry he always gave the best he was capable of giving at the time he gave it; that he never made compromises or concessions to public taste; that he was never consciously careless in his technique. If the results are of little worth it is because he himself was not at the time capable of better. He had not subjected himself to the restraint of an arduous discipline by which means only are great things achieved. He was unwilling to change the line of his vision toward the direction in which the light lay.

He was neither haphazard in his choice of subject matter nor was he without convictions as to how to present it. When he wrote a poem and thought he could improve it by casting it in a different meter, he did not hesitate to do so, even if the poem had reached the "fair copy" stage. Whether or not he sometimes forgot that behind every poem there is the art of poetry is a matter we must later consider.

It is common knowledge that one of the problems of any creative artist is first what to say, and then how to say it. What many persons forget, however, is that in the actual process of expressing himself the form of the poetry frequently alters the thought. This is obvious, of course, in some of the early Keats where the rhyme dictates the thought. It is apparent, too, in the evolution of a lyric like Shelley's "Lament." We have further instances in Graves, Housman, and Hardy. It was a technical problem in "A Spot," for example, that caused Hardy to change "trouble-tossed" to "transport-tossed" and "super-subtle soul" to "lonely shepherd soul." He realized, too, that poets need not be all of a pattern and that poets frequently wrote best in their later years. Hardy himself never ceased experimenting, hunting up old stanza forms that had not been used since the Middle Ages, or inventing new ones. The most poignantly beautiful of his lyrics belong to his later years. In looking over his papers after his death Mrs. Hardy found "quantities of notes on rhythm and meter; with outlines and experiments in innumerable original measures, some of which he adopted from time to time. These verse skeletons were mostly blank, and only designated by the usual marks for long and short syllables, accentuations, etc." [9]

In no poet writing over so long a period of years is there so little indication of chronology; in the work of none is it of so little importance. This arises partially, perhaps, from Hardy's belief that he could recall an incident fifty years after it had occurred as vividly as an incident of recent occurrence. His poetry lacks the brilliant

[9] These notes have apparently been lost or destroyed. Mrs. Hardy's executrix was unaware of them.

flame of youth that we are accustomed to associate with lyrical poetry; but we must not think the fire is out. Charcoal, for example, gives an intense heat even when it looks gray.

Yeats's poetry reveals a steady change in thought and rhythm from youth to age; Hardy's, little or no change in thought and some in rhythm. The greatest change lies in his greater sense of significant form. I do not mean to say that at any time in his poetic career does his poetry lack at least an outward structural pattern. He is apt, however, to weaken the basic structure by an ornamentation apparently designed to compensate for the lack of a vividly experienced emotion. In his later work I feel that he has strengthened the basic structure of the poem by substituting this vividly experienced emotion for more obvious ornamentation. He puts less of his dearly beloved Gothic into his work and more of Romanesque solidity. I should be the last person to suggest that we can divide his work into periods according to this tendency. In the poems that we most frequently encounter in anthologies, however, I think significant form largely accounts for their selection.

Since chronology is of so little moment in a consideration of his subject matter, it will not be a distortion of his achievement if we disregard it in Part I. In Part II it will in some measure, at least, force itself upon us.

Before considering the matter of form, or any of the technical aspects of his poetry, it is desirable to see what Hardy actually says in his poetry. It will not be possible, of course, except in a few isolated incidents, to see the bare materials to which he later gave form and emotional unity. Grouping the poems under the headings of love, woman, mutability, life, death, God, and so forth, implies no hard and fast lines of division, because, as I have already suggested, neatly to compartmentalize the work of a man of Hardy's caliber—or, for that matter, of any conscientious writer—does him an injustice. It is merely a convenience which will help to evaluate the statements in the poems that are more general in nature, more abstract, and less capable of resolution. We shall see into what his personal idiosyncrasy and the dictates of the poetic structure molded them. Of one thing we may be confident: the underlying idea is clear-cut, definite, and generally striking. Of another we must be careful. In any consideration of the subject matter it is not the objects mentioned in a passage that are important; they are subordinate to the quality, atmosphere, and flavor of that passage upon the imaginative palate.

⟫⟫ 2 ⟪⟪

LOVE

Compared with other branches of knowledge the fine arts are unique in that they are primarily concerned with the universals. More than any other branch of learning they seek expression for the permanent and abiding things in life—the struggle of man's spirit toward a greater consciousness, the ever repeating cycle of birth, love, and death, the conflict of man with and his attempts at adjustments to that environment. Of the arts, poetry surpasses all others in its ability to depict these universals. Of these universals, none has received more widespread interest than love, and we should expect that out of nine hundred-odd poems by Hardy some should deal with this phenomenon.

Love, in fact, interested him above all other subjects—love and woman—and he has explored almost every possible phase and has wrought permutations and combinations on each. I shall not here concern myself with the subtle nuances, but with the broader divisions of the subject. The reader must ever bear in mind that it was just the failure to realize the breadth and scope of Hardy's subject matter, however, that has led to much misunderstanding of him.

In order to vivify his impressions he makes frequent use of the fiction of the supernatural, a force pulling the strings of the puppet-lovers. And by "fiction of the supernatural," I mean just that. It irked Hardy to have this machinery cited as an example of his belief. No one criticizes Shakespeare for employing such devices in his plays and sonnets; he understands them as metaphorical expressions. Yet when Hardy makes a similar use of metaphorical expressions, they are presented as instances of his avowed convictions. This is both unfortunate and unfair. Whereas it is true (as Chapter 5 will show) that Hardy did write poems about fate, chance, God, and the workings of providence that were literal expressions of his beliefs at the moment, the use of these fictions in poems primarily about love or woman must be understood as a technical device for achieving an effective communication of the emotive impulse underlying the poem—that, and no more.

Nowhere is the poet's solicitude for nuance more carefully exhibited than in these poems in which love is an essential ingredient. No one can speak authoritatively of Hardy's so-called "pessimism" unless he knows this aspect of his work, and then the "pessimism" vanishes; but not the reality. Taken with the subject of women, love comprises over 400 poems, only a little less than half his total output. Much of this work is slight, and naturally so; but it is not so negligible as at least 100 poems on other subjects too trivial, too occasional for mention. Together, however, these poems on love and women reveal that nothing was too small for his interest or care. They amply attest his insistence on seeing his characters as they actually were, and not as they ought to be, or as they eventually might become. They also help drive home the idea that he sees the particulars of life as significant of life in general.

He realized as clearly as anyone of his age that one cannot flinch from a frank exploration of those constantly fluctuating moments of exaltation, complication, and depression in the relationships between the sexes that comprise the history of men and women. He had emancipated himself from convention (it is here that the influences of science are most apparent), and he had let his attitude in religion and morals be dictated by the inner light of reflection. He was never realistic with a moral purpose as was Crabbe, whose slight influence extended only to the novels, not to the poetry. He chiefly reserved his outstanding powers of irony and satire for convention and hypocrisy. In these poems on love in which he was most local and personal he achieves his greatest universality. They reveal the man behind the poems more clearly than any other one group, and help toward a complete picture of him.

He is tolerant, kindly, and charitable. The irony is not the poet's; it is Life's. He has been content to observe and record what he has

seen about him. Nothing in these poems indicates that he has re-
sented life or that he has had an unhappy one. If anything, the
converse is nearer the truth. He has the detachment that enables
him to hold the world but as the world, to ask of it no more than
the little he may rightfully ask and to enjoy every moment that
presents itself. He does not feel toward happiness as Hopkins did
toward peace—that piecemeal peace is poor peace; and that only
pure peace is acceptable. Happiness can be only piecemeal. By his
recognition of this, however, his piecemeal happiness more nearly
approaches pure happiness than that of those who shut their eyes
to reality. To have a passionate conviction of the blessings of the
good life we must have some conception of evil, a knowledge which
can come only from our contact with it in life; not as we view it
through telescopic lenses.

We find nowhere in the poetry a treatment of love or woman
such as we have in the novels. We have no Grace Melbury, or Giles
Winterbourne, no Tess or Angel Clare, no Sue or Jude, no Elfride
Swancourt or Stephen Smith. Nowhere is there the magnitude of
the novels. Nor should we expect to find such. What we do find is
an infinitude of crystallized moments in the lives of men and
women, chiefly nameless, whose stories, were they told at length,
would possess the dramatic interest of his better-known heroines.
They satisfy his love of the individual scenes which are often im-
perfectly joined in the novels. These vignettes in the manner of
Heine and of Wordsworth's Lucy poems are more than intuitive
flashes; they are the result of long and close observation; even more
than that. They are not the raw materials of poetry; they are those
raw materials beaten and shaped into artistic form until they have
a quality of general appeal that far outdistances the actual facts
on which they are based. They do not reproduce actual conditions;
they are the essence of actual conditions seen as proper material for
an aesthetic response. They are truer than the materials from which
they are made because their appeal no longer depends on an in-
timate knowledge of the milieu in which they occurred. The reader
should not complain that the ring that lovers hope for only rarely
brings gold, and, too often, sadness. He must constantly remember
that the chapters on love and woman are not Hardy's complete

statement. Although they may seem to lack the searching and profound qualities that we expect in the novels, they do not really do so. They are his most catholic view of the subjects.

Hardy found love a fit subject for study because of its historicity, its primal place in man's affairs, and its unaltering permanence.[1] He thought he saw fate's hand shaping the destinies of lovers—drawing them together, or keeping potential lovers apart, throwing the wrong persons together, and preventing the fulfillment of love; effecting any one and all of the possible combinations of which love is capable. He saw, too, Time in a similar role; and Death. His greater interest in the village Romeos and Juliets, the Gratianos and the Nerissas, in those who help to swell the scene, not dominate it, than in the town dignitaries, arose from the greater frankness of these lesser persons in the expression of their feelings.

No placid, well-bred exterior concealed their true emotions. Aesthetically, too, they were more interesting. Their stories lent themselves to a treatment in which the form was simple and pronounced. Psychological deviation did not conceal the simple outline behind a necessary mass of ornament. Quite possibly Hardy's treatment resulted from a natural reaction to the poetry of Robert Browning, whom he admired and realized that he could not surpass. He chose to depict the world he knew just as Browning did his. He liked the directness of love and its straightforward manifestation.[2] He was equally interested in the culmination of love, in its furtive and unapprehended beginnings, and in the unlooked for, unexplainable ends.[3] None of these poems, however, is movingly convincing.

He has also explored the theme when love has been realized.[4] These poems range from light to somber moods, from simple to complex stanzas, from early to late composition. The typical note is that if we knew that at the end of our journey happiness in love

---

[1] "In Time of 'The Breaking of Nations,' " "Two Clasped Skeletons."

[2] "The Third Kissing Gate."

[3] "In the Street," "A Man Was Drawing Near to Me," "As 'Twere Tonight," "Faintheart in a Railway Train," "Retty's Phases," "The Wind's Prophecy," "To Meet, or Otherwise," "First Sight, etc."

[4] "Before Knowledge," "The Night of the Dance," "I Worked No Wile to Meet You," "Why Be at Pains?," "At Casterbridge Fair," "I Was Not He," "A Thunderstorm in Town."

awaited us we could better bear the troubles that we can never evade, because to a man or woman in love, little else matters. The important thing is that love comes. When that which fanned the spark into a fire has served its purpose, it can be forgotten. For the most part the poems in this group are better poetry than those on other phases of love, although the effect is frequently marred by the use of an inept word or phrase or too clanging rhymes. In an occasional rare instance the movement of the verse so completely fuses with the thought that one poem rises above others in the same genre.

Although the poet sees everywhere fate manipulating the lives of humankind, it is not always fate alone. It is as often the functioning of an age-old psychological truth that long ago crystallized into the homely proverb about the greater greenness of the grass on the other side of the fence. Five poems,[5] each different in its approach to the idea and in its prosodic treatment, illustrate the theme. The earliest of the group is in reality a weak man's prayer, because only a weak man would hope never to feel a deep attraction for a woman simply because winning in love presents the danger of losing. The others reveal the power of the imagination in arriving at the final evaluation; or, as one spirit expresses it:

> Thou lovest what thou dreamest her;
> I am thy very dream!

It is the projection of a man's love on the beloved that colors her appearance to him. Hardy's young men may lack the brilliance of Shaw's Marchbanks, but they are equally aware with him of the power of love. Each must solve his own problem as to whether the presence or absence of the beloved strengthens his passion. It is only the sensitive and articulate young man who is as conscious of these processes as Hardy's young men; the average loses sight of the fact that more often than not it is his unconsciousness of being in love with love that moves him.

Hardy attempted an explanation of this phenomenon in his notebooks (October 28, 1891). He felt that it was the incompleteness that is loved, the less than perfection, when love is genuine and sincere.

[5] "Revulsion," "The Well-Beloved," "The Dream Follower," "A Thought in Two Moods," "I Said and Sang Her Excellence."

An ideal lover could possibly prefer perfection, but not the real lover. A practical man may well see, he says, "the Diana or the Venus in his Beloved, but what he loves is the difference."

It is evident that for Hardy prose and poetry were not instruments for different purposes. He merely developed more fully in his novels the ideas that abound in his verse. The novels aid in an appreciation of the poems, which are, however, capable of standing alone. They aid by showing us the complete working out of a situation that in the poems is etched with incisiveness. They serve as a guide to our imaginations as they reconstruct the suggested details of a crystallized moment.

Few, if any, facts concerning love were without interest for him. He found quiet amusement in the egocentricity of lovers like him of "To Carrey Clavel" who quietly wins his way by taunting Carrey about her prospective treatment of Charley. Her coyness only makes him bolder and before she realizes it (or does she?) he has won his way with her. The lyric measure catches the smile in the young man's heart as he rejoices in his cleverness.

This egocentricity likewise applies to newlyweds, he points out, so selfishly unaware that anything exists outside themselves. They can believe, for example, in "A House with a History," that their living in the house gives it significance, whereas the house has already passed its prime; has already witnessed far more important events than any they could offer. They like too, to foster the fiction that their love is greater than any other. One lover is convinced that his love for the daughter is more profound than the father's could possibly be; although, as the poet quietly observes, the father's love will persist long after the other is forgotten. He is realist enough, however, never to suggest that love is unalloyed delight, although his attitude depends largely on his mood at the moment of composition. At one time he suggests that the loneliness of not being in love is preferable to the cares that kisses bring. At another he is willing to accept whatever cares may come as long as she comes too, an attitude epitomized in

> How great my grief, my joys how few
> Since first it was my fate to know thee! [6]

[6] "Song to Aurore," "Come Not; Yet Come," "How Great My Grief."

Yet he knew that separated lovers are not wholly alone. They can still share many of the same things: the same wind, the same highway, the same ships passing them, the same moon. He can take an imaginative journey to other worlds so distant that the earthly spot where she is seems near. But however much each may desire the end of the separation, the moment of its close creates apprehensiveness arising from the knowledge that some moments are impossible of recapture.[7] Delay seems desirable, although it is sometimes dangerous. The average case more nearly resembles that of "Lover to Mistress." If she wants him near her, he tells her, she has but to give the sign and he will overleap all obstacles to be with her.

Hardy saw that love not only alters lovers' views of one another; but that it transforms, illumes, and gives significance to little nameless, almost unremembered trivialities of life, such as an unexpected kiss. A visit with or a letter from his beloved may immortalize for the lover a place of little distinction.[8] But Hardy sometimes loses his perspective, becomes oversentimental, and produces a poem of little intrinsic worth.

The reverse side of the picture is as common; and a scene, attractive enough in itself, remains unattractive because it is unknown to the beloved. When the poet fuses mood, thought, and observation into an harmonious whole the result is "A Wet August." In that earlier time, he asks, "were dim clouds, a dribbling bough, Gilt over by the light" he bore in him? He admits that the "then golden chances seen in things" may well have accounted for the difference.

Hardy crystallizes many of those moments when love hangs in the balance. The manner of his doing so depends on his mood; it can be tender, almost tragic, quietly humorous and ironic. He realizes that the scale may be turned for or against love by a feather,[9] and in the seven short stanzas of "The Week," he summarizes a common experience. When the young lover left his beloved on Mon-

---

[7] "The Musing Maiden," "In Vision I Roamed," "The Minute before Meeting," "On The Departure Platform," "Her Confession."

[8] "Love Watches a Window," "That Kiss in the Dark," "An Experience," "Midnight on Beechen, 187–," "Donaghadee," "The Letter's Triumph."

[9] "At the Word 'Farewell,' " "He Inadvertently Cures His Love Pains," "A Two Years' Idyll."

day, somewhat emotionally exhausted, no doubt, he thought she had changed and was indifferent as to whether or not he ever saw her again. Each succeeding day altered his feeling until on Sunday night life without her seemed worthless.

Hardy, sympathetic to lovers separated by misunderstanding, was keenly aware that a close physical proximity certainly does not mean spiritual affinity, the absence of which separates persons far more than miles and storms:

> But that thwart thing betwixt us twain,
> Which nothing cleaves or clears,
> Is more than distance, Dear, or rain,
> And longer than the years.
> —"The Division"

He sympathized, too, with the jealous lover, and recognized that it was the little rather than the major incidents which uncovered the lack of confidence that permits this emotion,[10] just as he sympathized with the devoted lover of Lizbie Brown who lost her because he waited too long to confess his love.

The fifty-odd poems dealing with the rather tentative beginnings of love, its false starts, its diversions and digressions are among the duller of Hardy's poems. Although none lacks some positive merit of tone, image, or astute observation, none has the passion or suggested implication—the quality of synecdoche, as Frost might say —that lifts it from the anecdotal or topical to the universal. This does not imply that the truth of the incident lacks a universal application, but rather that the described incident is of minor importance to the poem. To paraphrase one of Hardy's poems certainly robs the poem of some of its value. The residue, however, is still interesting and of worth. He differs greatly from Robert Frost in this matter and the degree of difference makes Hardy the lesser poet.

To say that Hardy wrote about life as he saw it about him is, of course, to labor the obvious. Many things in life struck him as being the workings of a blind power; but because of this we should not overlook the quality of graciousness that in a large measure in-

[10] "The Chimes," "The Face at the Casement," "Love the Monopolist," "To a Sea Cliff."

vests his poems as well as his novels. The poems in which this graciousness is most apparent are those in which there are several levels of meaning.

Nowhere is this quality more in evidence than in those numerous poems of understanding love between man and wife. Many of these belong to 1912 and 1913, after the death of his first wife, a period during which he wrote more than he had ever written before in the same space of time. He was "in flower," wrote the second Mrs. Hardy, and "his flower was sad-colored." He did not at the time prize to its full worth what he enjoyed; but once it was lacked and lost, he raised its value and found the virtue that possession did not show to him while it was his. These poems, bringing out as they do one of Hardy's deepest instincts, that of fidelity, form an impressive although unconventional elegy. They flowed from his pen naturally. As he remarked to Benson: "One looked back through the years, and saw some pictures; a loss like that just makes one's old brain vocal."

They cover almost all phases of a romance, but the emphasis is on the sense of loss when one of the partners has died. Such a point of view is not pessimistic. Man can only measure his achievement in anything by looking backward; it is as true of achievement in love as in work, thought, or ambition. True enough, looking back over too great a distance, one may tend to idealize the situation; but not Hardy. The apparent little annoyances that strike the observer go unnoticed by the couple themselves. They realize that the understanding is so deep that little surface ripples never penetrate to the subsurface calm. Nowhere in his works does one find so much beauty, passion, tenderness, and understanding as in those poems written during these years. He does not lash out in fury against a power that permits such things; he quietly attaches value to those things which were associated with the beloved. Mr. Frost has, I think, best represented the masculine point of view toward a love that passes understanding. Death was not necessary to arouse his poetic *daemon* to passionate utterance. With Hardy, however, the death of his wife was necessary to remove that natural English reticence and shyness which forbade his speaking. It is obvious that I cannot subscribe to the idea that Hardy's married life was an unhappy one even in the later years. The ecstasy had no doubt gone; little surface disturbances may have appeared; but more than that I cannot believe. Hardy had had experience enough to know that there is little black and white in life; he knew that the colors were essentially tones of gray. He also knew that one need not be blind to the weaknesses in a person in order to love that person. Mrs. Hardy must often have done little things that amused or irritated him, but certainly such trivialities are no basis on which to build the theory of a lack of love in later years.

The "Passer-by" is a fitting introduction to the poems on happy love. The woman, recalling her romance, noticed that when the young man first passed her house he was shy and blushed. Later, when love developed, she was the one who felt shy; but any girl, she believed, that could have known him as it had been her privilege would have loved him as did she. Readers of Hemingway's *To Have and Have Not* may remember the picture of Harry Morgan's wife at the time Harry's body was being brought into the harbor. A young man seeing her asked his companion if that bedraggled woman could ever have known love!

Hardy recognized that the romantic-looking youths who epitomize love in advertisements lack the innate sensitivity and possess too-inflated egos to be capable of the passion they are supposed to symbolize. He realized, too, that a superficial application of the Platonic idea that a beautiful exterior must reflect a corresponding soul-state does not accord with the facts, the persistency of the idea notwithstanding. His own clear vision had served him in good stead. At a time when common woman was neglected, when "no honors, praises, pleasure" reached women from men, when they were treated with stupidity and unreason, one had the power to ring him "with living light." Nor was he inclined to belittle the happiness of a couple whose plighting had been accomplished by "trite usages in tamest style," and who had seemingly been able to find happiness in the petty, simple things:

> Who could those common people be,
>   Of days the plainest, barest?
>   They were we;
> Yes, happier than the cleverest, smartest, rarest.
>   —"A Jog-Trot Pair"

Nor was he at a loss to understand that it is not always what a woman had within her that determined her influence over her husband. It could be a gift of "strange freshness" that brought new life and hope to him, that enabled him to find himself.[11]

His clear vision also enabled him to observe with sympathy those who from varying degrees of mental myopia partially or wholly lost their expected happiness. He had only compassion for a lover too early robbed of the object of an all-consuming love and could pity the young man's futile reliance on what he as a poet knew could never be. He understood the man who too late discovered that he had let slip from his grasp what would have enabled him to achieve a life "rarer than it figures among men." His own experience deepened the bond with others who when help was past realized what they had lost through a lack of the power to see. Rarely does Hardy write better than when his subject is the love that is fully realized only after death, particularly when it has been the death of someone close to him.[12]

Each place of association stirs him to reminiscence. Perhaps it was only the seasonal contrast in a scene reflecting the change in his own life ("The Prospect"); or a similarity in which the only difference is temporal. What, for example, would his reactions have been on a glorious earlier day had he had definite foreknowledge that at that very place fifty years hence he would be laying flowers on her grave ("If You Had Known")?

The poet's grief is much more convincing than the hero's grief in *Farewell to Arms*. He realized that a man of deep feelings does not rant and rave when his wife dies. The blow stuns him into silence. It is the person of superficial feelings that acts dramatically. "Just the Same," "The Wound," and "The Master and the Leaves" are three versions of a like emotion. In each the poet's economy of expression intensifies the tragedy of the protagonist. One man's world seems to have ended for him—"the beauty and dream were gone"—and he sought refuge in the outer world to discover that his tragedy went unheeded:

[11] "Her Apotheosis," "Without, Not within Her."
[12] "Unknowing," "Known Had I," "I Sometimes Think," "Your Last Drive," "To Louisa in the Lane," "Rain on the Grave," "Thoughts of Phena," "Lorna the Second," "To a Motherless Child," "1967."

> I went forth, heedless, whither,
> In a cloud too black for name:
> —People frisked hither and thither;
> The world was just the same.

He felt, for example, after his wife's death in the night, the great-
ness of her loss to him, although in the latter years they had com-
paratively little to say to one another.

> Well, well! All's past amend,
> Unchangeable. It must go.
> I seem but a dead man held on end
> To sink down soon . . . O you could not know
> That such swift fleeing
> No soul foreseeing—
> Not even I—would undo me so!
>
> —"The Going"

It takes little to arouse this lover's poetic daemon. A second sees in
the "crimson wound" of the setting sun a wound similar to his own:

> Like that wound of mine
> Of which none knew,
> For I'd given no sign
> That it pierced me through.

A third, too sunk in grief, sees but does not feel the mutation of the
seasons. The three men are one and the same.

Hardy's attitude toward a loved one's death steadily matures.
Instead, therefore, of the protagonist's trying to efface the memory
of the beloved by dwelling in a city she had never visited, he clings
tenaciously to his memories. Hardy eventually realized that the
grave was the last place to find the spirit of the dead wife. He con-
sciously sought but rarely could find it by visiting the places dear
to her. He sought it at morning prayers, at a lecture, by the sea; but
unsuccessfully. He found it only in those things in which they had
both shared, and then only when he was in the rare moments of a
mystical mood. Her picture, even a dead leaf blown on his hand,
evokes her spirit. She never quite lost the ability to rekindle in him
his early ardor, recalled by his reminiscence of her tastes and habits
and of tender moments in their courtship.[13]

[13] "After a Journey," "They Would Not Come," "A Night in November," "An Old
Likeness," "At Castle Boterel," "Lament," "The Frozen Greenhouse."

He recognized, too, that his wife opened many vistas. She revealed to him the beauty of the sea, of romance, of love, and (after her death) opened the door of the past to him, because little remained to which he could look forward:

> She opens the door of the Past to me,
> Its magic lights,
> Its heavenly heights,
> When forward little is to see.
> —"She Opened the Door"

She is never far from him. The creak of a small table stirs thoughts of her, its giver; a plunge of his arm into a basin recalls their visit to the spot. He hears her call to him over the wet meadows, sees her dwelling in the beautiful afterglow of the sunset, or in the shadow of a Druid stone, and finds her in the old churches he so loved to haunt. He visits the towns and places that she knew— Plymouth, Beeny Cliff, and others; he contrasts the meaninglessness of the summer after her death with the fullness of the one before, and experiences a general nostalgia for the things he did with her.[14]

To set these generalizations from the poems on happy love as a counterbalance to the poems on unhappy or unfortunate love would seem at first glance to be expecting too much of them. Reduced to the bare statement of factual data they do seem to fall short of their task. But no poems less lend themselves to abstraction than these. The thought is so intimately bound up with the form, the fusion of rational and emotive elements so complete, the overtones so much more important than in most of the poems that the reader must know them intimately in order to see their importance. The emotion is so profound that it has prevented the poet from indulging in any extraneous ornament to augment it. All the poems are not equal, of course, but they are of a surprisingly high level. These poems are remarkable for their understatement; but, as in "On the Doorstep," the reader has no difficulty in filling in the gaps. The last line of the second stanza—"And forth I stride"—is powerful in its simple di-

---

[14] "She Opened the Door," "The Little Old Table," "The Haunter," "Under the Waterfall," "The Voice," "He Prefers Her Earthly," "The Shadow on the Stone," "The Marble-Streeted Town," "Beeny Cliff," "Places," "I Found Her There," "Old Excursions," "This Summer and Last," "If It's Ever Spring Again," "The West of Wessex Girl," "A Spot," "After a Romantic Day," "A Church Romance."

rectness. When Hardy attempts the expression of grief in fanciful terms he is less successful. He seems unable to infuse his fancy with the strong masculine sense that is so necessary. On the other hand, when relating a story that has made a deep impression on him he gives us an excellent picture of the mind of a grieving man.[15]

Hardy realized that to the successful lover rain and storms are still fair; to him who has lost his beloved, summer is forever gone from his heart. In these poems of tender sorrow we can see as completely as anywhere else in his poetry the manner in which he has used the formless materials of nature to augment the form of his poems. "The King's Experiment" and "It Never Looks Like Summer" are interesting illustrations of this tendency. The first, written as a young man when he had only experienced in his imagination the loss he actually records in the second, is elaborate and minute in detail and possesses the qualities the nineteenth century academic landscape painter sought in his paintings. The second, with the quality of a Cezanne landscape, is sparse in detail, with striking simplicity in the handling of the masses. Its aesthetic impact on the reader is far greater, however, than that of the early work.

It is a truism—although like most truisms, frequently overlooked —that only a few rare poets like Shakespeare have the quality of imagination, of intuitive inspiration, that is accurate as far as experience permits one to judge. Hardy himself realized the incapability of the average person to pass judgment or correctly appraise another's unexpressed thoughts. He did not, therefore, adhere to a set plan in writing of the effects of death on those left behind.[16] But it would be folly to suggest that all the poems about death are autobiographical, even though we remember the large autobiographical content that he admitted his poems to possess. He did not confine himself to his own experiences or to observed ones. Old tales in which couples triumphed over obstacles that would daunt the less-determined and less courageous delighted him.[17]

Nor did he confine his treatment of late realization only to those

[15] "Her Temple," "The Fading Rose," "The Lament of the Looking-Glass," "The Phantom Horsewoman."
[16] "The Clock Winder," "When the Picnic Was," "A Duettist to Her Pianoforte," "The Figure in the Scene," "Paths of Former Time," and "A Dream or No."
[17] "The Elopement," "In Sherborne Abbey."

instances involving death. He was as interested when the problem was one of such wasted potentialities as those of spiritual kinship. The couple in "We Sat at the Window" is in many respects typical of the others. They spent a rainy day together and were bored. There seemed "nothing to read, nothing to see." Too late he sensed how much each could have given the other: "wasted were two souls in their prime." But speech is not always necessary.

He regrets, too, in "The Faded Face," that he was robbed of something vital because of his inability to recognize in his young wife those qualities that he came to appreciate only after they had faded. The theme of late realization is restated in "Penance," "In the Moonlight," "The Rambler," but most movingly in "His Heart," a poem which, though told from the woman's point of view, might well be Hardy's own analysis of his relationship with his wife. These poems are similar in tone, possessing an elegiac quality of restrained regret. Like most of his poems, each contains moments of close observation of life and nature that lift them above the commonplace. They do not startle the reader by overemphasis; they reveal themselves gradually with rereading.

It is interesting to compare two poems on the reluctance of couples of advancing age to be separated. One, "The Colonel's Soliloquy," was written early; "The Walk" is of later composition. One is sentimental in tone, the other realistic and of greater sincerity. The first is a picture of age as a young man might envision it; the latter, age as it is. The number of instances of inaccurate imagination in the poems is, however, relatively small. Hardy was aware that years of married life do not necessarily bring happiness; nor do they bring resignation. He clothes this knowledge in the irony of "The Curate's Kindness," in which an overzealous young curate thwarts the looked-for liberation of the husband. Theodore Dreiser has presented a similar situation in his much more bitter, more elaborately developed "Free."

So much for one phase of Hardy's treatment of love. It is clear that he did not write from an embittered heart. No one had a deeper respect for the finest aspects of love than did he. No one was more careful to preserve its bloom and rare flavor.

He was fully aware of the part played in love by pride and shyness. The couple of "The Dissemblers" certainly fool no one but themselves about their love. Each may profess to act as he does merely for his own sake, although it is clear that such is not the case. And it was shyness alone that kept the love from blossoming in "An Upbraiding." Only after death is each free to speak out.

His catholicity of interest in human nature was so great that nothing that happened in the world of real men and women lacked fascination for him. This real world lay for him, however, where it lay for Wordsworth—that is, the Wordsworth of the Preface to *Lyrical Ballads*—not necessarily in the world of the rustic, but in the world of the common man. Society neither awed him nor interested him. He saw that the real natures of persons in society were too much concealed by convention. In fact, Hardy, more consistently than Wordsworth, follows the latter's criteria for a poet. I would not even suggest, however, that he attempted to follow in Wordsworth's footsteps. No two poets are farther apart. Hardy was content to report his observations without moralizing upon them. He was frankly observing, yet his observations did not make him cynical.

No author could be less critical of characters than he. By this very fact, however, he has performed a greater service than many an author who attempts an evaluation. He has presented situations to us from which we can study the reverse side of love; and, even better, he has presented the incidents not from the outsider's point of view, but from the point of view of the actors in the poem.

That the majority of the poems deal with the reverse side of love need surprise no one, and for two reasons. The first is a purely technical one. As an artist he was constantly in search of subject matter. He found little that was new to say about the much publicized happiness of lovers. He thought he would be more effective were he to explore a new field. The second could be a personal one. He looked about him and saw the rarity of a marriage of true minds. He saw that from an apparently ideal beginning marriage often slipped into a satisfactory working agreement. He saw men and women refusing to be satisfied with a compromise of this sort and struggling to find a means for the consummation of the ideal. He saw the withering influence on men and women whose yearnings met with unimaginative response, and he was moved by the inherent tragedy offered by the situation. The young man of "The Echo Elf Answers" who will be inconstant, woo many, marry the wrong one, and find escape only in the grave epitomizes this not uncommon phenomenon. It makes little difference whether the trouble arises, as in the moving and poignant "The Ballad Singer," from a failure to accept the peace offering, followed later by infinite regret, or from an inability to forget the girl who brought him abundant sorrow, or from wounds each has inflicted on the other, or from the regret following upon the discovery that suffering has altered the ideal of his youth beyond recognition.[18] As often, it arises from infidelity, indiscretion, economic difficulties, or uncontrolled passion. This last cause motivates the most interesting poems.

The indiscretion of the heedless couple of "By the Runic Stone," for example, would bear less bitter fruit today than was the case when Hardy recorded the incident. The economic cause, receiving treatment in two poems of unequal quality—the early allegorical "Postponement" and the realistic "The Inquiry"—is still with us. But the fruit of uncontrolled passion is a more serious matter and the results are often tragic. Few of Hardy's men and women are thoroughly bad, although they do lack self-discipline. The men are vital, elemental, and overwhelmingly masculine; the women are innocent and trusting. And in that lies their trouble. In few of the poems is Hardy primarily interested in the situation from the man's point of view. Society does not condemn them as it condemns the women. Nor is he interested in their stories from a moral point of view. He never condemns, never launches forth into Jeremiads. It is rather surprising to discover in how many of these poems dealing with elemental passion we know little or nothing of the character of the man who has placed the girl in a difficult situation. Few, at least, have the engaging quality of Rake-Hell who, having become somewhat enamored of a girl at a dance, committed the sexual act with her, but later refused to marry her to save her name. There were, Rake-Hell knew, worse things than public opprobrium. He knew he was worthless; knew also that she would have an unhappy life with him and she would be better off without him. Rake-Hell's logic is incontrovertible:

[18] "The Peace Offering," "The Ballad Singer," "When Oats Were Reaped," "The Woman Who Went East," "The Discovery."

For is one moonlight dance,
One midnight passion,
A rock whereon to fashion
Life's citadel?
—"Rake-Hell Muses"

In spite of his apparent worthlessness there is something admirable about him, something fine, which is more than can be said of many of the nameless men in the poems who father illegitimate children.

I have suggested that Hardy's maidens are not bad girls; they are inexperienced. They have not had sufficient opportunity to learn about men while still under an understanding parental care. They are elemental enough to be swept away by passion, the results of which are unpredictable. One of the most moving poems in this genre—moving because it is wrought with the artistry that makes a perfect fusion of the thought in the form—is the two-stanza "The Seasons of Her Year." This is a good example of an architectonic device of Hardy which we shall later examine with some thoroughness. Stanza 1 expresses the girl's unbounded joy that the young man has finally expressed his love. Stanza 2 poignantly reveals her sorrow that she must bear alone the child to be born out of wedlock. "The Place on the Map," told from the man's point of view, and "Burning the Holly," both similar in theme to "The Seasons of Her Year" are less successful because marred by extravagance and artificiality. Hardy realized, of course, that an untimely pregnancy was not necessary to bring grief to a girl who has been indiscreet. Her conscience could punish her far more severely than could the censorious tongues of the villagers ("After the Club Dance"). He also realized that some girls, and among them Julie-Jane, have no consciences. Very different are the mood and quality of suffering depicted in "The Wedding Morning."

Although Hardy observes these wayward young men and women with tolerance and sympathetic understanding, he shows a quality akin to affection for those who will not surrender. The couples who refuse to conform to convention and refuse to be ashamed of their actions arouse his admiration, which, though never baldly stated, is subtly implied in the movement of the verse. "The Recalcitrants" is one example; "The Christening" an even better one, and a good instance of Hardy's association of himself with the character of the poem. The young man is deeply in love with a girl, although in many ways he is immature and certainly selfish. He does not want to marry because he believes it would rob his romance of its bloom. While watching the christening of his child, he muses on what marriage would bring:

> But chained and doomed for life
>   To slovening
> As vulgar man and wife,
> He says, is another thing:
> Yea: sweet Love's sepulchring.

Whether or not the young man is justified in letting the girl bear the brunt of social condemnation is not even hinted at in the poem. Nor do we ever find a hint of social condemnation in any of the poems. Hardy records the incident. His disapproval is not even suggested. It would be dangerous, I think, to suggest that the key lies in the movement of the verse. Reaction to that is too subjective, too much a matter of personal reaction to be of much positive value. In this very absence of criticism lies an element of weakness. Some couples have less courage to stand out against the social mores; they finally marry even though, like those in "The Conformers," they know that the passion whetted by the need of secrecy will die. Others are merely indifferent. Why should they bother at a late date —the theme of "Long-Plighted"—to go through with the marriage ceremony?

It is clear, however, that Hardy does not minimize the workings of conscience in a man. The sergeant's conscience in "San Sebastian," for example, is constantly stirred by the sight of his daughter. Occasionally, a man may act with surprising bigness, but the cases are rare and "The Husband's View" is Hardy's only poem of such an instance.

The theme of boy-meets-girl remains one of the most fertile subjects for an author. The popular writer has been prone to conclude his story with the wedding ceremony and the summary dismissal of his characters with the and-they-lived-happily-ever-after tag. The tendency of grown-up literature in any age has discredited easy generalizations of any kind and of this type in particular. Authors have always recognized with Byron that love for a man is a thing apart, and that it is so is the cause of man's frequent vacillation, arising from the conflict between passion and reason, passion and habit, or passion and freedom. Hardy has written many poems exploratory of this phase of man's life and of woman's inability to understand this conflict in him. He has presented woman's passionate challenge to the rewards of ambition above those of love, has pictured man's conflict within himself when love and ambition strive for mastery, and has seen that circumstances rather than volition sometimes keep a man from a girl. He gives, too, an ironic twist to a situation that leaves the husband upbraiding the early suitor for having rejected her. But the material of the poems in this genre never deeply moved Hardy and the result is weak poetry.[19]

Far more important to Hardy, and therefore more important to us because of the heightened poetic expression, is the moment at the end of love. The tragedy lies not so much in the fact that love ends, but in that love, not ending for each at the same moment, is heavy with pain and regret for one. The causes are many. Perhaps the most to be deplored is that when a couple simply let happiness slip away from them, uncognizant of what is taking place. More frequent is the discovery by the lover that the beloved is not as his imagination first painted her, that a girl is incapable of understanding his attitude or intentions, or that they have twisted the cord of their love till it breaks through too intemperate actions.[20] The situation of "Fetching Her" is peculiar to the idealist. He thought that in bringing his bride from the coast he brought with her

> The pure brine breeze, the sea,
> The mews—all her old sky and space—

only to find that in the new environment she quickly lost those qualities which had endeared her to him.

The drama at the end of love need be no less intense because of absence of histrionics. The simplicity with which the lover announces the discovery of a new object for his affections does not make the burden less hard to bear. There may be a premonition of

---

[19] "Her Reproach," "At a Seaside Town in 1869," "I Say I'll Seek Her."
[20] "Where Three Roads Joined," "That Moment," "The Dear," "The Dawn after the Dance."

the end as in "The Dead and Living One" or in "The Shiver," but
the statement of "The End of the Episode" more nearly summarizes
what each feels than would a more melodramatic manifestation:

> Ache deep; but make no moans:
> Smile out; but stilly suffer:
> The paths of love are rougher
> Than thoroughfares of stones.

And the "Last Love-Word" epitomizes the unsought, unwished for
close:

> I can say no more: I have even said too much,
> I did not mean that this should come:
> I did not know 'twouid swell to such—
> Nor, perhaps, you—
> When that first look and touch,
> Love, doomed us two!

In a few instances Hardy presents the drama of love's end in a
tragic, bitter, or ironic light: tragic when the son recognized his fa-
ther's wisdom in attempting to prevent his marriage; bitter when
the son recognized that his mother had better understood the girl's
character than he; ironic when, to her relief, his friends separated
him from the girl he loves; when he forgets his promise; or for
less obvious reasons.[21] He once wrote that "all tragedy is grotesque
—if you allow yourself to see it as such." Although aware that to do
so was a "risky indulgence for any who have any inspiration towards
a little goodness or greatness of heart," he wrote several narrative
poems that well illustrate that he was one who did indulge him-
self.[22]

In spite of fates being an active agent that makes awry things
that should have been straight, it sometimes does not alter the *status
quo,* and expediency will necessitate a behavior that implies at least
an outward harmony ("Side by Side"). Abetted by superstition,
however, the case may be tragic, evident in "The Catching Ballet
Wedding Clothes," and "The Dame of Athelhall," or if not actu-
ally tragic, movingly ironic, evident from "At Tea."

[21] "The Forbidden Banns," "Rose-Ann," "Cross Currents," "The Lost Leaf," "The
Month's Calendar," "Singing Lovers," "The Two Wives."
[22] "The Newcomer's Wife," "A Conversation at Dawn," "The Burghers," "The Duel,"
"The Moth-Signal," "In the Days of Crinoline," "The Telegram," "The Rash Bride,"
"Her Secret," "The Re-Enactment."

Hardy's notebooks are, in fact, filled with stories he had heard of strange tricks of fate in the lives of star-crossed lovers, and particularly those with an ironic twist in which one almost hears the demonic laugh of the puppeteer as he manipulates his puppets through the intricacies of their tangled lives.

In his later years, he was interested in recording the moments when the bedrugged lovers regain consciousness. He looks with amused pity at them, aware that what seems peculiar to themselves has been of constant recurrence throughout mankind's history. His aloofness and his general attitude toward life give him perspective and provide him with the means for personal happiness that is denied most persons. Many of the situations would be matter for amusement were not the protagonists themselves too dreadfully serious and concerned over hurt pride ("In Her Precincts"). "Let Me," expresses every lover's desire:

> Let me believe it, dearest,
> 　　Let it be
> As just a dream—the merest—
> 　　Haunting me,
> That a frank full-souled sweetness
> 　　Warmed your smile
> And voice, to indiscreetness
> 　　Once, awhile!
> And I will fondly ponder
> 　　Till I lie
> Earthed up with others yonder
> 　　Past a sigh,
> That you may name at stray times
> 　　With regret
> One whom through green and gray times
> 　　You forget!

This realization of the end, however, is not always willingly acknowledged, and the unwillingness arises, no doubt, from the natural reluctance of a person to admit even justifiable inconstancy. The monument maker in the poem of that name awakens to his new state at the moment he is about to place the beloved's statue in the church, but he refuses to accept the fact completely. The same phenomena operate on him, no doubt, that operated on the young lover who talked himself out of love, only in this case the work of the chisel accomplished what talk had done in the other.

Hardy is careful, however, to make it perfectly clear that the pain is not always to the lover. He does not sugar-coat the philosophic pill that the beloved must frequently swallow—the tardy realization of what she had missed. Any one of a number of causes may jar her from her rather smug assurance of having behaved properly. The severest jolt is to the pride of one making the simple discovery that another has gained his affections, a discovery ironically treated in "Two Serenades." The poet depicts a less usual instance in "Every Artemisia," in which the chanced death of the slighted lover stirs the beloved's conscience to regret and her imagination to an idealization reaching to the point of a godlike reverence. But is it actually a less usual instance? Is it not rather an extreme example of a common observation? The survivor, indifferent in the manifestation of his affection in lifetime, regrets his defection when no one remains toward whom to manifest what he never under any circumstances would reveal.

It is only natural that Hardy, interested as he was in the reverse side of love, should explore the effects of disillusionment. As fertile a field as any for such a study are those already mentioned moments when the lover regains consciousness; when, in other words, reality and his imagination or wishful thinking—call it what you will—clash, and reality triumphs. "Misconception" is the story of one such idealist. Although the poem has little intrinsic merit because of the highly wrought diction that prevents a direct poet-reader relationship, its subject is useful for throwing additional light on the microscopic intensity with which Hardy examines love. A young man has slaved to find a "smug hermitage" where his beloved could dwell in peace and security far from the din, strife, and perturbations of the city. The only result of his labor is the discovery that those very things from which he wished to shield her were for her the breath of life, the things in which she found most pleasure.

Disillusionments of any kind are bad enough, even though inevitable. The most bitter of all, however, are those that come after the consummation of the marriage vows, and they may display themselves under many guises. Could the husband of "She Charged Me" have seen that jealousy of another woman and the resulting insecurity were the causes of his wife's tactless nagging, he might well have behaved with greater tolerance. But being an average husband, he could only see that the result would sever their love, that soon the curtain would fall on their play of slave and queen. More bitter to bear is the disillusionment arising from the discovery of a wife's pettiness, whatever the cause ("The Homecoming"). The result is regrettable. Hardy, however, never censures, never blames. He associates himself so closely with the person from whose point of view the poem is written that more than once we weigh the possibility of another side to the question. With difficulty we confine ourselves to the strict limits of the poem. The older woman of "The Homecoming," for example, might well have been one of the noble women about whom we shall later know more.

Hardy realizes that physiological or biological conditions also have much to do with the awakening to reality. He saw that, in marriages of less than true minds, those moments are more frequent than one willingly admits, when following the marital act a man does not have enough emotional reserve to sustain the projection of his beloved as he had done before. At such a time man sees—or thinks he sees—the woman with his mind and not with his heart, and the sight is not pleasant. She may be, as the man in "At Waking" said, only "one of the common crowd," although for his soul's sake he tries to rid his mind of the thought. To what a state this disillusionment can grow is well epitomized in the relatively early, frequently quoted "Neutral Tones." He suggests, too, in "In the Night She Came," that even a dream could produce a similar reaction.

Bitter, too, are those incidents when the love that should flower with the consummation never does. It brings frustration to the man or woman, and often induces a fixation that haunts him and drives him to despair.[23]

Hardy saw enough in life to feel that it was fortunate that no one can foresee the sage and shallow things that will happen between the first note of tenderness and the last note of pain ("Read by Moonlight"); nor are all the results of fate's cold-featured actions visible to the world. Each of us may unsuspectingly at any time

[23] "At an Inn," "Her Love Birds."

and in any place be witnessing the enactment of a tragedy more profound, more poignant, more decisive than those that are storied to the world ("At the Wicket Gate"). But one thing is certain: neither the man nor the woman has all the good luck. The best that we can ask of them, therefore, is honesty, directness, and frankness when the end is at hand.

> Face unto face, then, say,
>   Eyes my own meeting,
> Is your heart far away?
>   Or with mine beating?
> When false things are brought low,
> And swift things have grown slow,
> Feigning like froth shall go,
>   Faith be for aye.
> —"Between Us Now"

Is the clean ending, however, so easy to achieve? Can an effort of will eradicate from the mind the mental scars caused by deep emotional experience? And is love worth the risk of disillusionment? Hardy had his moments of doubt. He recognized that one who has deeply suffered from love or from any cause could never again be quite the same. He also recognized that one such experience carried blessings in disguise. A man who has once suffered the agony of a great loss can never again undergo quite the same pain. Through this loss he has achieved an invaluable freedom.

Less convincing because of its tone is his further statement that men can exist without love.[24] He may exist without it, but only for a time. And no man that has lost his love because she has turned from him (and not he from her) willingly admits that she has wholly ceased loving him. He quite possibly interprets her reluctance at not wanting to see him as a lingering affection for him. The young man of "She Did Not Turn" typifies those who have never examined their own actions under similar conditions.

Hardy did not overlook the importance of place in poems connected with love. Nature as an illumination of the moment at the end of love or the moments of reminiscence of the end of love gives him the opportunity for indulging his propensity for seeing "countenances and tempers in objects of scenery," and provides him with

[24] "I Thought, My Heart," "In Tenebris I," "I Said to Love."

the fragmentary and incomplete materials he can fuse into organic form. The reflection of the moon in the pond can be the wraith of the departed beloved, as in "Rushy Pond." The two opening stanzas, accurate and vivid as they are as an example of Hardy's mastery of infusing emotion into a landscape, serve a subsidiary purpose. They are a means for heightening the mental state of the lover whose love had not remained steadfast. The indelible impression may be one of happiness, of dejection, or both. It may arise from the reminiscence of the manner in which the thistledown, brushed by her petticoats, rose behind them; from the bleakness of the day when she left never to return; from the empty place on the wagon seat; or merely from the sight of a faded flower.[25]

The important thing is the freeing of the imagination for the purposes of idealization. But the one left behind must be careful not to be unduly critical of himself for having taken the other too much for granted. Hardy's own recollection ten years after his first wife's death reveals in its tone that the heavy sense of immediate loss gives way to a somewhat sentimental recollection ("Ten Years Since"). Loss also stimulates fancy to the point where the poet imagines he sees his beloved glancing at him from a twinkling star, or feels her ghost haunting him and does not wish it away. But when fancy gives way to a sterner imagination the result is better poetry.[26] The overtones become more important than the story itself and a slight incident conveys the lover's preoccupation with thoughts of his beloved better than a detailed account could have done. Alone he is free, too, to muse on life's tricks of denying foreknowledge of the separation that can only bring sorrow, and of time's permitting changes that make early moments impossible of recapture.[27]

The interest for Hardy of the theme of too late realization is apparent from the many variations to which he subjected the theme, although as in "She Who Saw Not," he sometimes fails to present the theme with conviction. He links it, too, with that of Keats's "La Belle Dame Sans Merci," but never with great significance. Its

[25] "Days to Recollect," "The Carrier," "The Flower's Tragedy."
[26] "Molly Gone," "The Phantom," "Something Tapped."
[27] "The Last Time," "We Say We Shall Not Meet," "A Wife Comes Back," and "A Second Attempt."

best expression is in a familiar poem from his first published volume of poems ("Her Death and After").

One group of poems about love and marriage deals with violence. Among them is "The Trampwoman's Tragedy," which Hardy regarded as one of his best. Although these poems throw little real light on Hardy's thought, they do reveal his interest in the action of characters of differing types under the influence of passion. They illustrate the limits to which passion in sexual matters manipulates lives that are undisciplined. They interest him as violence often interests persons whose lives are the acme of self-control. Knifing, hanging, drowning, poisoning, shooting, financial ruination, witchery, robbery, seduction followed by murder in cold blood, going mad, suicide, and the macabre in general are the ingredients.[28] Many of these are excellent examples of Hardy's powers of condensation. Others are less violent in their details, but are equally motivated by passion, chance, and fate.[29]

A second group is less violent but equally impersonal. It reveals the poet's constant alertness to the dramas of life being played about him and his curiosity in trying to penetrate through the appearance of things to reality. Everyone interested in creative writing exercises this faculty, but only the imagination of the artist is able to fathom the truth. One evening, for example, Hardy encountered a couple walking slowly and talking earnestly. He surmised that they were lovers, although their love was no longer of the springtime. What was their story? Thirty years later ("Beyond the Last Lamp") he still wondered what it was. Being a poet, however, he was not often content with wondering. He resolved the story in his own imagination, and invested it with the sincerity and passion that made it an even greater reality than the facts might have permitted. "At Mayfair Lodging," "On the Marquee," "At Wynyard's Gap," and "Near Lanivet, 1872" could easily be examples of the way in which his imagination reconstructed the stories, although their basis probably rested on a foundation of fact.

[28] "A Trampwoman's Tragedy," "The Flirt's Tragedy," "The Vampirine Fair," "The Mock Wife," "The Tree," "On the Death-Bed," "A Sound in the Night," "The Sacrilege," "The Single Witness," "The Workbox," "The Second Night."
[29] "The Memorial Brass," "Her Second Husband Hears Her Story," "The Contretemps," "The Brother," "The Whaler's Wife," "Mad Judy."

One instance, "Near Lanivet, 1872," we know was based on an actual occurrence in his own life. This rather weak, ineffective, and prosy poem indicates the danger of versifying an anecdotal experience that has been insufficiently subjected to the powers of imagination. It is a verse record that lacks significant form. Unfortunately for Hardy's stature as a poet, there are too many such poems when he reminisces without creating. They may be interesting for the biographer, but they are of little moment to the person interested in the poetry as poetry.

Allegory is a difficult instrument for a modern, although often a tempting one. It is unfortunate that Hardy so often succumbed, because he is rarely successful. "The Spell of the Rose" is overshadowed by the naturalism of "The Revisitation" which carries the genuine Hardy stamp with the old soldier's remark that "love is lame at fifty years."

Hardy noted, too, the difference in attitude toward love in youth and age. Of the two persons who strove in youth for the love of a girl did it make any difference in the larger problem of life which won? Age can see this better than youth. To the older person the thorn murmurs about the difference between the seasons, to the youth it is but a reminder that a girl had once almost broken his heart at the spot.[30] But we should never try to turn back the years; we would regret it, even if we could. We must accept our lot. Age has its compensations in love as in other things. A careworn wife reveals vestiges of beauty when she is moved to joy; a loving husband fails to see the changes in his wife that are visible to everyone else. Age may not bring the passion that attends love in youth, but it continues to lure life on and remains a constant.[31]

In spite of the unhappiness of the lovers and the married couples he saw about him, Hardy realized that he had himself experienced what comes to few. More to him than dinner invitations, acclaim, and visitors from afar, was the realization that

> Whatever his message—glad or grim—
> Two bright-souled women clave to him.
> —"A Poet"

[30] "The Young Churchwarden," "The Voice of the Thorn."
[31] "The Clock of the Years," "Wives in the Sere," "Faithful Wilson," "Lines," "She, to Him I–IV."

In 1883 he wrote that, after twenty years' occupation with love, he was going to abjure it; the subject continued to occupy his attention, however, for twice twenty years longer.

Such, then, is the subject matter of love in Hardy's poetry. We must remember always that we have seen, not the raw materials from which he worked, but the finished material transmuted in the mind of the poet. For an understanding of Hardy this is more important. He has not looked only at those phases of love which might coincide with some particular aspects of his own experience, but he has looked searchingly at any aspect of love that has crossed his vision. Although he has touched on the moments of ecstasy in a new and untried love, he has preferred to pay most attention to those moments of love that are fraught with greatest significance for the protagonists. He has not merely suggested the emotions of love found in life, but he has added something to those emotions that in his best poems lift them into the realm of aesthetic emotion by their sheer rightness of form. It is true, of course, that Hardy works best in his poems about love, as with his poems about life in general, when he is directly inspired by the concrete rather than by abstract thinking.

Hardy's sanity is refreshing. When other Victorian poets were loudly shouting their optimism to cloak the terror in their hearts at changes in their knowledge of the world that they would willingly conceal, he looked at this new world and was not terrified. He realized from the beginning that only by strenuously concentrating on the object could one see the object as a thing unworthy of fear. He could see that with the expansion of our knowledge of the universe man has been liberated from fears that constantly beset an Elizabethan.

With age and maturity one is less subject to the steep gradients that he suffers in youth. Instead of a *Romeo and Juliet* we get an *Antony and Cleopatra,* instead of a *L'Allegro* and a *Lycidas* we get a *Paradise Lost,* a *Paradise Regained* and a *Samson Agonistes,* instead of a bright star we get a thought that lies too deep for tears. But is the exchange an unfortunate one? I cannot think so. Nor would I willingly exchange one of Hardy's measured later lyrics for an earlier one in a more ecstatic vein. Nor would I exchange a later lyric on the same theme as an earlier one for that earlier one. I have suggested that chronology is of little importance in understanding the thing said, in understanding what we may well term the secondary material of the poetry. From the point of view of the primary, the ingredients that go to make up his way of saying it, I think chronology is more important than is generally assumed. We must delay our consideration of this matter, however, until we have further examined what the poems say.

» 3 «

WOMAN

Any valid treatment of love necessitates a center of experience from which to argue. This does not mean that a writer is restricted to a literal exposition or interpretation of his own immediate experiences. It may be so, if his own experiences are shaped by his imagination; but they must have form if their plausibility is to be convincing. Call this shaping process emotion recollected in tranquility if you wish, always remembering, however, that neat labels—the result of oversimplification—are at best but partial truths. The experiences may also be those observed in the actions of others. In such cases the effective treatment depends on the writer's possession of that state of correspondence known as empathy. Here the novelist, dramatist, or poet is apt to go astray. He not only comes to believe that the women who have stimulated his imagination about love represent all women, but he is gradually seduced into thinking that he understands what he observes in the actions of other men toward women. If, for example, he is of the temperamental type classified by Dr. W. H. Sheldon as extreme cerebrotonic he will have great difficulty in understanding the type classified as extreme somatotonic. Unless he is scrupulously honest, and not only honest but understanding, he will begin to indulge in sweeping generalizations on the relationship between the sexes and freely judge all women.

Hardy's reluctance to moralize and to say that what he says of one woman represents all women lends sanity to his observations. He examined woman with the same objectivity that he examined love; that is, he subjected it to the same simplifying process that we expect in a poem and not as we might find it in a history that would sacrifice form to verisimilitude. We have seen, too, particularly in many of the later poems when he had attained the calm that comes from a well-lived, well-rounded life, that he achieved this simplification in the manner of a serious and intelligent artist. By discarding irrelevant detail and striving for significant form he secured a heightened communication by the combination of two emotions: one arising from form—an aesthetic emotion—and one arising from the fundamental emotions of life. Let us follow him, therefore, on more dangerous and treacherous ground.

Snobbery, it has rightly been said by a well-known critic of art, makes acceptable the portrait of a great lady, though it be by a second-rate artist. When we approach the subject of woman in Hardy's poetry we shall find few portraits of great ladies and the snob will feel justified in rejecting those we do find. Hardy has unjustly been called the nineteenth century John Ford; unjustly, because his vision is broader than Ford's and certainly more democratic.

We must constantly bear in mind in any discussion of Hardy's women that he is not giving us or attempting to give us a picture of woman as if she were existing apart from her environment. He knows better than to attempt what could only result in cold lifelessness. By environment, however, I mean something broader than the village in which, and the village folk amongst whom, she finds herself; although he does that, too. I think it is impossible to overstress the fact that Hardy's portraits of women are portraits of women in a man's world and of women seen through the eyes of man. Portraits of women by women are apt to be more acid than those by men. We need only recall the women of Jane Austen, of George Eliot, or Clare Boothe to realize that it takes a woman to penetrate into certain realms that remain concealed to men. Only a woman—unless it be a George Bernard Shaw—has the courage and hardihood to rip open the curtains (not draw them apart) to surprise another woman in her Duessa-like nakedness. If we remember this we shall not be surprised at certain reticences in Hardy's portraits. Perhaps, on the other hand, it is a quality of abstraction rather than reticence. He portrayed what a man can see and understand—certain broad outlines of character without the ungracious details.

He invested his portraits with a man's idealism about women, although it may sometimes be an outraged idealism. One may be truer than the other, but both are distorted. He further colored his portraits of women of a higher social stratum than his own by his consciousness of the stratification. Of this, however, we shall speak later.

A comparison of Shakespeare and Hardy as interpreters of woman has frequently been suggested, but I do not think the suggestion wholly pertinent. It is true that since Shakespeare, woman has had no more profound sympathizer, one more willing to understand her as she is, than Hardy. He seems to have understood her inner qualities better even than he has understood those of his men. Seems to, but only seems. At least he felt deeply enough to feel passionately about her and to be able to imbue poems about her with passionate feeling. We must remember, however, that Shakespeare's women and Hardy's are from different social worlds. We must also remember that Shakespeare's creation of women was limited by the necessity of their being portrayed by boys. Shakespeare succeeds where Hardy goes astray—in the portraits of women of the *haute monde*. Meredith understands women in this world better than Hardy and has a closer affinity with Shakespeare than his contemporary. Whether or not the difficulty arises from Hardy's own early social experience is difficult to say; but certainly he is too prone to let the superficial surface irrelevances blind him to the solid qualities of the woman which pulsate behind the conventional exterior. Again we must have recourse to a woman's interpretation of such women. Amy Lowell lets us see in "Patterns" what no man can show us, no man, that is, unless it be Shakespeare.

In his treatment of love, Hardy has, of course, given us many glimpses into woman's soul, and women have acknowledged that the glimpses have, in general, been accurate. The selection of poems for a more detailed picture of woman may well be questioned; but since our only purpose is to get as catholic and as comprehensive a view as possible of Hardy's subject matter, it will make little difference. Any division of the poems will add up to the same thing. We must remember, however, that since woman throws herself more wholeheartedly into her emotional relationships than does a man, much of the present discussion of woman will supplement the material on love rather than strike out in new and uncharted directions. The freshness will be a change of emphasis rather than a change of direction.

The matter of love, we have seen, is a tricky business. It frequently blossoms when it should wither, and it disappears when it should flourish. The causes vary, but one of the most potent is the arrival of that moment when the imagination of the man no longer projects his image of the beloved's character onto her body, and he sees her, not necessarily in her true light, but high lighted—and distorted. Such was the situation of the young man in "Outside the Window" who, returning to his sweetheart's house for his cane, overheard her berating her mother in a vixenish voice. Whether or not he saw her undraped soul as he thought he did, he believed he had had a narrow escape. This satire of circumstance is but a brief and unimportant flick of the brush in Hardy's portraiture. The relationship of mother to child stirred him far more. The continuous love of the mother for her child from the cradle to the grave, in times of misfortune as well as good, was a mystery of life which he wished to understand. Why is it, he asked himself, that with all the examples before her of parents whose children were as fair or fairer than hers, with her knowledge of the thousands of cases where the child's life is destined for tears in "new thoroughfares in sad humanity," the young mother can derive such ecstatic pleasure from the contemplation of the newborn child and from the pride of motherhood? He poses the mystery but does not penetrate it. Years later it still haunted him and again he attempted a lighthearted expression. He had learned in the meantime the lesson of the acceptance of life without the necessity of understanding it. He is content to report. The interpretation is the task of others. This love manifests itself in strange ways which would embarrass the mother did she know she were observed. Although she might know little of her immediate neighborhood and nothing of spots ten miles away, she knows and cherishes details of the distant ports to which her son has sailed. To contrast the unemotive atmosphere of the relatively early "Geographical Knowledge" with the highly wrought mood of the later "The Sailor's Mother" is interesting solely from the point of view of Hardy's development as a poet, not from any intrinsic difference of subject.[1]

He saw that the impulsion to motherhood was sometimes powerful enough to drive a woman to desperate and unusual measures, even to committing adultery to gain a healthy child. He saw, too, that a child born out of wedlock may bring troubles that overshadow the joys of motherhood, or seem to at the time. The realization of the transcendence of the joys over the sorrows may, it is true, come too late, but not necessarily so.[2]

Only with difficulty can a man fully appreciate a woman's attitude toward her child, and the difficulty often leads to jealousy. He might be shocked to find, if wooing a widow with a child, that whatever her love for him, her love for her child was greater. He would be wholly unable to understand the mother who, unable to convince her daughter's "betrayer" that poverty in marriage was not worse than shame, poisons her daughter. He could better understand the daughter who on her way to tell her mother of her betrothal asks herself if her marriage will come between her mother and her. Hardy suggests, however, in the lighthearted movement of the verse that the question was essentially a rhetorical one, and could make little difference to her plans even did she know that her mother might object.[3]

But for Hardy at his best in the depiction of this mother-child relationship we must turn to two short poems, the sonnet "By the Barrows" and the rondeau "The Roman Road." The locale of each, although the scene of memorable historic incidents, is hallowed for the poet for other reasons. The first, because a woman had "fought singlehandedly to shield a child—one not her own—from a man's senseless rage"; the second, because it was at that place that his mother walked guiding his infant steps.

In two other short pieces—"In Weatherbury Stocks" and "The Nettles"—he portrays the loyalty and devotion of mothers who remain steadfast and devoted when a sweetheart jilts or a wife forgets, even though he gives a wry, ironic twist to the theme in the trenchant "In the Cemetery," one of the fifteen satires of circum-

[1] "In Childbed," "The New Toy," "The Whitewashed Wall."
[2] "A Practical Woman," "The Dead Bastard," "The Dark-Eyed Gentleman."
[3] "The Widow Betrothed," "A Sunday Morning Tragedy," "News for Her Mother."

stance. Of the women weeping and quarreling over the exact loca-
tion of their children's graves—actually the children had been re-
moved to a common fosse to make room for the main drain—the
poet says:

> As well cry over a new-laid drain
> As anything else, to ease your pain.

He treats the theme from a different point of view in "In the Room
of the Bride-Elect"; but incisive as the expression is, the poem some-
how misses fire. So, too, does that of the overwrought story of the
father who spurns the daughter who has succumbed to the easy
ways of the town.[4]

More interesting to Hardy than the parent-child relationship was
that restless period of a girl's life when she is passing from late
adolescence into young womanhood, when she is longing with a
mad impulse for larger, freer life. He can sympathize with the girl
who is fully aware that from every reasonable point of view she is
better off in the country, yet longs to madness that she might par-
ticipate in the follies of the town. He works out the theme more
satisfactorily in a later poem by making the young man in love the
pleader. But whatever her age, it is always as an emotional being
that he thinks of her.[5] This emotionalism is a dark abysm across
which man cannot pass, and his inability to do so promulgates mis-
understandings, sorrows, and tragedies. With his keen vision and
strong poetic sensitivity Hardy can watch with amused tolerance
that which baffles the less fortunately endowed.

Innocence also interested him. Tess was a pure girl, and in fact,
the betrayed girls in his poems are generally innocent, although they
may act foolishly and unreasonably. The seeming innocent ones
are a different matter, compared with whom men are mere children.
Hardy himself once said that it had never struck him "that the
spider is invariably male and the fly invariably female." Hardy saw,
too, that man's idealism limits his understanding of women, and
he shows the limiting process at work by highlighting different as-
pects of the problem created when affected innocence completely
fools the man. He shows, too, that it often takes years for man to
realize that he has been duped; or that he has not been. But the

---

[4] "A Daughter Returns."   [5] "From Her in the Country," "An Expostulation."

misunderstanding of women is not confined only to the inexperienced. A man of experience, for example, frequently wants too much; he wants all women in one. He seeks for one person that will be his perfect complement; that will play the Cleopatra to his Antony. It requires an Edna Millay to make a man realize that this is not a unique characteristic of the male.[6] To emphasize this idea Hardy frequently endows his men with his own poet's sensitivity, as in the widely different moods of "The Chosen" and "The Protean Maiden." He saw that the average man and woman compromise on a general approximation of the ideal; the poet never gives up the quest. In unusual cases the Ernest Dowsons and Don Quixotes are able to metamorphose their barmaids and Dulcinea del Tobosos into women who are for them what the Indian maid was to Alastor.

When men worship ideals so unrelated to reality it takes comparatively little to kill the love which rests on quicksand foundations. The weapon that kills love takes many forms, one of the most common being a lashing tongue. The young man of "In the Vaulted Way," for example, cannot understand how the girl can kiss him a vehement good night after she had roundly berated him for what she thought he had done. He *knows* that his love can never again be the same. Did Hardy's knowledge of women go no deeper than that of the young man we could not justly credit him with the understanding of women that we do, because the described phenomenon is of too common occurrence not to be accepted. Only the extreme idealist would let such a flare-up mar his happiness. The phenomenon does no credit to women, it is true, but it is frequent enough to be characteristic. Actually, the poem tells us more about the young man than it does about the girl; or rather, more about Hardy. Were Hardy he, the outrage to his sensibility would be enough to kill his love.

A less common form of weapon for killing love, although not an unusual one, is man's discovery of a woman's hypocrisy, and the hypocritical attitude need not necessarily be directed toward him. The mere fact of its presence is enough. For example, the meaningless words of a woman who slept during her friend's playing, awoke

[6] "The Sweet Hussy," "The Caricature," "Gallant's Song."

only in time to mutter "Beautiful!" and "Heartaching!", and a week later blandly expressed the joy she had experienced from the playing, "gave love pause and killed it."

He also saw what Strindberg would call her unconscious instinctive dishonesty and her dishonesty and scheming. He saw her willingness to use her lover to hurt another woman, unaware that by so doing she killed his love. He saw her resort to blandishments merely to win a favorable decision from a judge at an agricultural show. He saw her steal the sweetheart of her best friend with only slight compunction.[7]

Hardy pondered, too, the question that has puzzled many men. Why does a woman close her eyes when being kissed? When she sighs at the same time, he suggests, the problem is even more perplexing. But whether she sighs when being kissed or whether she even refuses to be kissed, he saw that certain women like to play the role of cat to a man's mouse; that she derives a subtle pleasure in stringing the man along. But if he turn, she feels injured. She may repent too late. He recognized, however, the other extreme —the too possessive wife who kills what she tenaciously clings to, and treats the theme in parable.[8]

A man fears woman's tears because he instinctively knows they are a weapon against which he can make no firm stand. They are at times the only means, too, by which a man can eat humble pie without loss of face; the only time when he can be the brave, strong male and yet the tender sentimentalist beneath the bold exterior. The woman who refuses to use the traditional weapon of tears, scorning these visible signs of weakness is "less feebly human" than her sisters. Unfortunately, suggests Hardy, the "deep strong woman is weakest, the weak one is strong" and she pays the price of grief for her strength.

> You felt too much, so gained no balm for all your torrid sorrow,
> And hence our deep division and our dark undying pain.
> —"Had You Wept"

A noble soul is not, nor is the willingness to hold her "life's blood" at the call of her friends, sufficient to win man's love. More

---

[7] "What Did It Mean?" "A Pat of Butter," "A Military Appointment."
[8] "The Sign," "The Prophetess," "One Who Married above Him," "The Ivy Wife."

is necessary. Rare indeed is the man who is realist enough to rise above outward defections of look or manner for the sake of inner worth. The noble soul may be a wife who waits outside the dance hall to see that her unfaithful husband gets home safely. She may have the courage to realize and accept her outward changes; she may desire remembrance only for her inner qualities, not for her beauty; she may have the qualities of the wife of the actor who failed when he attempted a comeback; or she may be like the woman who having heeded her father's selfish admonition not to marry, found herself disconsolate and alone after his death.[9] But whatever she may have been, her nobility is its own and her only reward. Nor is that reward insufficient; because, as Hardy suggests in "A Self-Glamourer," we get from life what we *demand* that life give us. The protagonist's "trusting daring undoubt" helped her achieve happiness. Hardy did not withhold sympathy from the woman less fortunate because she lacked the determination or courage to force life to her will; nor from the woman who suffered because of her unfulfilled desires for husband and children and for her greater loneliness because convention denied her the right to move as freely as a man. Into the mouth of the city shopwoman he puts the cry of the class, a cry which can be as profound although less audible in the woman of the village ("Lonely Days").

> O God, that creatures framed to feel
> A yearning nature's strong appeal
> Should writhe on this eternal wheel
> In rayless grime;
> And vainly note, with wan regret
> Each star of early promise set;
> Till Death relieves, and they forget
> Their one Life's Time!
> —"Dream of the City Shopwoman"

He can understand, too, the woman who, realizing that her youthful dreams of a prosperous husband were futile, took the middle way and married a man whose financial position could never be good. This did not prevent her continuing to dream the dreams that she knew could never materialize ("Imaginings"). She is only an earlier

[9] "A Wife Waits," "Circus-Rider to Ringmaster," "The Beauty," "The Noble Lady's Tale," "The Orphaned Old Maid."

manifestation of the women in the cinema audiences who drug themselves into an ecstatic escape from reality in the arms of the Cary Grants, Gary Coopers, and Robert Montgomerys of the moment, and into a sense of things that they know can never be, say the dancing partner of Fred Astaire. The minister frequently supplies the place of the movie hero, but even he, according to the oft-quoted "In Church," can have feet of clay.

Because love is a more completely absorbing quality to her than to a man, her sterling qualities sometimes lead her closer to the ideal of love expressed in Shakespeare's "Let me not to the marriage of true minds" than is possible for a man. The heroine of "A Woman's Trust" is a case in point. Scorn and derision heaped on her beloved do not touch her loyalty to him. But should we blame a woman for not being overscrupulous, when she can take little interest in a world where it is sometimes necessary to pretend to feelings one does not possess? Certainly no opprobrium should attach to her because she lied to lighten the last moments of a dying man; nor should she be censured for a spontaneous, generous deed impossible of conventional approval. Noble action in woman toward her husband and a second woman is rare, and dramatists have made capital of women who divorce their husbands because of infidelity and realize too late that they have paid an incommensurate price for the offense to injured pride.[10] Of the many expositions of this theme in literature, "Over the Coffin" probably most effectively encompasses in small space its essential ingredients. Nobility, amounting almost to the ecstasy of martyrdom, lies in the action of the wife who buried her husband by the side of his beloved; whereas she requests that she be buried with her family as though never married. This was a single instance! Hardy saw that too many women were like her who lacked

> That high compassion which can overbear
> Reluctance for pure lovingkindness sake.
> —"A Broken Appointment"

But that Hardy neither set women on a pedestal nor in the mire, although he knew that some women would adequately fit such places, is readily apparent. He attempted to be a realist, nothing

10 "Her Dilemma," "A Wife and Another."

more. A milkmaid was for him no Maud Muller, nor a disguised princess of Fontainebleau. The setting might be as idealistic as in either of the former cases, but the mind of the maid is not immersed in the charms of divine philosophy; she was thinking of a new dress and her jealousy—although she did not think of it as that—of the girl to whom her Fred has paid attention. She is concerned with the practical. Hardy realized that a woman is not necessarily unhappy because of a prosaic husband, if her economic position permits her to satisfy her social thirst. A poet may satisfy her romantic youth, but, on the whole, he is too curious about a woman's reactions for her own comfort. He is not only too curious, but he is just as apt to be wrong. His insistence on the projection of his ideal endows her with a romantic imagination which she simply does not possess; or which, if possessing, she lacks the circumstances permitting her its indulgence.[11]

I stressed that we must remember that we are dealing with woman in a man's world. It is more restricted even than that. It is not only woman in a man's world; it is woman through a poet's eyes. The poet attempts to be impartial; attempts to report, not judge; but the very fact that he is a poet militates against him. His livelier sensibility is like a seismograph. However slight the disturbance to his ideal, the needle responds to the impulse. "The Moon Looks In," an inconsequential poem, illustrates this. Instead of experiencing a romantic reaction to the moonlight, she was prettying herself, getting ready for a party at which she thought the men might be sweet and the women sour. Men are apt to be disconcerted to discover that the average woman is not as susceptible to moonlight as they, and read into the fact things that should not be there. In the poem in question, it is jealousy.

I have mentioned that Hardy has attempted few portraits of great ladies. He was wise in not attempting more, because it is evident that he knows them only superficially as he met them in their London drawing rooms after he had become famous. Never can such a woman, he says, in "The Leader of Fashion," experience the great pleasures and sorrows of rural life and its minutiae. Although the basic statement is open to question, the poem presents with feeling,

[11] "The Milkmaid," "I Rose Up As My Custom Is."

accuracy, and fine selectivity those missed pleasures and sorrows of rural life. The woman is what Hardy might well call a "no character." Lady Vi is another such who subscribes to the dicta of well-bred conversation:

> While griefs and graves and things allied
> In well-bred talk one keeps outside.
> —"Lady Vi"

Her portrait, however, has no more depth than has one of Sargent's society ladies.

Hardy's intense curiosity about women leads him astray in other than portraits of great ladies. One beauty grown to womanhood where there were few to admire her is purported to have come too late to the realization of her great beauty and that she has untimely thrown herself away on a poor plain man whose pride in her, manifesting itself as it does, makes her petulantly remark to herself:

> O damn, don't show in your looks that I'm your chattel
> Quite so emphatically.
> —"The Beauty's Soliloquy during Her Honeymoon"

I cannot vouch for what went on in the woman's mind to give her a disgruntled look, but I cannot believe that it was resentment at her husband's pride and attention.

Man is as incapable of understanding some of woman's values as a woman is of understanding a man's poetic sentiment. And not understanding them, he interprets them in the most unfavorable light. The question of furs is a case in point. Few men can understand the sense of well-being the average woman derives from the possession of rich furs. Hardy attempts an analysis in "The Lady in the Furs," but his own sensibility intrudes. He sees the coat as a manifestation of cruelty to animals and as cheating of poor natives, and puts those ideas into the lady's mind where they have no place. If the truth be known, it is probably little more than an atavistic tendency which crystallizes as an indefinable sense of self-confidence from well-being.

Hardy carries the idea of woman's concern over clothes to the utmost degree of absurdity in "The Satin Shoes," a poem in which the protagonist must have been incipiently weak-minded, although outwardly beautiful, to permit a trivial incident like her inability to wear her new satin shoes to her wedding, because of the mud, unbalance her mind. So, too, must have been the woman in "Henley Regatta." He reveals the apotheosis of woman's triviality, however, in his portraiture of two women whose husbands lay at death's door. The one picked out her mourning clothes before his death; the other was concerned that his death would deny her the pleasure of being able to wear her new pink dress ("At the Draper's," "The Pink Frock"). Poems on trivial subjects necessarily remain as trivial as Dr. Johnson's satire on the ballad of "The Babes in the Wood."

Hardy's concept of history has a definite bearing on his attitude toward people. We might as easily restate it conversely and say that his attitude toward people affected his attitude toward history. He believed, and I think time has confirmed him, that events and tendencies are not "rivers of voluntary activity," but are "in the main the outcome of *passivity*—acted upon by unconscious propensity." Later, he expanded his idea:

History is rather a stream than a tree. There is nothing organic in its shape, nothing systematic in its development. It flows on like a thunderstorm-rill by a road side; now a straw turns it this way, now a tiny barrier of sand that. The offhand decision of some commonplace mind high in office at a critical moment influences the course of events for a hundred years. Consider the evenings at Lord Carnarvon's, and the intensely average conversation on politics held there by average men who two or three weeks later were members of the Cabinet. A row of shopkeepers in Oxford Street taken just as they came would conduct the affairs of the nation as ably as these.

Thus, judging by bulk of effect, it becomes impossible to estimate the intrinsic value of ideas, acts, material things: we are forced to appraise them by the curves of their career. There were more beautiful women in Greece than Helen; but what of them?—*Early Life,* 225.

The *passivity* of history in the larger sense might equally be said to be true of individuals in private life; it explains Hardy's attitude toward the subject matter of his poetry. He knew, for example, that the reasons underlying one's actions are frequently trivial, stupid, or completely incomprehensible. Why, for example, did a girl not at all interested in livestock choose a big animal fair as the place for her holiday? And why should a slight experience of an idle moment long remain in one's mind? Less puzzling is the reason for the frequent miscarriage of the best-laid plans, especially when the actual consummation depends on another person.[12]

Woman's false pride both intrigued and embittered him. Four women will not marry the men they love because of the difference in social position: one is willing to perform the marital act with him and to bear his child, but refuses to marry him; a second, having been similarly intimate, throws him over for a brilliant match; a third meets her lover a week after her marriage, reaffirms her love, then continues on her honeymoon; a fourth submits to a dull boring life with a husband who is her social equal and enviously watches the rejected suitor and his wife win fame and popularity.[13] Of these four poems only the second is of much poetic worth, in spite of excellent touches in the others. Basically I think the poems are essentially autobiographical and reveal as clearly as "A Pair of Blue Eyes" what is difficult for an American to understand—the stratification of English rural life: the difference between village and "county," and so forth. Mr. Blunden, who understands the subtleties of this world, has helped us to understand certain qualities in Hardy that would otherwise puzzle us. Hardy knew in his mind that he was greater than these differences, but his early life left too deep an impression for him ever to free himself from the emotional consciousness of these differences. Although these poems help us in understanding the scope of Hardy's portraiture of women we must not forget that they give us an even better understanding of the poet. The number of portraits of woman colored by class-consciousness are fortunately few because otherwise Hardy would have little stature as a poet. It is also fortunate for women.

As I have already mentioned, these poems are not basically poems from the women's point of view. They seem to be, but they have the same effect as Clare Boothe's *The Women*. When you lay the poems aside, as when you leave the theater after her play, you remember only the men, although there were none in the cast. Hardy associates himself so closely with the men in his poems that unless we are careful we are unlikely to detect the disguise. Even in his por-

[12] "Expectation and Experience," "Sitting on the Bridge," "By Her Aunt's Grave."
[13] "A Hurried Meeting," "A Poor Man and a Lady," "Four Footprints," "A Question of Marriage."

trait of Rake-Hell, as I have elsewhere suggested, there is a large admixture of Hardy. When he said that there was more autobiography in a hundred lines of his poetry than in all his novels I think this is what he meant. The external incidents may well have been suggested by his observation and experience; his treatment of them colored by his own spirit. Actually, he does not give us a true picture of the rustic. He rather gives us a picture of how the rustic would behave and what he would say were he possessed of Hardy's sensitivity and his command of language.

The conventional-minded persons would call some of his young carefree village girls loose. But not Hardy. He sees them as unselfish. One is indifferent to marriage so long as nothing comes between her lover and her; another, fallen upon evil days in Rou'tor Town, cares less for what happened to her than for the evil she brought upon her lover; a third is the type of woman difficult for a man to understand. She just is not interested in marriage, will not be tied to one person, and is satisfied with episodes of "comradeship." Hardy understood what Shaw has brilliantly portrayed, that few women are ever "ruined" who are not willing to be and that few are ever subjected to the manhandling to which Richardson made Clarissa Harlowe submit. He also knew that the average young man is a babe-in-the-woods compared to a smart woman. He is the gullible one.[14]

The power of passion fascinates the person who is not passion's slave; and it fascinated Hardy under whatever guise it appeared, but never more than when it was powerful enough to make women defy conventional morality, particularly when it was powerful enough to impel a woman to adultery. The ironic possibilities of the theme, particularly the bondage that may come to those less directly concerned challenged him. The variations are numerous, with sometimes the men, but more often the woman, the chief protagonists.[15] The phenomenon of unhappy wives and husbands attempting to find some bliss in imagining that the person embraced is the desired rather than the actual person is not unusual.

[14] "A Maiden's Pledge," "I Rose and Went to Rou'tor Town," "The Mound," "At the Altar Rail."
[15] "At a Pause in a Country Dance," "On Martock Moor," "In the Restaurant."

But one wonders at the attitude of the husband of "In the Nuptial Chamber" when he learns that he is playing the role of substitute. The situation is ironic, but not necessarily tragic, depending on the degree of his sense of humor and the extent to which his passions are engaged. Nor is the phenomenon unusual of a woman who is willing to sacrifice everything for love, and of a man who is not ("In the Restaurant"). Hardy saw that pride and loss of social position may make a woman less willing to face the world; but where loss of high social position is not involved, the case is different. On the whole, man is actually a little more conventional than most women, or at least more idealistic. He may profess to set little store by chastity and virginity, but actually, he cares greatly about it. His basic, unconscious reactions overbalance his intellectual attitude, because more primal, more deeply rooted than the later encrustation of the intellectual. A wise woman, he says, will at least pretend to virginity. She should not make herself common, lest she find that, having surrendered to her lover, he will no longer approach her with the eagerness he had earlier shown. Or lest she find herself in the sorry plight of another girl who paid too dearly for winning the young man against his reason. Of the poems on this and closely allied themes the latter ballad is the most convincing, being a bare and objective statement of the situation without the undue elaboration of which the poet is sometimes guilty.[16]

We must remember, however, that Hardy never criticizes his characters nor consciously moralizes on the incidents; yet a moral is possible, just as a similar moral is possible from an observation of the extensional world. With no axe to grind, he yet furnishes enough examples to warrant the induction that one cannot flaunt the social mores without paying the price. For everyone who escapes, many are caught. The least one pays is worry and fear of discovery; the greatest death.[17]

Late nineteenth century melodrama is full of betrayed girls driven from home with their bastard children. But Hardy knew that worse than parental wrath can be the workings of conscience, especially if, as in "The Ballad of Love's Skeleton" and "Reluctant Confession,"

---

[16] "The Tarrying Bridegroom," "The Supplanter."
[17] "The War-Wife of Catknoll," "At Shag's Heath, 1685."

a child's death may be the prompting instrument. In both poems he captures the mental torment of the woman, the ballad carrying more overtones because of the strong contrast of the setting and situation, with the woman's mental state intensified to the degree that her love for the young man is an all-embracing one. He only rarely suggests, however, that woman's price is the higher.[18]

He realized long before Shaw in *Mrs. Warren's Profession* that drudgery is not the best inducement for a young girl's happiness, and in "The Ruined Maid," with its lively anapestic rhythms and its humorous touches, gives evidence that some of the ways to free oneself are easier than long hours of digging potatoes until one's hands are like paws and one's face blue and bleak. He compresses the plight of many such women in the narrow compass of "The Fight on Durnover Moor," a typical Hardyesque poem in the ironic manner in which fate deals blindly, without respect to alleviating conditions. A blind god acting blindly makes through two men a similar pattern of the lives of two girls, both expectant mothers without benefit of clergy. Whereas the lover of one is on the way to see about having the marriage banns published, the other acts cruelly to his woman. The couples meet and instinctively the generous man goes to the aid of the badly treated woman, engages her tormentor in fight, and is killed when he strikes his head against a stone. The world sees little difference in the two women.

But however much Hardy may see women as frivolous, foolish, or flighty, he is also aware that they are often noble and self-sacrificing, and have refused to cheapen themselves to gain their men. When such a woman marries she loves deeply; when widowed she sorrows in the same way. If a widow, she listens unconcernedly to the raging gale, knowing that it can no longer frighten her because of her concern for her husband. She has attained the peace of Maurya at the close of *Riders to the Sea*. She can be brave at parting; she may even maintain an outward air of conventionality which falls away when she thinks she is unobserved.[19]

Hardy watched pride prevent love's blossoming and marriage. He was fascinated by its occurrence in other moments of life when

[18] "The Man with the Past."
[19] "She Hears the Storm," "On Stinforth Hill at Midnight," "Seen by the Waits."

it sometimes won his commendation. Nothing, in fact, about women really failed to interest him. He noted their frequent superstitious susceptibility, especially where it concerned the death of a beloved; he was amused at their reasons for marriage; the manner in which a woman consciously or unconsciously sets out to catch a man; and the operation of fancy. He saw that a woman does not always conform to the masculine idea that she lives for love alone; and he can understand the woman of "The Chapel Organist" willing to sacrifice everything for the sake of her music. He sympathized with the surging uplift of soul of the heroine of "Heiress and Architect" who could ill brook the prison of practicality; and he found matter of interest in the ironic situation of a girl's destroyed happiness in the age before the dentist when by a "dream's nervous bite" she broke her front tooth and thereby lost the new-won favor of the prince. He was aware, too, that for some unfortunate souls youth is a time for happiness and old age a time for sighs; but he also realized, as did Yeats in a different way, that Jenny has many spiritual sisters and brothers.[20]

Hardy's portrait gallery is full of different types; and he fails only when he sees with an unconsciously jaundiced eye—when, for example, he looks at the women, or the men, he met in the fashionable world, or high society, call it what you will. Only then are his portraits unconvincing. This is as true in his novels as in his poems.

In a note of December 10, 1888, he gives us the clue to his treatment of men and woman and why he blames them for their actions. They are merely puppets of a greater power. "He, she, had blundered; but not as the Prime Cause had blundered. He, she, had sinned, but not as the Prime Cause had sinned. He, she, was ashamed and sorry; but not as the Prime Cause would be ashamed and sorry if it knew."

Hardy's woman frequently shows up best in the poems where she does in life—after the death of her beloved. Quite possibly she will react slowly to the news of his death and say things that might indicate that she did not care, although already her heart had begun

---

[20] "The Woman in the Rye," "The Inscription," "The Harvest Supper," "O I Won't Lead a Homely Life," "A Watering-Place Lady Inventoried," "A Woman's Fancy," "The Gap in the White, 178–," "The Singing Woman," "The Dance at the Phoenix."

to break. She may lose all interest in life, or she may even wish death for herself; she may try to recapture through dreams some of the past moments together by looking in the direction she last saw him; or by cherishing mementoes. The greatest sorrow is that of the woman who must conceal her sorrow and must deprive herself of the comfort of sympathy.[21]

I suppose there are some types of women that Hardy omits. Most of those he writes about live in small villages and market towns. They are largely elemental creatures not altered by too much education. They are natural creatures. I think, however, he was little interested in the superficial variations resulting from difference of economic strata. It was the basic qualities in women that interested him. I can think of no man in recent years who possesses his understanding of them. In fact, we must look at the women in Meredith, Shakespeare, and Donne for a comparable understanding, although their women, as I have already mentioned, are of a different social world. In Hardy, however, they do not become highly individualized and vitalized as do Cordelia, Goneril, Lady Macbeth, Cleopatra, Viola, and others; we do not even know their names. We recognize their relationship with their earlier sisters, in spite of their being village rather than court-bred. They blend into their setting, and few, seeing them in the village street stopping to look into a shopwindow, would fathom the qualities behind the appearance, or in which one lay the passion, the hate, the cruelty, the love, the power of self-sacrifice, the capacity for sorrow that Hardy found in them.

When we finish the poems we realize that the only valid generalization about women is valueless: women are women. We cannot speak of them as strong and weak because, as Hardy pointed out, by one set of standards a woman may be weak, by another strong. The great diversity in nuance arises from the fact that he shows woman as motivated by emotion rather than intellect. Much of the misunderstanding between the sexes in life as in his poems arises from a difference of motivation in the actions of each. A man is capable of a detachment to a problem that permits an objectivity

[21] "The Slow Nature," "Signs and Tokens," "Bereft," "Bereft, She Thinks She Dreams," "The Riddle," "The New Boots," and "She."

which can eliminate or simplify its difficulties. Just because a woman is incapable of this intellectual approach she needlessly complicates her life. This does not mean, of course, that there are not exceptions in both sexes, nor does it mean that in something that does not touch her emotions closely a woman is incapable of using her intellect. Lawyers know, for example, that in cases involving women, women jurors are more penetrating, more objective than a man. But the norm of women is more emotionally motivated than the norm of men.

But what of the men in these poems that help us to an understanding of women? If we study them carefully in their inconspicuous roles I think we can learn much. Frequently it is the unerring accuracy of the poet in capturing their exact mental attitudes that gives the poem its permanent value. Hardy understands man's imagination far better than he understands that of a woman, if we can judge by the portraits of women other women have given us. Perhaps I should say he better understands one man's imagination, and that man is himself and a ubiquitous personage in the poems. He has frequently invested his women with more imagination than they can rightfully claim to possess; he endows them with the imaginative power of a sensitive poet rather than with the imagination of a person of restricted point of view.

But of one thing we may be certain. He has broadened our sympathy and understanding of the type of girls Tess knew at the dairy farm. We know them not only as they appear at the farm, but as they appear on the streets of Dorchester, or when they have gone to London to work. He does not give us studio portraits, but incisive line drawings and occasional genre pictures à la Breughel, but a refined Breughel. The theme of women who retain their romantic ideals about sex until it is too late for a realistic attitude to be of any help is capable of many variations, and Hardy exploits them all.

⋙4⋘

A MISCELLANY

T<small>HE</small> QUALITIES in Hardy's work which have brought upon him the charge of pessimism most frequently manifest themselves in poems dealing with his conception of God, Free Will, Fate, and other imponderables—the subject matter of Chapter 5. To see those conceptions in their true light we must first understand the conditioning process which made such ideas possible. Hardy was not one who could look at life without passion; yet he was wise enough not to strive against those things against which striving would be vain. He was objective as few persons have been. He looked at the evanescence of youth and saw too truly that youth, like the leaves that come in the flowery springtime, has no to-morrow and lives but as a sunlit afternoon. He saw the unceasing mutations about him and could not see that they carried with them any gain. He experienced age and found in it no particular cause for rejoicing. He read the Bible, studied art and architecture, and listened to music. Their story was the same. He looked at love and woman and cherished few illusions about either. Everywhere he looked a glory seemed to have passed from the earth, and he lacked Wordsworth's faith in the value of the obstinate questionings of sense and outward things that occupied his attention. He not only looked at the many diverse and unrelated matters about him, but he spoke about them. What he said helps explain his general statements on nondebatable and therefore most hotly contested ideas. A study of his images (Chapter 8) will by implication throw as much or more light than the direct statements. We must never lose sight of the fact that Hardy's absolutes, as Mr. Blunden has observed, "were conjectural first and last from a profound submission to the diurnal visible microcosm of Wessex." (*Thomas Hardy*, p. 3.)

His intimate acquaintance with the Bible, for example, is more evident in the images taken from it than in any of the poems dealing directly with Biblical subjects; his attitude toward youth, mutability, age, and death has already received partial treatment in the chapters on love and woman; his attitude toward art, in the discussion of his aesthetics. His interest in architecture and its basic form manifests itself in the structure of his poems, his handling of detail, his images, as much as in poems with a direct architectural bearing. This being so, the reader must constantly remember that this chapter, like that on nature, cannot tell the whole story any more than could a chapter on Hardy's humor, basic characteristics of which I have suggested in Chapter I, and details of which every reader can and must supply for himself.

What the present chapter intends, then, is a treatment of those poems which fall wholly in any one of several categories such as Youth, Mutability, Age, Death, and so forth—that is, as far as any poem can ever fall wholly into any category. We shall find in these poems that Hardy's approach to his subject is a mature one. He achieved what only a few succeed in doing; because only a few have within themselves the divine spark of discontent that keeps them forever struggling forward in their attempt to penetrate the barriers of the unknown. Only a few persons, indeed, have the courage to examine themselves with sufficient minuteness and objectivity to see the fetters of selfishness that hold them back and retard their development. Only a few have a scholarly attitude toward life or the enviable philosophy of a Henry Ryecroft. Because the scholarly attitude and maturity are synonymous. Each is the ability to examine dispassionately the facts of a problem under consideration and from such an examination arrive at a judgment justifiable by those facts, even though it mean that the effort has been fruitless and the results negative. Few persons are willing to admit they have barked too long up the wrong tree and have worried but a squirrel.

Hardy was a scholar in the true sense of the word—a scholar of life. Throughout his long years of literary activity he examined and reexamined the minutiae of life as he could find them. He had a catholicity of interest akin to that of Goethe. Music, art, science, history, and philosophy moved him profoundly. He was not afraid, however, to say that he found few judgments about life possible. His poems report, but rarely do they judge. The reader of his poetry who is emboldened to judgments that Hardy carefully refrained from is the lesser scholar. And yet Hardy did arrive at some conclusions. Before talking about them, however, it will be well to examine with some detail his individual reports. Admittedly, the subject division is arbitrary, and will be unsatisfactory to many. Much overlapping blurs the outlines. The thoughts of a man who embraces all phases of life are not easily compartmentalized and therefore puzzle those who like to save themselves the anguish of thought by using inaccurate and stultifying terms that attempt to reduce a creator to their own level of impoverishment. No poet writes with such things as classicism and romanticism in mind. He attempts to make lucid his inward thoughts, nothing more. He is not, naturally, always of one mood; Hardy least of all.

I. Youth, Mutability, Age, Death

Hardy reveals his attitude toward children in "In the Waiting Room," a poem recounting an incident that happened one day in a railway waiting room. In a copy of the Gospel of St. John which was lying on a table, the narrator found some figures—multiplications, additions, and so forth. These led his mind along devious paths; first, to the soul of the man who had used the Testament to figure his profits and loss, then to a soldier and his wife about to separate, and, finally, to their children in high spirits. The innocence of these carefree children spread, he felt, a "glory through the gloom."

He also saw, however, that youth, secure in its own estimation of self, frequently has a tolerant and patronizing attitude toward age; that it imagines things about it that never are and never can be, just as age in retrospect distorts that early period, highlighting it according to the islands of joy and pain that rise from the sea of memory. Age, for example, delights in distorting the happiness and suffering of the sensitive rather than of the average person. Youth thinks it sees clearly, and, considering its limited experience, frequently does. It sees, for example, with surprising lucidity the means for the attainment of an immediate and selfish end. Rarely is it capable of a view sufficiently distant to assure itself increasing happiness and satisfaction. Nor can youth be blamed, because it has before it the life patterns of persons older in years but of no greater maturity.

This attitude of children with only the future to look forward to accounts for the difference in their and the poet's attitude toward the present. "Experience," said Hardy (December 12, 1885), *"un-*teaches." Two weeks later he continued: "The Hypocrisy of things. Nature is an arch-dissembler. A child is deceived completely; the older members of society more or less according to their penetration; though even they seldom get to realize that nothing is as it appears."

The difference between a child's fancy and a poet's vision is an almost unbridgeable gulf. The child sees only a quiet house in the midst of a shady lawn. The poet, possessing the "visioning powers of souls who dare to pierce the material screen" sees a constant activity; figures that dance, music and laughter, a place

> Through which there pass, in fleet arrays
> Long teams of all the years and days,
> Of joys and sorrows, of earth and heaven,
> That meet mankind in its ages seven,
> An aion in an hour.
> —"The House of Silence"

Age is not, however, a time for memories; or should not be. It is a time for a realistic attitude. The young man of twenty, as we all know to our own discomfort and occasional dismay, has no hesitation in expressing his views about the purpose, tendencies, and shortcomings of life. He has the confidence of ignorance. The thoughtful person is less certain than are so many of these young men of "what Earth's ingrained conditions are." At best, life can be no more than a steady progress from youth and innocence to old age and experience; from cocksureness to inquiring skepticism, although the things about which one is cocksure alter from generation to generation.[1] Hardy thought much of what youth misses. He saw that the clarity of vision with which youth seems to himself

[1] "Seventy-Four and Twenty," "After Reading Psalms XXXIX, XLV, etc.," "Boys Then and Now."

to walk is only relative. Instead of seeing and enjoying the world about him, instead of luxuriating in the sensuous milieu which nature provides, he loses himself in a world of reveries. He dreams of the great things he will accomplish, of his triumphs and successes, and thereby shuts himself from the glorious reality about him. A sense of what he has missed, of what he has only half-apprehended, comes too late to be of any real service:

> O it would have been good
> Could he then have stood
> At a clear-eyed distance, and conned the whole,
> But now such vision
> Is mere derision,
> Nor soothes his body nor saves his soul.
>
> —"Self-Unconscious"

Hardy resembles Wordsworth in his tendency to look back upon a scene and invest it with more than it could possibly have meant to him at the time ("The Voice of Things"). Their difference, however, is that Wordsworth is always careful to let us know that perhaps he has read too much into his earlier feelings; Hardy, too little. Both only do what mature persons tend to do: evaluate early sensations in the light of mature ones.

Readers of Wordsworth vividly remember the poet's consternation when he discovered that he had *crossed* the Alps; that he had finished what he thought he was only beginning; that a moment that he had expected to be epochal in his life of sensation had passed unobserved. Frost generalizes on this in "West-Running Brook"; we can only see how far we have come by looking back. Hardy, too, dwells on this oft-recurring phenomenon in poems of unequal merit, sometimes recounting specific moments; sometimes making a general statement. Even when one grasps the significance of a rare moment that must stand out as one to be cherished, he knew that its effect is apt to be impaired by the intrusion of the saddening thought that an equal ecstasy is incapable of recapture. "O value what the nonce outpours" is indeed good advice, but few can heed it.[2]

Hardy is not only interested in the islands of memory of youth

[2] "The Temporary the All," "Best Times," "You on the Tower," "The Lady of Forebodings," "The Musical Box."

as things of unusual luminosity; he is fascinated by the changes they undergo with the washings of the steadily flowing years. The changes are as much in the observer as in the things observed. The mutation is in the imponderable relative as well as in the ponderable object under observation; the mutation of youth succumbing to age, or the invisible mutation in an inanimate object. Hardy gives an upward swing to the saddening thought of time's mutations in the last line of "The Second Visit," conjuring before us a living picture of the young lover who attempted to win his way by chiding the girl that she no longer loved him, and her impulsive response—"You know I do." Such occasional lines vitalize a whole poem and punctuate its calm revery. The poet repeats the theme of mutation, or rather subordinates it for an atmospheric effect of desolation in "The Selfsame Song" and "Where They Lived."

Anniversaries serve little purpose except to remind one of the mutational process, and to the unpracticed eye no change may be visible. The artist detects the minute differences: the tree has become wind-cracked, the walls overgrown with moss, the eyeballs sunken. He not only detects the difference, but he recaptures in his rhythms his different reactions at different times to the same phenomena. A tree frequently serves as the symbol of the never-ceasing changes. It may be a little sycamore tree that becomes the long-limbed sycamore tree; it may be a wind-break that only reaches a point of effectiveness when the planter of it is about to die; or it may be an elm tree to whose rings life may be compared. A child, however, still untaught by life is incapable of grasping its steady changes, and cannot conceive of a time when the beech woods were not there.[3]

Hardy realized that the processes of mutation worked unequally on different persons and in different ways. That is why he knew that a return to the haunts of one's earlier years must be disillusioning and unsatisfactory. It is these returns that emphasize the changes, because he sees at one glance a decade's rather than a gradual day's exaction of its toll—the outward changes and the weakening of the will. What any person may fail to realize, how-

[3] "An Anniversary," "The Ageing House," "Everything Comes," "The Felled Elm and She," "At Day-Close in November."

ever, is that the way of life of those left behind has so far altered
as to make him as uninteresting to them as they are to him.[4] In
poems of this nature the prosodic form must control the nostalgic
mood, but Hardy sometimes mars the effectiveness of his com-
munication by the choice of a wrongly attuned metrical pattern.
That of "His Visitor," for example, has too facile a lilt to be wholly
effective.

Man's attempt to force his way across the rushing waters of time
to the little islands of memory whose outlines are softened by the
engulfing mist is a disillusioning or a saddening task. Wise is the
person who never returns to his alma mater for a class reunion or
pays a belated visit to the schoolhouse so provocative of pleasant
memories. Never return in the flesh, says Hardy. One should wait
until he can return as a ghost. Then he will avoid the realization
of being out of place.

> But to show in the afternoon sun,
> With an aspect of hollow-eyed care,
> When none wished to see me come there,
> Was a garish thing, better undone.
> Yes; wrong was the way
> But yet, let me say,
> I may right it—some day.
> —"He Revisits His First School"

He tempers the bitterness by the humor of the last line. "The
Strange House" shows that he has learned the lesson. He waits
until the year 2000 before returning to Max Gate.

In spite of return being undesirable, its avoidance is sometimes
impossible. Merely to hear the viols playing an old dance tune may
force one into the association of that melody with an earlier and
happier occasion when friends now dead were in their prime, and
oneself at an age when to ask

> O what's to me this tedious Maying,
> What's to me this June?
> —"Song to an Old Burden"

would be impossible. He elsewhere accentuates change by stressing
the absence of passion arising from ignorance of the associative

[4] "His Visitor," "In a Former Resort after Many Years," "Welcome Home."

powers of a melody played by street musicians that a century earlier had caught dancers in an impassioned swirl. He knew that heard melodies are sweet and can be a potent link with the past, but that those unheard, stimulated by the mere sight or thought of the family violin, are sweeter and more powerful. Once freed from auditory and visual limitations, his imagination recreates the vigor and exultation of released passions at a dance or the tender moments of a choir rehearsal, of a church service. So moved he ponders on death, and experiences the loneliness of a sole survivor and the ceaseless modification to which everything is subject.[5]

He is most vividly aware of the sense of mutation in the presence of old women he had known as young girls, although, as I have elsewhere shown, the basis of comparison adopted in "The Former Beauties" is unfair. It is the fault similar to that of which Goldsmith was accused when in "The Deserted Village" he chose an English village for the earlier picture and an Irish village for the later. He is also aware of it in the romantic setting of moonlight when his thoughts are of his earlier years before his metaphorical lute was "strewn with years-deep dust," thoughts from which he would gladly escape.[6] He is no less insistent on the immutable changes in "One We Knew" and the almost hypersensitive "At the Royal Academy" in spite of their quieter mood. So aware was he of this constant progress that he could not even look at a landscape painting without realizing that the limp grass, the new and soft leaves belonged to last season.

Yet beneath this welter of mutations he found some permanence; perhaps only a forgotten miniature, one of time's cold pastorals, or the spirits that throng the deserted market place after the fair, the same breed of men that thronged the spot in Roman days ("After the Fair"). In the novels as well as in the poems, he employs this theme of the essential stability of mankind as a continuous bass for the melody of individual man's change. The least changing thing to the poet, however, is the church, not the institution itself, but the places of worship. He captures in two poems—

[5] "Music in a Snowy Street," "A Merrymaking in Question," "To My Father's Violin," "In the Small Hours."
[6] "Shut Out That Moon," "Seeing the Moon Rise."

"She Revisits Alone, etc.," "The Self Unseeing"—what many persons acutely feel about the small English village churches.

Hardy recognizes that age adjusts itself to change much less readily than youth. The ruts of custom are too deep to be easily got out of, even when the matter is no more than a discussion of parish problems with the new rector. Rather than try to get out, age acquires its stay-at-home propensities and luxuriates in the past, and in the if's of life.[7] What would life have been like without his Florence, Emma, Mary, who had meant so much to him? The order in which he arranges the names—from his second wife to his first to his mother—indicates the route he has traveled from the present to the past, and it certainly is not an order of diminishing importance.

Before too readily accepting Hardy's dicta we must be cautious on one point. He is aware of the mutating processes about him, and seems to be aware of them within himself. But is he? He prided himself on his ability to recall vividly after fifty years the exact mood and proportion of an early incident. But has not time softened the outlines? Has life actually become the hopeless thing he sometimes finds it to be, or is it merely that he cannot face the harshness and brutality of life with the youthful confidence that made him unaware that life is harsh and brutal? Has not the girl become more appealing over the years? Is it not natural to think as one grows older that earlier New Year celebrations were more joyous and carefree than present ones? And is not the seemingly more desolate landscape of today in contrast to the bright and joyous ones of his youth only an indication of age? Hardy was at times fully aware of the affirmative answers to the foregoing questions, but with the passage of years he forgot or chose to forget what he once so clearly realized.[8]

It is a truism that a trifling incident of childhood or youth frequently stands out more clearly in our lives than a later and more important event; in fact, it gains clarity with the years. With Hardy it was the missing of a train because of a girl (a universal incident), a snatch of old song, the scene of a tryst. It requires little to ignite

[7] "The Old Neighbor and the New," "Paying Calls," "Conjectures."
[8] "Green Slates," "At the Entering of the New Year," "At Middle Field Gate in February."

these recollections, and the match need be no more than the slightest associative contact.[9]

However much he might be aware of the outward changes wrought by time—the death of friends, growing bodily infirmities, the vanishing of familiar landmarks, the increasing tendency to dwell in the past—Hardy shared with the aging Yeats and almost every aging person the realization that, in spite of our consciousness of having passed inevitable milestones along our route, our hearts and our spirits remain as young as ever. The paradox of a youthful heart in a withering frame makes life more difficult to bear. It is apt to make a man more crotchety than he would otherwise be if younger men press too eagerly at his heels to share the responsibilities and the rewards for those responsibilities that the world metes out with an unequal hand. He may give way, it is true, but only reluctantly; even then his courage never deserts him.[10] Like those of Yeats, too, Hardy's early poems on age have a sentimental rather than a realistic quality. Writing on age in his prime and vigor, he catches a confident lilt and robustness that he fails to achieve in the later poems.

However young the heart may be, or however much the world and we have changed to outward view, he recognized one inescapable fact—our inevitable dissolution. Does anything remain of us? Are we able to leave an imprint on those material things with which we have come in contact, so that persons not yet born will unconsciously notice our presence ("The Strange House")? Or are we such things as dreams are made on? Those thoughts occupied Hardy early and late and are inextricably bound up with his thoughts of other imponderables of life and with his thoughts on death.

Actually, Hardy on the subject of death is at first disappointing until we realize that he has written on the subject as a careful reader of his other work would expect him to write. His attitude is one neither of negation nor affirmation; it is essentially an attitude of indifference except as he feels the loneliness experienced

[9] "The Missed Train," "A Bygone Occasion," "The Man Who Forgot," "Logs on the Hearth."
[10] "In a Eweleaze Near Weatherbury," "I Look into My Glass," "Superseded," "An Ancient to Ancients."

by the survivor. His attitude toward graveyards—not very different
from that of a healthy extrovert—may throw a flickering light on
the larger subject. His frequent references to them never suggest
morbid connotations. Their proximity to the church and the fre-
quency with which any village inhabitant must necessarily pass by
or through them tends to remove the oppressive quality that is
sometimes associated with those in America. The churchyard in
England, as in America, is a communal meeting place and the pres-
ence of graves and tombstones does not stifle sociability. From an
artist's point of view the parish church is more often than not the
most picturesque object in the village, the best view of which is
from the adjoining graveyard. If not intrinsically beautiful it yet
affords the best composition because it is inflected with its sur-
roundings and serves as a focal point. Hardy confessed that the
pleasant hours he had spent working with another friend amid
these surroundings had robbed churches and churchyards of any
sense of gloom.

He often mused, for example, not only on Death's strange trick of
leaving alone those who do not fear him, but of the persistency with
which some persons visit the cemetery. His own feeling was that
nowhere did one less feel the presence of the departed; he found
it only in association with their customary surroundings.[11]

He was, perhaps, occasionally inclined to become a little impa-
tient with death because it seemed to take away the things we enjoy
most and leave only the undesired pain, age, and suffering; but
such moments were short-lived and gave way to the realization that
death or time shows no discrimination; that it removes the evil as
well as the good; that it is an ever active force that feeds life. Man
returns to dust, for example, fertilizes the earth, and is transformed
into new life; and even though death come in formidable strength
under the guise of war, destruction, or pestilence, it cannot ex-
tinguish certain activities. It may destroy individual men but not
man; it will take this or that particular tiller of the soil, but tillers
of the soil will remain; and lovers. In this knowledge lies comfort.[12]

[11] "The New Dawn's Business," "Her Haunting-Ground," "The Marble Tablet," "My
Spirit Will Not Haunt the Ground."
[12] "Going and Staying," "Transformations," "Life and Death at Sunrise," "In Time of
'The Breaking of Nations.' "

Nor is the worst that can happen the sudden cessation of "Time's enchantments." Harder to bear for many is the gradual day weakening the desire for living—the problems of life, the death of friends, hatred. The man who endures these dies piecemeal and not with epic grandeur. Madness is worse than death; it intrudes upon persons in all walks of life and assumes many different forms.[13]

Without placing an overemphasis on premonitions about death Hardy found them appealing. He is not concerned with those vague premonitions that come to naught; they are of little interest in poetry. He is only interested in their dramatic potentialities, and they need not be personal experiences to start his imagination. For the most part, even when they are personal, they do not foment a strong reaction.[14] But, as elsewhere in Hardy, we do not know what the reasoned conviction of the poet is toward these phenomena. He has reported the incidents; that is all. They are moods of the moment, and I think he would be the first to object if we looked at them in any other way or attached any greater importance to them.

He was also interested in the role of death as the great leveler. "Clamor dogs kingship" (he says in "The Coronation"); "afterwards not so." He could likewise have said the same of beauty and grace. Even so, death is no cause for regret or sorrow, and the idea manifests itself in many ways. We should not mourn nor abstain from our joys, because the departed has escaped from the world's slow stain into a dreamless slumber. Death has liberated him from the cell of Time and from his many wrongers. Or rather death will liberate him when he is no longer misrepresented on the earth, when the world will look behind his deeds to the more important motives that prompted them.[15]

Closely linked with this was his admiration for the person who could meet death with a stoic's fortitude, be it a close friend, Squire Hooper, or a farmer who wanted to be buried on Sunday in order

[13] "The Dead Man Walking," "The Interloper."
[14] "In the Garden," "The Pair He Saw," "She Saw Him, She Said," "The Announcement."
[15] "The Coronation," "A Winsome Woman," "Louie," "Regret Not Me," "After the Last Breath," "Spectres That Grieve."

that his friends could leisurely drink the ten bottles of rum he had liberally provided for them.[16]

Association with death can be and often is the awakening into significant life. Once the mystery has seized the imagination it never relaxes its hold. Whitman and Lawrence have associated themselves more intimately with death than have most poets, and their association has born rich fruit. Hardy, too, rubbed shoulders with death, but he never became absorbed by its mysticism. He remains calm and temperate in its presence. He was generous and compassionate, and therefore free from the rhetoric of judgment. Too often, however, I think, he was merely indifferent. Only occasionally did death jostle him into passionate expression, and rarely did he concern himself with death as an abstraction. He is more apt to think of the brevity in a man's mind of the memory of the death of a close and valued friend, of the disintegration in a household that death causes, or of the imminence of death itself. Life, in fact, is little more than a series of farewells at which it is unwise to show the grief we feel.[17]

To the poet's question "Why did the Immanent Will crown Death king?" the Immanent Will could give no satisfactory reply. It had no meaning as far as It knew. The poet did not ask why death came differently: unnoticed by the watcher, silently, to the unexpecting rather than the expecting. He was content to know that it inevitably came to all.[18]

If we turn from the foregoing poems on death merely to glance at those by John Donne on the same subject we have a point of reference from which we can better estimate Hardy's achievement. I am not primarily interested in which are the better, but the difference of approach is readily apparent. Hardy never gives the impression of wrestling with his subject, of exerting a fiery energy to wrench the utmost from its potentialities that he at other times displays. This lack of exertion is a clue to the small number of great poems by one so prolific. Is he calm in the presence of death

[16] "After the Death of a Friend," "Squire Hooper," "Farmer Dunman's Funeral."
[17] "Unrealized," "A Last Journey," "The Death of Regret," "The Five Students," "Exeunt Omnes," "During Wind and Rain," "Saying Good-bye."
[18] "An Inquiry," "A Watcher's Regret," "The Coming of the End," "After the War," "June Leaves and Autumn."

because he knows it not, or calm because he knows? Or was it merely a universal that lent itself to treatment in verse, a universal to which he could not give his best because he had found no satisfactory answer to the more challenging subject of God?

II. Spiritual Leaders

A great man's greatness seldom exists in his personal relations, but it is from these personal relations that his greatness stems. It is these that keep him linked with reality without which greatness cannot survive; that remind him of his humanity and not his divinity; that keep him to the personal "I" rather than the imperial "We." Hardy has written two groups of poems that bear such a personal relation to the poet that they deserve particular mention. One group treats of Christ and the apostles, the other with the poets whom he admired. Both have their basis in an early enthusiasm that persisted throughout his life. He expresses in the fragment "The Wood Fire" a subject of perennial interest that has inspired poems, short stories, and recently a novel. What was the attitude of the average person among Jesus' contemporaries to his crucifixion? Was he aware that the executed person was destined to shed a light of such magnitude over the world that even those dwelling in the shadows and darkness claim to be suffused in the light lest they be scorned by their fellows also dwelling in the shadows? The fragment tells the story of the burning of the crucifix. It is cheaper to burn, at least the cross-arm which is apt to be split by the nails, than to repair. Hardy wisely left this a fragment; it is better so. No ending could improve its suggestive potentialities. He also recreates in modern dress Peter's thrice-denial of Christ. The picture has the subtle appeal of Breughel's *Massacre of the Innocents* with its reenactment of the Biblical story in a Flemish village with a sixteenth century populace.[19] He imparts a sense of immediacy to the tragic realization that in any period Christ would fare the same. He rejects the story of the virgin birth, so dear to those who need magic rather than impressive truth to be aroused even to a faint emotion, and explains Mary's incapability of understand-

[19] "In the Servants' Quarters."

ing her son.[20] Why should so handsome a young man neglect his personal appearance, talk so wildly and confusedly about things? Why associate with publicans and sinners immediately after charging persons to obey the commandments? When he asks Mary, "Woman, what have I to do with thee?" or "Who is my mother?" knowing very well, he must, she says, be mad.

> He might have said, "Who is my father?"
> —and I'd found it hard to tell!
> *That* no one knows but Joseph and—one other, nor ever will;
> One who'll not see me again . . . How it chanced!—I dream-
> ing no ill! . . .

Distance has likewise lent enchantment to St. Paul just as it has done to Christ. Is there anyone, Hardy asks in "In St. Paul's a While Ago," who, if he heard St. Paul preaching on the steps of the cathedral bearing his name, would not brand him as an "epilept enthusiast?"

Hardy's clarity of vision enabled him to see and to feel passionately what few persons wish to. The spiritual barrenness of the age, however, effected a relaxation in his will to fight. It may be true that following Darwin's publication of the *Origin of the Species* he read with interest, understanding, and sympathy the reactions of men of vision in *Essays and Reviews,* but it is not clear that he was fired with the same enthusiasm as the authors. Hardy was no Milton, no young Wordsworth. In spite of his faith in Tom, Dick, and Harry, and the graciousness he was able to maintain in his personal relations, when he looked on mankind as a whole it was not with an outraged idealism such as we find in the poets of the nineteen twenties and early thirties, but it was with an idealism, the fire of which his sensitivity demanded that he cover over. From time to time when he thought the world was improving he uncovered the smoldering coals and a flame licked forth. The circumstance was short-lived and he laid on more ashes.

He expressed a sentiment in "A Christmas Ghost Story," inspired by the Boer war, which was equally appropriate twenty years later, and were he alive today he would find it as fitting now as when originally expressed. When, asks the phantom of the dead soldier,

---

[20] "Panthera," "An Evening in Galilee."

was Christ's message of peace ruled to be out of place? Why do we continue to count the years "Anno Domini" when the cause for which he died has not triumphed and men are still slaughtered? The poet is not embittered, he is saddened. He is past the age when he can be moved to the passionate exhortation of the thirty-seven-year-old poet who cried out against the selfishness of the church, the army, the writers, against every class of persons, in fact, who had lost sight of their spiritual goal, in the soul-stirring "Milton! Thou shouldst be living at this hour." He is past the age, too, when he is capable of the passionate utterance of the fifty-year-old Milton. Although not wholly content to put only his own house in order he felt the futility of attempting to help men who prided themselves on being realists, not aware that an idealist not only sees all that a realist sees, but sees farther, to the ultimate rather than to the immediate results.

Yet he realized that the spirit of Christ did not exist in isolated cases. He saw a laborer standing before a stone from the Areopagus thrilled by the thought that that stone once echoed the voice of St. Paul. He knew, too, that many others besides Christ had been persecuted for their beliefs although their deaths have not been celebrated in Good Fridays. Like some strange bird these persons mingled for a while with the barn-door brood and then vanished.

In a world where lip service is paid to spiritual values and a deep knee-bending reverence to materialistic ones, it is no matter for surprise that the great spiritual leaders of any age are not, nor ever were, recognized by the masses. They are not recognized because of the simplicity and the humility which resides at the heart of religion. It speaks well for the vitality of the spiritual values, however, that even the uncomprehending feel that they gain in respectability by acknowledging their worth and position—at least, if Time has had the opportunity by its slow incremental powers to raise them to their proper place on the heights. Hardy found in the stories of the poets substantiation for his poems on Christ and Paul. Is it not likely that the same situation has always existed? It takes the united work of the small groups of several generations to counteract the limiting powers of the majority of any generation. It is one of the ironies of life, and a fortunate one for the minority, that the work of the materialists of one generation is completely lost sight of by the materialists of a generation a few times removed, whereas the work of the minority is never lost, but steadily gains new adherents.

Think of Shakespeare, the least capturable of themes. His contemporaries of Stratford saw only his material prosperity and had no conception of the reaches of his imagination nor of the influence he was destined to exert. Keats is another. Had anyone seen him in 1820 when he landed at Lulworth Cove for a day, he would have been unimpressed. He could not have imagined the depth of emotion aroused in the young man by his observation of the evening star. Yet a hundred years later people visited the house in Rome where he had died, visited his grave in the Protestant Cemetery, and paid visits to his house on Hampstead Heath, now a museum. Hardy saw the irony of the situation of his and Shelley's grave in the shadow of the pyramid of Cestius. Who was Cestius? Perhaps one of the rich men of his day, a materialist. But who now remembers him except as his tomb guides visitors to the graves of the poets? One instinctively recalls the fate of Ozymandias. More recently dull officialdom with its narrow vision has denied Swinburne a place in the Poets' Corner, Swinburne the poet who had pierced the drabness of Victorian sham:

> —It was as though a garland of red roses
> Had fallen about the hood of some smug nun
> When irresponsibly dropped as from the sun,
> In fulth of numbers freaked with musical closes,
> Upon Victoria's formal middle time
> His leaves of rhythm and rhyme.
> —"A Singer Asleep"

Meredith fared somewhat differently and to him Hardy gave different praise.

> He was of those whose wit can shake
> And riddle to the very core
> The counterfeits that Time will break.
> —"George Meredith"

How effectively can be seen in Meredith's novels and poems; with what directness of untransmuted feeling, in his letters.[21] To believe

[21] "To Shakespeare," "At a House in Hampstead," "At Lulworth Cove," "Shelley's Skylark," "Rome," "A Refusal."

as Hardy does that Time will riddle counterfeits to the very core strikes a note of optimism which he cannot, however, always sustain.

What Hardy saw must have had some effect on his attitude toward the great abstractions. What is the nature of a God who can let such things be? Is there justice in a being who can withhold the light from ten thousand and give it to one? Such problems have always confronted thinking man and each age has attempted a solution.

God has been variously appraised and interpreted. Seventeenth century poets found the solution in predestination; earlier peoples in tribal deities in conflict with one another; Hardy, inductively, in an unknowing, conscienceless God. Have not all missed the truth, and Hardy as much as any?

That he attempted by inductive means to arrive at the truth is abundantly clear. Whether or not his final inductions are correct is disputable. But what was the nature of those inductions? Did he become so immersed in the relatives that he overlooked the absolutes? The question is not a rhetorical one. It is the question of the nature of Good and Evil which is again stirring the world. Are these relatives or are they absolutes? Hardy's literary fate depends on the answers.

⋙ 5 ⋘

SOME IMPONDERABLES

Any ATTEMPT at a neat synthesis of the accumulated data of the foregoing chapters must necessarily fail, because these data do not result from an integrated philosophy of life. They are exploratory. Hardy could not make such an integration and he was honest enough to admit it. His poems were, he said, "merely . . . a confused heap of impressions, like those of a bewildered child at a conjuring show." That they are only that constitutes his weakness. But he was not a person to surrender easily. He observed life carefully, thought about what he saw, read the philosophers, believed he had learned a lesson from their "contradictions and futilities," and came to this:

Let every man make a philosophy for himself out of his own experience. He will not be able to escape using terms and phraseology from earlier philosophers, but let him avoid adopting their theories if he values his own mental life. Let him remember the fate of Coleridge, and save years of labor by working out his own views as given him by his surroundings (December 31, 1901).[1]

This, of course, is what every thoughtful person does and must do. Before accepting others' ideas he must feel them emotionally, else they cannot become a part of him. They will be superfluous bits of decoration that mar the essential form of the original. Nor is feeling them emotionally sufficient. He must subject them to close scrutiny, correlating them with other ideas he has fused into a harmonious whole. The process will involve a merciless scraping out of certain colors from the picture in order that cleaner tones of the palette may be introduced without destroying the essential

[1] Italics added.

form. Too many persons tend to muddy the painting by overlaying the colors. If the tones of the new palette do not clash with the old, but differ only in tonal quality, they must still be worked in with care. There must be no sense of patchwork.

Another jotting (May 5, 1902) reveals the strong element of chance he found in life:

Life is what we make it as Whist is what we make it; but not as Chess is what we make it which ranks higher as a purely intellectual game than either Whist or Life.

We must believe Hardy in such statements. He was moving in the right direction, but two obstacles kept him from his goal: the limitations of his age and the limitations within himself. They are not easily separable. I suggested in Chapter 1 possible influences on his development. Hardy had to struggle with himself before he could accept those influences. He had first to reject the easy generalizations about God, man, and the universe with which he had grown up; he then had to move forward with these new ideas that were under constant attack from all sides. To do this meant that he made the mistake of many persons under similar conditions; he began to overstress the power of reason and to deny those transcendental values necessary for a complete life. He could no more accept than could his thinking contemporaries Pippa's depressing optimism that "God's in his heaven. All's right with the world."

Since he was forced into the line of most resistance, since he had to fight every inch of the way, it is little wonder that he could not reach far enough. The same expenditure of energy in the thirteenth, seventeenth, or mid-twentieth century would have sent him higher.

Unbeguiled by wishful thinking, he examined every straw that might possibly sustain him through a difficult period. He grasped at many, but even those he clutched tightly could not long sustain him.

When he saw science pushing back the limits of the universe, saw psychologists making discoveries in human behavior, had ample evidence to support the theory that fate acts blindly, felling alike the innocent and guilty, a childhood or adolescent faith was little comfort to him. He would have liked to believe attractive theories that might lend an inner security, but he was not easily beguiled.

> ——And dwell you in that glory show?
> You may; for there are strange strange things in being,
> Stranger than I know.
>   —"He Prefers Her Earthly"

He struggled to formulate his own philosophical system but finally confessed that the sum total of his struggle was only a series of impressions. We must not, however, minimize his achievement. He has been a powerful influence on the present age. Although he failed to reach the goal himself, except perhaps once in "The Absolute Explains," a position to which he did not cling, he has helped others to greater heights. They have profited from his failures. He has taught us that negation, useful as it might be in definition, is not sufficient. He never transcended negation as did Dante and Milton. He was born too late to be able to have the vision of the early Wordsworth. Unlike the later Wordsworth, however, who refused to forge a new instrument of expression for his ideas and thereby became dull, Hardy did not refuse. His trouble is more serious. He began too late to perfect himself in the manifold subtleties of the smith's art.

The actual distance traversed by Hardy in his thinking is as great as or greater than many who have traveled higher. The regret is that he had to begin so low. He rightly rejected loose generalizations about God and the universe and attempted by the inductive method and a deep sincerity to arrive at concepts firmly enough founded to give him support. He gives us a clue to an insurmountable difficulty in the phrase "development according to perfect reason" taken from a jotting made in 1880: Since he lived, he wrote, in

a world where nothing bears out in practice what it promises incipiently, I have troubled myself very little about theories. . . . When development according to perfect reason is limited to the narrow region of pure mathematics, I am content with tentativeness from day to day.

He was subject to the limitations for which Descartes has been largely responsible—the insistence on an interpretation of life and the universe limited by reason.

This exaltation of reason had not only persisted, but had grown during the eighteenth and well into the nineteenth century. Tom Paine, the young Wordsworth, and the young Coleridge exalted it with enthusiasm. Hardy was under its influence. It had been rejected by some of his contemporaries, it is true, but their manner of rejection was unconvincing. Their distrust of reason arose not from the probings of minds that could go no further; but from minds afraid to go far enough. The hollowness of their affirmations of success implied defeat rather than victory. Had Hardy not distrusted himself he might have reached the goal, so near he was to it.

Since, therefore, Hardy lacked a philosophical system but depended on his observation of diverse phenomena for his conception of any absolutes, it would be foolhardy to attempt to find what he admitted was not there. We may attempt, however, to give some element of form to the generalizations which he felt justified in deducing from his observations over a long span of years. Nothing can be omitted, because he believed that his poetry could not be truly judged until its last line was written; until, in other words, he had finished his observations, a matter about which he had definite ideas. On July 1, 1892, he wrote:

The art of observation (during travel, etc.) consists in this: the seeing of great things in little things, the whole in the part—even the infinitesimal part. For instance, you are abroad: you see an English flag on a ship-mast from the window of your hotel; you realize the English navy. Or, at home, in a soldier you see the British Army; in a bishop at your club, the Church of England; and in a steam hooter you hear Industry.[2]

He thought that a too widely appreciative mind could fail to achieve its work from "pure far-sightedness":

The very clearness with which he discerns remote possibilities is, from its nature, scarcely ever co-existent with the microscopic vision demanded for tracing the narrow path that leads to them. (June 19, 1867.)

Everywhere his poetry attests his keenness of observation. A note from the *Early Life* shows his inclination to view other persons as being in a "somnambulistic state, making their motions automati-

[2] It is interesting to compare this statement with Frost's about the importance of synecdoche.

cally—not realizing what they mean." A late observation (August 21, 1888) affords a parallel: "Society consists of Characters and No-Characters—nine at least of the latter to one of the former." The "no-characters" not only jealously protect their self-importance but seek to enhance it. They reject anything that would tend to diminish it, and, because they do, Hardy did not expect a favorable reception of his *Moments of Vision,* which contained poems, he said, that "mortify the human sense of self-importance by showing, or suggesting, that human beings are of no matter of appreciable value in this nonchalant universe."

Hardy needed no gestalt psychologist to convince him that we all have many facets. "I am more than ever convinced," he wrote on December 4, 1890, "that persons are successively various persons, according as each special strand in their characters is brought uppermost by circumstances." A teacher, for example, shows one facet to his students, another to his family, a third to his larger acquaintance, a fourth to the few intimates with whom he can share his dreams, a fifth to the woman who has helped him realize certain aspects of his emotional nature; and other facets to others. He knows which facet is appropriate to which group. He dreams of the person to whom he will be able to reveal all and not be misunderstood; but he knows that unless he is blessed above others, he dreams in vain, that some of the things most precious to him must remain his own secret because the terminology he would be forced to use would give the wrong impression. He knows, too, that these many aspects are not contradictory, however much they may appear to be so; often they are but the reverse side of the same facet.

Hardy realized, too, that his sincerity placed him at a disadvantage. He knew that few readers could appreciate all the facets that as an artist he felt impelled to show; knew that conditioned by what he had already shown them, they could not approach the new facet without prejudice. Yet he persisted. He tried to prevent distortion in the reader's vision by cataloguing in "So Various" the many facets he characteristically revealed in his novels, poems, and notebooks. To understand the catalogue is better to understand him. Even this, however, is not enough. Each facet is colored by the emotion that plays on it; by the frequent dominance of the heart over the head ("He Follows Himself"). We have an example of this in the theme of "Concerning His Old Home." In one mood he remembers an early dwelling as a dismal place he would willingly forget; in a second, as a memorial place he would be faintly glad to see once more; in a third, as a friendly place he would willingly see at any time; and last, as a lovable place that drives regret away. For a reader unwilling to recognize the multiple moods and characteristics, the poet's thought is bound to be distorted, in the manner recorded in "A Poet's Thought."

The distortion arises, too, from a yet deeper cause. The reader fails to grasp the poet's symbolism. Time, God, Fate, and Chance are symbols for evoking associations as well as for stimulating new thought. These symbols often fail in their purpose, however, because they fail to stir in the reader the profound recognition of fundamental truths. They may have done so for Hardy's immediate contemporaries, but the chances are that responses of later generations to his symbols will be fainter. Hardy will hold the anomalous position of a poet who will need a commentator to show his relation to his age as well as to furnish a commentary on that age.

A preliminary glance at Hardy's images on Time supports the theory of the importance of his moods. It is not enough to say that he has a "saddened sense of Time" or of the "vastness of Time." He subordinates his conception of Time to the emotional unity of the poem. He does the same for his conception of Fate, Chance, God, and so forth. Time is a productive force, an evil force that separates lovers, or "dooms man's love to die." It is a condition, a builder and destroyer, a sportsman that "but rears his brood to kill," a spirit that destroys the good as easily as it destroys the evil. It is an unthinking force that holds man in bondage or in prison, and mistreats him as a puppeteer might mistreat his puppets. Time is likened to a soldier, the Fair's hard-hitter, to a cruel tyrant, a sleepless sculptor, a philosopher, or a weaver. Time is a cynic, a derider, a scoffer, and a mocker. Time has human features: hands, fingers, tongue, but lacks teeth. It is a housemistress, can swing us around, and has power of cure. Time is kingly and sublime. Time possesses "untraveled space," a den, vaults, a cell, and an hour-glass. It also is likened unto a horse to be "reined back." [3]

Now, how is it possible to select any one or any several of the foregoing conceptions as truly indicative of Hardy's thought? They are poetic impressions, and must be looked upon as such, which have no significance apart from the poem in which they occur. They help to key the emotional tone of the poem and rightfully deserve consideration in the study of the organic structure of the poem. I cannot, therefore, stress too greatly the absolute necessity of distinguishing between the essential idea in the poem and the poet's use of metaphor for bolstering his thought. The examination of his metaphors, however, properly belongs to the consideration of his technique.

In spite of the danger of constructing a philosophical system, it is possible, I think, to observe the general tendency of his musing on life because, unlike Housman, his periods of composition did not correspond to periods of illness. And since the greater corpus of his work does not deal with God but with love, woman, youth, and hope, these poems are important to any attempt at an analysis of his complete thought. Hardy has not primarily written much on immortality, although many poems on death touch upon the subject. But his few poems on immortality reveal a pretty consistent view from his early to his last years. In "The Occultation," for example, he wonders if the joyousness of his soul lives on after it has left him, and in "Heredity" he speaks of the immortality of the family features; but his most consistent belief is one held by many moderns, including a few advanced members of the clergy. He can find no support for the conventional idea of an afterlife nor for thinking that death is not the end-all ("A Sign Seeker"). Our immortality lies in the memories of us carried by the living,

---

[3] "A Philosophical Fantasy," "The Faded Face," "The Inquiry," "She, To Him, I," "God's Education," "Lines," "At Castle Boterel," "The Bedridden Peasant," "In Child-bed," "A Broken Appointment," "A Forgotten Miniature," "In a Eweleaze Near Weatherbury," "Panthera," "After a Journey," "At the Piano," "My Cicely," "The Flirt's Tragedy," "At the Entering of the New Year," "The Blow," "The Ghost of the Past," "I Worked No Wile to Meet You," "Lonely Days," "Freed the Fret of Think-ing," "To an Impersonator of Rosalind," "A Plaint to Man," "After the Last Breath," "Near Lanivet, 1872," "The Minute before Parting," and *The Dynasts*.

memories which, unfortunately, steadily fade, then die, lasting at most only unto the second or third generation. Such is the theme of "Her Immortality," "His Immortality," and "The To-Be-Forgotten." It is true, of course, that Hardy repeatedly uses concepts of survival after death as machinery for his thought, but, as I hope will be apparent, those devices are machinery and nothing more.

The problem of the nature of God was not so simple of solution as that of immortality. He pondered the question again and again. "I have been looking for God for 50 years," he wrote January 29, 1890, "and I think that if he had existed I should have discovered him. As an external personality, of course,—the only true meaning of the word." "Personality" was a dangerous word to use. Repeatedly he was driven back upon himself until, as in "Waiting Both," he arrived at the calmness of the stars and was willing to wait for Time to go by. Fitfully he thought he saw an answer to his problem, but the illumination was short-lived.

Every deeply religious person has experienced Hardy's perplexity. Only the unthinking or half-thinking on the subject find ready answers which rest easily on their hearts. The problem was not an abstract one for Hardy, any more than it is for anyone who uses his eyes for the purpose of seeing things as they are and not as he wishes they might be. Those who have not believed that conditions such as are portrayed in *The Grapes of Wrath* exist or existed only in the West, or that environmental conditions such as are represented in Farrell's *Studs Lonigan* are endemic only to the south side of Chicago, or that the conditions in *Dead End* are only the figments of a diseased imagination will find in Hardy's attitude many points in common with theirs. That does not mean, however, that a person need stop where Hardy stopped, nor that Hardy's generalizations were the only ones possible. But it does mean that Hardy pursued the right route—the route of arduous intellectual endeavor. In a different age a St. Thomas Aquinas could go higher; and the renewed interest in the work of that great theologian who made possible the exalted vision of the *Paradiso*—a work dull only to those who have not been able to travel so far and a thrilling one that overshadows the *Inferno* to those capable of grasping Dante's vision—points to a dawning age that may well look upon Hardy's age as one mired on the plains.

Looking back over a period of fifty years he could see little improvement in man. However patiently a few held steadily to their purpose of straightening "visions wry and wrong," their efforts produced little good. Faced with such "truths" he could understand a child's unwillingness to grow up, a man's reluctance to be born. Could, in fact, a child have any conception of the nature of the universe? These "truths" more completely engulfed him at Christmas than at any other time, when the contrasts between what Christ taught and what people did in his name were most vivid to Hardy's mind. The misery of the world was almost too much for him. He wished that for one day at least he could feign that earth is Paradise, and still retain his consciousness of Death, Time, and Destiny.[4] Easter worked a similar reaction. Christ may be risen, but the world remains much the same: suffering, pain, want, wars, strain are the rule rather than the exception. Why cannot man learn from experience? Why must he continue in his old way?[5] The world does not grow better. Life is only

> A senseless school, where we must give
> Our lives that we may learn to live!
> A dolt is he who memorizes
> Lessons that leave no time for prizes.
> —"A Young Man's Epigram on Existence"

Men continue to build churches and cathedrals to glorify God and act in such a way as to defame Him. Hardy has much truth on his side. Not one of his observations of details is falsified. His only trouble, as I have elsewhere suggested, is not the breadth of his vision, but its narrowness. He was not as far-sighted as he liked to think he was.

That he sometimes doubted whether or not Christianity could be a religion of permanence is not surprising; although few persons sought with greater diligence than he to practice the Christian ethic. Just as it had supplanted paganism, he thought another

---

[4] "The Jubilee of a Magazine," "Childhood among the Ferns," "Midnight on the Great Western," "A Necessitarian's Epitaph," "The Reminder," "To Life."
[5] "A Drizzling Easter Morning," "A Night of Questionings," "Channel Firing."

religion may well supplant it. Attempts in our own generation have been made; that they have any chance of ultimate success only a minority still believe.

He recognized the necessity for a perspective on life if he were to see it whole and wondered whether, if he were far enough from the earth, the apparent differences between the seeming and the real would disappear. Would all the earth-torn strife show but as a regular curve ("At a Lunar Eclipse")? No answerer, he.

He did realize that few things of life can be shared. Each has a darkening hill to climb—and alone. Take, for example, the girls in a ballet linked in "a one-pulsed chain, all showing one smile." Each rustling bit of flesh outwardly so like the other can share nothing with her fellows; to each her own world. Among them are "daughters, wives, mistresses; honest or false, sold, bought;/ Hearts of all sizes" ("The Ballet"). Or, even if experiencing something in common—say the magnificence of a drive to Great-Orme's Head—an extraneous element may superimpose itself on the "eye-records" to the extent that it will widely separate them: his recollections will be commonplace, hers, "tragic, gruesome, gray" ("Alike and Unlike").

Although Hardy was a willing listener to the scientific ideas of his day he could not completely shake off the shell of much that passed for theological thinking. It weighed on him and harassed him, just as it harassed Meredith whose letters cry out against the pronouncements of the contemporary clergy. He believed that God did not create man in His image, but rather that man created God in his. The final state, however, of the evolution of man's concept of God remained inadequate.[6] Men may know a "phasm" which they call God, but it has none of His qualities. This being the case, man should face the fact that he has long evaded:

> The fact of life with dependence placed
> On the human heart's resource alone,
> In brotherhood bonded close and graced
>
> With loving-kindness fully blown,
> And visioned help unsought, unknown.
> —"A Plaint to Man"

[6] "God's Funeral," "Not Known."

Hardy found no comfort in his inability to accept the current ideas of God; or to rely on a simple faith. Quite the contrary, in fact. He would like to have escaped from the bonds of reason that held him earth-chained:

> Loosed from wrings of reason,
> We might blow like flowers,
> Sense of Time-wrought treason
> Would not then be ours
> In and out of season.
> —"Freed the Fret of Thinking"

This regret is not the matter for a moment but is consentaneous with his whole poetic life. He expresses it in the early "The Impercipient" and in the late "Yuletide in a Younger World," and under many guises. When those of simple faith seemed to sense heaven he could hear only the dark and wind-swept pine. He could picture the martyrs imaged on the cathedral façade sighing regretfully over the steady weakening of faith under the stress of Reason's movement. He was hurt when persons said he preferred skepticism to this simple faith.[7] Hardy's regret, however, bears a strong sentimental cast and should not be taken too seriously. It is a nostalgic regret that gives pleasure rather than pain. No one would want Hardy to have remained in his childhood faith. We should rejoice in his obstinate questionings of sense and outward things, in his insistence on hard thought and in his reliance on reason. He performed a salutary service to his age and a greater one to ours. We can regret, however, that he could get no farther than he did, that he could not quite attain unto that state of grace which is the greatest realism.

Could he have done so, doubts would not have assailed his justification for disturbing from their own beliefs those who find happiness therein; nor would he have been concerned that his friends looked upon him as "a thinker of crooked thoughts upon life in the sere"; nor could he have believed that one should not concern himself too greatly with the wherefore of life, nor that those who indulge in little speculation are the happier. He would have been able to give a new spirit and meaning to the idea that those who seemingly care little enough for life do not seek to evade it, and

---

[7] "The Impercipient," "In a Whispering Gallery," "The Lost Pyx," "The Oxen," "Yuletide in a Younger World."

his persistent thinking on God and the changes in the philosophic
concept of the universe from Thales to the moderns would have
given him an even greater pleasure. Many times he was not far
from the goal.[8] He knew that the traditional opinions of the priest-
hood and press, being the undigested, unapprehended appropria-
tions from the great spiritual leaders, were not the truth, even
though widespread. Could he have grasped the reaches of one of
the small groups who remain quiet because they know the words
they would have to use to express their concept are a debased coin-
age, he would have valued their serenity that beats no drum. He
would have been reassured. That he could not grasp those reaches
makes him the spokesman for the group which cannot sense or
can only dimly sense the greater meaning of the *Paradiso,* of *Para-
dise Regained,* of *Faust, Part II,* or of *St. Matthew's Gospel.* He
knew that good motives are ever subject to misunderstanding; if
one is to rise in the church he must possess other qualities than
those of true Christianity.[9] He knew, but was not bothered by the
knowledge, that however great a person's incompetence, he can
always find a greater to applaud it. He was less patient with the
person who recognized the greater incompetence of his fellows and
yet catered to it. He asked honesty and sincerity, not cleverness,
alike from parishioner and priest. More important than the actual
result was the attitude of mind. Whether it meant foregoing church
in order to read "that moderate man Voltaire" or whether it pro-
duced no perceptible change in the vicariate made little differ-
ence.[10]

The difficulty of the problem of God varies from age to age ac-
cording to the ability of peoples to maintain a vital sense of a tra-
ditional and powerful mythology. During the mid-nineteenth and
early twentieth century all vitality had evaporated from this sense
of spiritual tradition, leaving only a placid outward manifestation
in social taboos. The revolt against this debilitated religion broke
out in many quarters, with the scientists in the vanguard. Agnos-
ticism, long kept closely under cover, gradually emerged into the
light. Men sought avidly for an anchor that could take the place

[8] "The Problems," "Before Life and After," "For Life I Had Never Cared Greatly,"
"Drinking Song," "Mute Opinion."
[9] "The Peace Peal," "Whispered at the Church Opening."
[10] "A Respectable Burgher," "An East-End Curate."

of what they had hollowly called faith. The young Matthew Arnold chose love; Hardy could not even accept that. He pondered long the nature of God but could find no answer. He rejected utterly, as most persons have done, an anthropomorphic concept of deity, just as he rejected the concept of God as a quality within oneself. No one thinks more about God than a sincere agnostic. An unsettled problem permits no peace of mind. It is not until he passes through agnosticism to a confirmed knowledge of God that he attains serenity, that he no longer feels the necessity of arguing about it, trying to convince himself. Since Hardy never reached the point of distrusting reason, never reached the point of suspecting that truth is more than a closely observed interaction of outward phenomena on oneself, he never passed beyond the necessity for revolving in his mind the problem of God. To what conclusions did he come? Generally, only to the idea that God is a blind creator who may eventually develop through man's insistence a consciousness and, perhaps, a moral sense.

He warned Alfred Noyes in 1920 against picking isolated passages from the poems to represent his beliefs. A vast gulf separated the expression of his fancy from that of his belief.

My imagination may have often run away with me but all the same, my sober opinion—so far as I have any definite one—of the Cause of Things, has been defined in scores of places, and is that of a great many ordinary thinkers; that the said Cause is neither moral nor immoral, but *un*moral: "loveless and hateless" I have called it, "which neither good nor evil knows." . . . This view is quite in keeping with what you call a Pessimistic philosophy (a mere nickname with no sense in it), which I am quite unable to see as "leading logically to the conclusion that the Power behind the universe is malign."

Several years earlier he had differently expressed a similar view:

My own interest [he wrote in 1901] lies largely in non-rationalistic subjects, since non-rationality seems, so far as one can perceive, to be the principle of the Universe. By which I do not mean foolishness, but rather a principle for which there is no exact name, lying at the indifferent point between rationality and irrationality.

And the following year:

So you cannot, I fear, save her [Nature's] good name except by assuming one of two things: that she is blind and not a judge of her actions, or that

she is an automaton, and unable to control them: in either of which as-
sumptions, though you have the chivalrous satisfaction of screening one of
her sex, you only throw responsibility a stage further back.

This latter statement explains Hardy's poetic tendency at times to
treat Nature and God as synonymous and at other times to dis-
tinguish sharply between them. He poses the question in "Nature's
Questioning." Is God, ask the objects in Nature, a "Vast Imbecility"
that can create but not tend its creations? Is it an Automaton un-
conscious of what he has created? Or are we "Godhead dying down-
ward"? Or is there an unapprehended plan? The poet gives no
answer. Many poems would seem to give the answer; but if we
observe carefully we find that although several affirm each of the
questions, he finally admits that he is "no answerer."

"A Philosophical Fantasy" is a focal point for many of his poems
on the nature of God the Creator. He builds the poem on Bagehot's
statement that "Milton . . . made God argue." God having the
whole universe in its care hasn't much time to devote to "frail Earth
—life shotten/ Ere long, extinct, forgotten." God confesses to lack
of forethought, admits that "it is all nonsense/ That I mind a fault
of manner/ In a pygmy towards his planner!" and that it is aim-
less, revealing "no heart-scope for faint feeling," is a "purposeless
propension . . . along lines of least resistance." At least twenty-
five other poems support this view in whole or in part. Xenophanes
of "Xenophanes, the Monist of Colophon" receives no satisfactory
answer to his insistent demands as to whether or not the Prime
Mover is a conscious force, because the Prime Mover is under a
spell. The only note of hope is that some day it [11] might break
the spell. When it does awake will it, he asks in "The Sleep-Worker,"
out of shame destroy its creation, or will it "adjust, amend, and
heal" it? When the poet does not think of it as under a spell, he
thinks of it as a logicless, blind creator unaware that it has created
an intelligence that can question the rightness of its ways. If he
grants it consciousness it either regrets its creation's lack of ap-
preciation of its methods, or thinks man's consciousness one of its
mistakes. It has physical as well as mental blindness, and is totally

[11] For purposes of consistency I have employed the neuter pronoun although the poet
uses all three genders according to the way it suits his artistic purposes. Hardy when
using the neuter pronoun often capitalizes it.

at a loss to imagine its Nature. The foregoing poems agree that God either has no ethics, or at least one that differs from that of the intelligence it has created.[12]

Hardy further expands the concept of a being, force, or will lacking intelligence, in those poems which speak of Nature as one who, although harming the bodies or souls of its creatures, yet loves them. Why should Nature, for example, rob a woman of her beauty? Is it to hoard those sweets for her until another day, as Hopkins depicts God doing in "The Golden Echo"? The idea is proposed in "The Absolute Explains." More often, however, Hardy takes a different attitude. "I bid Time," it says, throw those sweets carelessly away. Surprised that man can see the act as cruel, it confesses that man's is the teaching mind. The harm may result, too, from the impact of a still greater force that has jarred the creator's hand.[13] Pursued to its source, the Prime Mover seems to be Necessity. Of course, this is only a poetic fancy not to be taken literally. Nor should any of his other representations of God. We must remember that this "logicless creator" uses pretty convincing, straightforward English and has a penetrating consciousness.

Hardy exploits the many roles that Chance plays in man's life. He believes that the person who can accept its importance and inevitability is less apt to be embittered than one who sticks to the Panglossian theory that everything happens for the best in this best of all regulated worlds. Once man understands the role of "crass casualty and dicing time," those "purblind Doomsters" who would as readily strew blisses in man's path as pain, he can better steel himself to the unmerited ire that frequently overtakes him. If he achieves objectivity toward the world he will realize the impossibility of the Earth's grieving for anyone. Nor will he expect the great forces of the universe to pay more attention to him than they would pay to the least inanimate things.[14]

It would be a great injustice to Hardy to say that the foregoing,

---

[12] "New Year's Eve," "The Mother Mourns," "I Travel as a Phantom Now," "Doom and She," "Agnosto Theo."

[13] "The Lacking Sense," "Genetrix Laesa," "The Blow," "God's Education," "Discouragement," "On the Portrait of a Woman about to Be Hanged."

[14] "Hap," "The Subalterns," "Autumn in King's Hintock Park," "At the Mill," "Coming up Oxford Street: Evening."

although not a reasoned philosophy, presents even the sum of his impressions. Many poems breathe a more hopeful spirit. Nor is it possible to say that the foregoing ideas present his less hopeful thoughts at one period and that he presents the more favorable concepts at another. Different degrees of confidence are about evenly distributed throughout the published works. He sometimes combines a strong social note with the religious, as in "The Bedridden Peasant."

Hardy has moments, as in "Fragment," when he believes that God must eventually arrive at a conscious state when he will "know how things have been going on earth and below it." Man is God's pioneer who has reached the "consciousness of Life's tears" sooner than God. Eventually, however, God must overtake him. He poses a different problem based on God's consciousness in "A Dream Question." Does God care about his creatures' deeds and opinions even when He is their subject? Nonsense, "Rail and blaspheme all you want to. Why I act as I do must remain my mystery. It lies within the ethic of my will. Do not think that I keep a dossier of your every word and deed." If any philosophical concept can be formulated from the foregoing poems it is little more than a negative one. Do not be too curious about the ways of God, but rather concern yourself with the problems of everyday living.

Hardy injects a moral note in "God Forgotten," in which God admits that he had forgotten he had created the earth. Man was to blame, however; not He. For a man to know good and not ceaselessly to strive for it is inexcusable. *Not to Mend* is the same as *Not to Know,* although God should not let man continue to suffer.[15]

The problem of free will has early and late absorbed the attention of philosophers and continues to do so. At no time have scientists been less prone to grant its existence than at the present time. Digging for the fundamental truth along the horizontal path reaching from the ego to observed phenomena they have unearthed fragments of the truth, but not the truth. Poets as well as scientists have prospected along the same route; a few have sought the uplands. Before writing his *Paradise Lost,* Milton pondered the nature of

[15] "To the Moon," "By the Earth's Corpse."

free will in his *De Doctrina Christiana* and solved for himself certain problems that obstructed him. Hardy, too, providing himself with some of the prospector's tools, undertook to unearth valuable ore. Having too great confidence in his scientific predecessors, he was content to carry out his explorations on the horizontal level. He unearthed many interesting and valuable things but he did not discover the truth after which he had set out. His ore was only flecked with gold.

Since man, he finally concluded, is incapable of molding his fate, it is as well or better to have the lot of the average man than that of a king, because even a king cannot hold himself true to his first thoughts however good they may be. Nor will fate permit the lover to break with his beloved even though he acts against his intellect:

> But against what I willed worked the surging sublime
> Of the thing that I did—the thing better.
> —"The Thing Unplanned!"

Fate directs even the least important incidents in life. It dominates, orders man, is often unfriendly, unaccountable, and as capricious as a maid. It gambles recklessly with him and sets little value upon him.[16]

I think it is possible to look upon Hardy as performing in a very minor degree the same function for his age that Plato did for his. He poses the questions, examines them from many points of view, but does not solve the problems raised. It is useful to know the questions. Hardy's unsettled state of mind is everywhere evident. He admits he is torn in his beliefs as to whether man acts as he does because of his ancestors or because of free will. And is man as clearsighted as he thinks? Can the birds and flowers, for example, have a perception into the heart of things that is impossible to man? They are able to find happiness in the presence of desolation, cruelty, and pain. Is man justified in his self-complacency over his superiority to other living things in this world? Can he, for example, know as

---

[16] "The King's Soliloquy," "On the Esplanade," "In a London Flat," "The Torn Letter," "The Pedestrian," "The Lost Chrysanthemum," "I Met a Man," "The Reminder," "The Colonel's Soliloquy," "Paths of Former Time," "The Change," "Four in the Morning," "The Turnip Hoer," "Hap," "The Bedridden Peasant," "The Graveyard of Dead Creeds," "Panthera," *The Dynasts* (pp. 49, 75), "Leipzig," "The Opportunity," "By the Runic Stone," "At Waking"; and many others.

much about the secrets of the earth as the ant? Is not man more impotent in the face of natural forces than the birds? [17]

It is possible, of course, for these questions to serve a more definite purpose than merely to pose unanswerable riddles. They caution man to be humble. We, like the beasts of the field and the birds of the air, are but of dust. A year ago the thrushes, finches, and nightingales now singing in the copse as if all Time were theirs were but particles of grain, earth, air, and rain. Only a little longer ago the trees in the churchyard were pulsating men and women. In this constant mutational process we are all part of the general will, but only in our most optimistic moods can we believe that we have in us sufficient power to make things develop as we would have them.[18] Most of the time we are powerless. Actually, life offers little to most persons. We are born; we die. In the interim we act like puppets. We are not moved by wisdom, far-sightedness, or reason to a greater honesty with ourselves, but rather by unreason and lack of prescience into self-treason. The unborn think of this world in their ignorance as a place of pure delight. Were they wise they would not willingly come into this welter of futile doing, this place of foiled intents and vain lovingkindness where little that we see of our actions is a cause for pride. How can we think the world is growing better or that man will refrain from destruction when our leaders—the statesmen, teachers, physicians—are so blind? Is there no one who can "lead the nations forward from gloom to light"? [19] Hardy's difficulty was that of every person who places a great value on the efficacy of reason. He was impatient. Godwin made the mistake of thinking that human nature was perfectible within the span of an ordinary life; Shelley, that reason was an instrument of such power that man had but to be shown the truth and his reason would make him embrace it. In his calmer moments Hardy knew that truth must be advanced slowly, "but in phrase

[17] "The Pedigree," "The Year's Awakening," "The Blinded Bird," "The Darkling Thrush," "The Head above the Fog," "An August Midnight," "The Caged Thrush Free and Home Again."

[18] "The Wind Blew Words," "Proud Songsters," "Voices from Things," "He Wonders about Himself."

[19] "What's There to Tell," "Thoughts at Midnight," "The Unborn," "In Tenebris, III," "Copying Architecture in an Old Minster," "I Have Lived with Shades," "We Are Getting to the End," "Murmurs in the Gloom."

askance." He could understand and give an affirmative answer to Gibbon's questions:

> Still rule those minds on earth
> At whom sage Milton's wormwood words were hurled:
> *"Truth like a bastard comes into the world*
> *Never without ill-fame to him who gives her birth?"*
> —"Lausanne"

Aware as was Hardy of the misery and suffering in the world, and anxious as he was to do something about it, he realized that alone he could do little to ameliorate conditions. "No man," he said, "can change the common lot to rare." In his youth he could bear the misprision of his fellow men because of the gleam he carried with him in his breast. He could see it in other young men, too, and often wondered if they had been able to sustain it or whether the realities of life had quenched it. A clue to the inadequacy of Hardy's own vision, however, creeps into his poetry. Youth, he suggests, because it is blind and heedless can sustain this inner light. Prescience of the realities necessarily extinguishes it.[20] What kind of a light did Hardy carry in him that could be so extinguished? What kind of fuel fed that light?

I have no quarrel with the details of the picture that Hardy drew of life, nor with their arrangement. But has he seen behind the surface phenomena to the something that lies deeper? It seems to me that he has restricted himself to a horizontal vision. He prided himself on a sense of history, but I cannot think he read his history accurately. He had not measured the distance his age had actually advanced beyond earlier ages, nor could he see the real changes that the leaven working in his own age was leading to in ours. He saw the surface eruptions. The mere fact that he could feel as acutely about the problems as he did marks a great advance.

Blindness is not a requisite to happiness. But a vision that moves in all directions is. To see into the depths and up to the stars is as necessary as looking toward the east and west. We must remember that to look *about* us suggests a vertical as well as a horizontal axis. If we do look *about* us we have rid ourselves of fear. Nothing can surprise or overwhelm us. We can find pleasure in the passing mo-

[20] "To an Unborn Pauper Child," "In the Seventies," "The Youth Who Carried a Light," "A Nightmare and the Next Thing."

ments and minutiae of life when the illusion that the world is collapsing becomes a common belief. We know otherwise.

Hardy had a happy life. He accomplished what he had set out to do; or he thought he did. He did not shut himself in a quiet backwash of life, and he saw that most persons about him experienced little real happiness. Had he lived in the seventeenth century he might, like George Herbert, have explained it by predestination. In the nineteenth he did it by belittling God. It is to his credit that he did not belittle Him in the way his pseudo-pious critics did and continue to do.

From his visions of the world's suffering he frequently apprehended the gleam of a finer future. He once dreamed, for example, that a germ of Consciousness from another planet awoke the earth to a realization of the cruelty and misery that here exist hand in hand and of which it had never before taken cognizance. Too many of earth's so-called seers were not anxious for this knowledge. From the imperfect creeds, however, finer ones must certainly emerge. Evolution in thought is as possible as evolution in material things. In the dead creeds of the past there must lie some germinating influence that will flower forth a creed of enlightenment and vision. At times, he senses that the change has almost gathered enough momentum to dispel the darkness that has clouded men's eyes, but such moments are rare. More often he can see little regret over the fact that his family dies with him. These moments of hope coming to him late in life differ greatly from those he experienced in his younger years. He utters the earlier moments with a voice of confidence touched with ecstasy; the later ones in quietly measured rhythms.[21] In spite of all the discouraging aspects of life, he finds encouragement in many of man's activities. He admires, for example, in "Rome: on the Palatine," the spirit that enables man, even though he has tangible evidence that everything built by him passes, to continue to move forward and to build as if for eternity. After all, time counts for little. To the philosopher it is only a thought and of little importance ("Rome: Building a New Street, etc.").

More persistent in the poems is the view of life as a lottery where

[21] "The Graveyard of Dead Creeds," "There Seemed a Strangeness," "Sine Prole," "A Song of Hope," "Let Me Enjoy."

the cast of the dice brings no prizes. Any happiness necessitates the attitude that sufficient unto the day are the evils thereof. To muse on the meaning of life is a futile occupation. According to Hardy, the one who muses is no better off than those who spend their time in church in mindless outpourings. The most one learns is not to complain when misfortune comes, but to expect it. And do not set much store by things valued on the earth. They distract man and delay his attainment of a god's composure. Since all things belong sooner or later to Death, the wise person will seize the happiness of the moment, he will embrace life eagerly, and he will surrender it as willingly, because he who seems most kingly is the king.[22] I am afraid Hardy tended to undervalue the doubts that beset him because he could never quite emerge into the pure serene. Born a generation later with the same inquiring mind he may well have found that for which he sought. He was well aware that fame was no plant that grows on mortal soil nor could it spring from materialism nor from anything connected with it. Only spiritual achievement could give it and God was the only giver. His difficulty lay in his conception of God.

Hardy had moments of vision, as do most of us, when he could see himself bare, moments when he could see aspects of himself that normally are hidden to us. What is the power that enables us to have these moments of self-knowledge and who holds the mirror for us is the theme of the title poem of *Moments of Vision*. Elsewhere in the same volume he gives us a glimpse of himself as a youth with a Shelleyan light in his eyes that was "the radiance of a purpose rare/That might ripe to its accomplishing."

Such are the ideas of Hardy on the subject of God and man's position in the universe as revealed in the *Collected Poems* and *Winter Words*. For a more complete picture we should see these ideas in relation to the basic conception underlying *The Dynasts*, always remembering, however, Hardy's statement in his Preface about his use of the phantasmal Intelligences and the nature of the Immanent Will. These "Intelligences, called Spirits,"

[22] "Afternoon Service at Melstock," "The Child and the Sage," "Friends Beyond," "The Bullfinches," "A Commonplace Day."

are intended to be taken by the reader for what they may be worth as con-
trivances of the fancy merely. Their doctrines are but tentative, and are
advanced with little eye to a systematized philosophy warranted to lift
"the burden of the mystery" of this unintelligible world.

He used the impersonal pronoun instead of the masculine pronoun
in allusions to the First or Fundamental Energy as a "consequence
of the long abandonment by thinkers of the anthropomorphic con-
ceptions of the same." A further reason is essentially an artistic one.
Just as he felt he had a greater field if he chose to write on the ugli-
ness in life and on the reverse side of love, so too was there a greater
field if he selected a concept of the creator which had not already
become threadbare. An artist is conscious that there are some de-
velopments beyond which he cannot go if his work is to have fresh-
ness and vitality. The great artists in any field, be it painting, sculp-
ture, music, dancing, or poetry, are not content merely to repeat.
"The old theologies," wrote Hardy in this vein, "may or may not
have worked for good in their time. But they will not bear stretch-
ing further in epic or dramatic art. The Greeks used up theirs: the
Jews used up theirs: the Christians have used up theirs. So that
one must make an independent plunge, embodying the real, if only
temporary, thought of the age. But I expect that I shall catch it
hot and strong for attempting it." And he did!

Examples are numerous enough to discredit the assertion that
Hardy has postulated a malignant and fiendish God. He has done
nothing of the sort. At most he has thought that at the back of
things existed an indifferent and unconscious force. One can dis-
agree, in fact, with Mrs. Hardy's statement that her husband be-
lieved that "neither Chance nor Purpose governs the universe, but
Necessity," although he was willing to grant a certain measure of
freedom of will. But the poems dealt with in this chapter do not
give a complete picture of Hardy's thought. They illustrate his grap-
pling with the problem that confronts every thoughtful person:
the nature of man and his place in the scheme of things. To have a
well-balanced personality requires that man must have the courage
to strive to know himself. Yet he cannot know himself unless he has
some sense of his relation to the universe; and to know this he must

attempt to come to some conclusion about the nature of God. This attempt has many amusing aspects, as Hardy frequently recognized.

It would be an amusing fact, if it were not one that leads to such bitter strife, that the conception of the First Cause which the theist calls "God," and the conception of the same that the so-styled atheist calls "no-God," are nowadays almost exactly identical. So that only a minor literary question of terminology prevents their shaking hands in agreement, and dwelling together in unity ever after.

Mrs. Hardy better indicated Hardy's attitude than did the critics when she said that instead of

Non-conformist, Agnostic, Atheist, Infidel, Immoralist, Heretic, Pessimist they might more plausibly have called him Churchy; not in an intellectual sense, but insofar as instincts and emotions ruled. As a child, to be a parson had been his dream; moreover, he had had several clerical relatives who held livings; while his grandfather, father, uncle, brother, wife, cousin and two sisters had been musicians in various churches over a period covering altogether more than 100 years. He himself had frequently read the church lessons, and had at one time begun reading for Cambridge with a view to taking orders.

What led Hardy to his views? Observation played an important role, the germ of which observation may well have been planted by words of Shelley that he consciously or unconsciously remembered from *Prometheus Unbound:*

> Yet thou art more than God
> Being wise and kind.

To most of Hardy's contemporaries these were indeed words of an ineffectual angel beating his wings in the void. The words were the trumpet of a prophecy unto which the average man of his age, or the man with vested interests, was afraid to hearken. Hardy was more fearless; he longed to see the end of winter. It is our age, however, rather than his, that can glimpse the spring. Did Hardy never share in these glimpses?

Before bringing to a close the discussion of what he has said in his poetry we must examine his positive statements on his general philosophical position, although under no circumstances must we confuse this with a well-integrated philosophical system. These positive statements, like those of negative implication, are impressions; and even these will not bring comfort to everyone. The person who could write as he did to Galsworthy—"that there seems no ultimate reason for existence, if not a staggering idea, does not make most of us feel that, if there could be a reason, life would be far more interesting than it is"—is not one who could bring comfort to more than a few. He was close enough to life and the people to see that everything does not always work out for the best, and that a deafening of oneself to the rumble of discontent by blatantly screeching that it does, wrought more harm than good. The least a person could do was to be honest with himself.

Honesty and sincerity in the face of ugliness, superstitious credulity, and hypocrisy, he said, could effect a greater good than a blind denial of the existence of these forces. It may be that life is gradually decaying, but it does no good to conceal the grief arising from such knowledge by false protestations of rejoicing. If man were to cast aside his delusions and face life bravely, quite possibly this resolution would itself bring a condition of life that would better the promise of circumstances. We now know, of course, that Hardy was right. Had his contemporaries at the end of the century been willing to take the full look at the worst, which he held necessary if a way to a better was to be found, we might not be in the muddle we are now in and have been in for some time.[23] For some years we have been reaping the rank growth of weeds permitted to gain a strong foothold in the 1880s and 1890s. It is significant that those poems in which Hardy challenges the optimistic complacency of his age were written at a time when, had they been heeded, they might have altered the course of world history. It is possible, of course, that their not being heeded at the time may be productive of greater good in a shorter period. Personally, I am not one who sees cause for despair in the seemingly cataclysmic changes the present age is undergoing. The changes are long overdue.

That Hardy did not become embittered by the rejection of his warnings was to be expected. Bitterness only follows upon too great expectations. Recognize that ecstasy comes to but few, and you will not mind overmuch if it passes you by. Hardy confirms in a poem written on his eighty-sixth birthday an impression gathered from poems spanning his period of literary activity: One must never ex-

[23] "In Sincerity," "In Tenebris, II."

pect too much from life.[24] He best expresses this attitude in a somewhat earlier poem:

> I never cared for Life: Life cared for me
> And hence I owed it some fidelity.
> It now says, "Cease; at length thou hast learnt to grind
> Sufficient toll for an unwilling mind,
> And I dismiss thee—not without regard
> That thou didst ask no ill-advised reward,
> Nor sought in me much more than thou couldst find."
>
> —"Epitaph"

Hardy maintains that however great our good fortune has continuously been, the wise person will not only accept the proffered joy, but he will at the same time realize that he has not merited his good fortune and will accept without complaint its cessation which must assuredly follow. He must realize that life offers only to deny.[25] My own reaction to such ideas is that they tell us more about Hardy than they do about life. But an interesting if not novel idea emerges from the foregoing poems. Read in the reverse order of time of composition the poems tell us that, in the light of greater experience and maturity, events that disturbed him at the moment lose with distance that quality which placed them apart from ordinary happenings. Since, then, joy and grief are the lot of every person, youth with its stress on the immediate moment will take joy early and put off grief until "surly Time has dulled their dread" of it. By the time it arrives they may be dead ("First or Last").

Hardy early found in Darwin's *The Origin of Species* an idea capable of poetic treatment and one which some of our younger poets are making capital of: the idea that the struggle for survival is in as constant progress in Nature as in man.[26] Although he early realized it, he generally chooses to forget it. More often than not the woods afford him refuge from the burden of the world.

An important element in Hardy's thinking that impinges on the foregoing ideas is his recognition of man's responsibility to live life as fully as possible even though he has not solved the riddle of life itself, a "giddying place with no firm-fixed floor, a great surging space" with only two doors—Birth and Death. It is as useless for

---

24 "He Never Expected Much."
25 "He Fears His Good Fortune," "Yell'ham-Wood's Story."   26 "In a Wood."

man to complain that he must do what he does not understand as it would be for the pen of an author to complain because it does not understand the words it must write. No good comes from lashing out against reality, although that, too, is sometimes necessary. Real solace comes from the adherence to one's dream, one's ideal.[27] His difficulty lay in his inability, the farther he traveled from the east, to maintain the freshness and brightness of this conviction. When one surrenders to the idea that the world is falling about one's head, cleaving to the stern ideal is not easy. Milton never for a moment surrendered his ideals nor swerved from their firm prosecution; he remains, therefore, sublime to the end; Wordsworth only until his surrender.

One of the difficulties in the way of the faithful prosecution of ideals is the inability of the world to distinguish between the aim and the results and hence the necessity of struggle without encouragement. The world makes little distinction between effort and achievement, disregards the workings of chance, and neglects the person who has ruined himself in an unselfish deed.[28] The fact that Hardy understood the difference should have persuaded him that others, too, may have understood. The plaudits of the multitude may sound sweet in one's ears, but they bring little real satisfaction. True fame is not set off in a glistering foil. It lies in the knowledge of honorable work well done. The only man who understood that was Hardy's old stonemason; and understanding it, he had all the reward he needed.

He also deals elsewhere with the matter of fame. To the wise, fame is as nought compared with the properly evalued commonplace lives that are lovely and true ("The Souls of the Slain"). In particular, the ambitious "raking riches into heaps," the able pleading of lawyers, the heralded deeds of statesmen are small things to the poet who has lived in quiet with opportunity to drink deep of the natural phenomena about him,

> Tasting years of moderate gladness
> Mellowed by sundry days of sadness.
> Shut from the noise of the world without,
> Hearing but dimly its rush and rout,

[27] "The Masked Face," "On a Fine Morning."
[28] "The Two Men," "The Casterbridge Captains," "The Old Workman."

> Unenvying those amid its roar,
> Little endowed, not wanting more.
>   —"A Private Man on Public Men"

His tolerance undoubtedly kept him from achieving certain masteries, but had he lacked tolerance he would have forfeited, so he thought, the things most precious to him. He never lost sight of his humanitarian interest in man. And this interest gives him a vision which he is not always able to sustain in the more important aspects of his thinking.[29] He is always humble and aware that pride, however disguised, is littleness; that it is the obstacle keeping us from enriching experience. We can never know, for example, from what source a beneficent influence may descend upon us. It may be from a casual acquaintance, from a wanderer resigned to his miserable existence, from a sodden tramp who in the face of adversity can maintain his cheerful outlook, or it may be from the sudden realization that the conditions about which he is grumbling were to the earlier generations the rule rather than the exception.[30]

His aim was truth. As he once said ("To a Lady"), knowing that truth is truth, he did not resent his books being banished for smugger things. The question we must later face is whether or not he did recognize and understand truth. Even he was sometimes beset by the doubt that he had not lived up to his determination to uphold truth, justice, beauty, love, and above all, charity. The reader, too, is beset by this same doubt. His frequent lack of ardor, his growing indifference, his vaunted placidity are not the best ingredients for moving poetry. Poetry may appear to be calm, but beneath the surface must surge a creative intensity. Too often Hardy forgets to be the artist when attempting to reproduce a quality, assumes a layman's attitude, and immediately becomes dull. Such is the trouble with the following. He is more concerned with the problem arising from the choice of a single rhyme than with the problem of infusing emotion.

> As for my life, I've led it
> With fair content and credit:
> It said: "Take this." I took it.
> Said: "Leave." And I forsook it.

[29] "Then and Now," "Often When Warring."
[30] "The Casual Acquaintance," "The Wanderer," "Christmastide," "A Wet Night."

> If I had done without it
> None would have cared about it,
> Or said: "One has refused it
> Who might have meetly used it."

And such is the trouble with Hardy and with his age. Lacking the will to believe and unable to see in the vague surface movements a powerful leaven at work soon to burst into changed concepts of man's political destiny, their calm did not rise from electrified hope but from a fatalistic despair. It was not the charged calm preceding battle, but the benumbed calm following defeat. Is it strange that in this age the most vibrant poems—those of the later Hopkins or of Francis Thompson—were by a convert and the son of a convert to Catholicism, by men to whom religion was more than outward form, and the world of spirit of greater significance than the world dominated by materialistic values?

PART II

THE WAY
OF SAYING IT

The fullest pleasure occurs when, having realized the general idea, the main relations of the members of a building, the main composition of a picture, the disposition of the links of a sculptural figure, we are able to consider the interior relations of the parts, proceeding always from larger to smaller relations, without finding any point at which the informing idea breaks down, until we come to the matter of the work, the grain of the stone or the canvas.

ROGER FRY

❊6❊

DICTION

IN THE FOREGOING chapters the subject matter of Hardy's poetry has been of prime importance and critical evaluations were held to a minimum. We have witnessed his wrestlings with the perennial and unsolvable questions of whence, whither, and why, have observed the notes of sadness, frustration, and nostalgia accompanying these questions, and have sensed a gradual relaxation of the will. We realize that Hardy was moved by the pity of the world rather than by its folly, that, more keenly than most, he sensed the greater significance of obscure tragedies that were apparently only local, that he found the loves, hates, and sorrows of his simple Wessex folk of the same nature and same degree that are found elsewhere. In the present section I think we shall find more. We shall have occasion, for example, to test the truth of the assertion that a flash of insight is worth more than a ton of experience, and that creating a work of art is, as Clive Bell has suggested, "as direct a means to good as a human being can practice." We shall observe in Hardy, for example, the phenomenon of the same thought twice-garbed. In one it is attractive and appealing, in the other—well, who except the social worker even noticed it? When he is a poet he illumines the obscure joys and tragedies of Wessex with the light of the universal and we value him for showing us what we should otherwise have missed. Then he is Wordsworth's man of livelier sensibilities speaking to men.

That he has upset traditional modes of thought by showing the unimportance of impedimenta hitherto thought indispensable has disturbed many readers. But at no time does he approach the pessimism of Ecclesiastes, of Jonathan Swift, nor, for that matter, even of Thomas Gray.

It is a truism that the best poetry is successfully communicated emotion of man's significant experiences. The emotion must be common to all ages, although clothed in the thought and idiom of the poet's own. The communication of this vision, universal in quality and coming from his passionate understanding of the living human record as he has had opportunity to observe it, to be successful, cannot ignore the entire stock of time-tried poetic devices, although he may alter, change, and add to them. The degree to which he does these latter things will be the extent to which he will be misunderstood by the general run of readers, even critics. Hardy, who believed that there was no new poetry—only the new poet—has paid the price of being misunderstood for those qualities which made of him a new poet. He was not generally content to put new wine in old bottles, nor old wine in new bottles. He wanted the new vintage in fresh containers. He wanted that, but only partially achieved it. He has been accused, therefore, of agnosticism (to which he confessed), atheism, pessimism, misogynism, and a host of other -isms (which he has denied), of being harsh, crabbed, rough, and stilted in his style. He has been misunderstood on every count, and the fault has lain largely with the reader rather than with the poet, and chiefly for two reasons. The reader has insisted on looking on the poems as comprising Hardy's reasoned philosophy, although to do so necessitates the neglect of a large part of his poetry. Time after time, as I have pointed out, he insisted that the mission of poetry was to record impressions, not convictions—and the impressions never appear in their nudity. The reader neglects the clothing of the thoughts. In Hardy's case it is not manners but clothes that "makyth the man."

A poem is something like a snail with its house on its back. The house has little real value to anyone except the snail, who cannot live without it. Just as inseparable are the thought and the form of a poem. Often, in fact, the form is the poem, or practically so. In Part I we have examined Hardy's thoughts; now we must examine the form—the houses. Several methods are possible, none of which is entirely satisfactory. Every valid method will accomplish the same

ends. I am beginning with the grains of sand and shall follow them
to the finished structure, from words, to phrases, to images, to
stanzas, and then to the finished poem, although in poetry as in any
art, we become aware of the details in the reverse order.

Hardy has frequently been criticized for his predilection for
learned words, especially his use of them in close conjunction with
those of a colloquial nature. The charge is justifiable, but more so
when aimed against his novels, particularly the early ones, rather
than against his poetry. In the opening chapters of *A Pair of Blue
Eyes,* for example, many of the sentences possess the stilted quality
common to much Victorian fiction, although nowhere does Hardy
have the wooden quality so frequent in Bulwer. The first sentence
of the novel illustrates the point: "Concerning the beings categor-
ized above, it may be premised that the aim and meaning of their
appearance upon the earth, of what, in its highest sense . . ." To-
day a writer would avoid such latinized words as "categorized" and
"premised" as used in the sentence. A worse case is his use of "syn-
thetized" in the following: " 'Dear me, the shaft of the carriage
broken!' synthetized Elfride." Unfortunately, there is too much of
this in the poetry. Learned words occur, and frequently give a sense
of stiltedness. Their use becomes a unique characteristic of Hardy's
poetry. Rhyme, rhythm, alliteration, and accuracy of thought gen-
erally dictate his choice. The level of the word was unimportant to
him as long as it afforded him a sharper notation for his observa-
tions. Hardy more nearly resembles Browning, I think, in this mat-
ter than any other poet. Several poems have a decidedly Brown-
ingesque flavor. He knew Browning well, met and talked with him
frequently, and during his trip to Italy in 1887 was more under the
spell of Browning and Shelley than of anyone else. "It is rather no-
ticeable," wrote Mrs. Hardy, "that two such differing poets as Brown-
ing and Shelley, in their writings, their mentality, and their lives,
should have so mingled in Hardy's thoughts during this Italian
tour, almost to the exclusion of other English poets equally, or
nearly so, associated with Italy, with whose works he was just as
well acquainted."

This may have been true in 1887, but the poet I am most con-
scious of in reading Hardy is Wordsworth, but Wordsworth with a

difference. Whereas Wordsworth wrote of the northern rustic, the independent man of the Lakes region, Hardy has written of the southern rustic, a different breed of man. Whereas Wordsworth's poetry teems with moral reflections, with saws and sentences, Hardy's is free of them. By avoiding them he has robbed his poetry of one of its most effective instruments; he has denied himself the use of a factor that distinguishes and raises poetry beyond any of the other arts. For Wordsworth's austerity of language and his genius for the inevitable word, Hardy uses the accurate but only rarely the inevitable word. And yet everywhere I find Wordsworth's influence. I cannot catch in the early *Domicilium,* as does Mr. Blunden, the rhythms of Coleridge's blank verse. To me the rhythms as well as the subject matter stem from *The Prelude.*

But to illustrate Hardy's use of aureate terms in short quotations is difficult if not impossible. I seem to sense their inappropriateness in the earlier work more than in the later, although he never entirely frees himself from the tendency at any period. Too persistent reading of his poetry dulls one's sense of incongruous or unfelicitous associations of strange bedfellows. He is correct but not always apt in his selection, and his failure in this latter quality tends to destroy the inherent dignity of the word. In many instances the critic has erred. He has forgotten that however much a word may have been vulgarized by misuse the poet's apt use of it restores or invests it with dignity. Wordsworth is supreme in this; Hardy felicitous only upon occasion. Nonetheless he helps prevent the impoverishment of the language. When Hardy is at his best—and his best is found in those poems where he struggles to understand life —his language is pure Hardy, a perfect fusion of seemingly contradictory elements.

More important than learned words, however, for imparting a sense of strangeness—one might almost say the Wessex village quality—are those which the *Oxford Dictionary* classifies as archaic, obsolete, rare, poetic, coined, and dialect. The tendency of critics constantly to harp on his use of local Wessex words as being obsolete irritated Hardy. "But," he said to William Archer, "they are not obsolete here; they are understood and used by educated people. And if they supply a want in the language—if they express an idea which cannot otherwise be so accurately or so briefly expressed—why may not one attempt to preserve them?" He was, moreover, a stout adversary of those who would impoverish the English vocabulary by subjecting it to arbitrary rulings. In his introduction to the *Select Poems of William Barnes* he enlarges upon his reluctance to see a useful word disappear. "The process," he says, "is always the same: the word is ridiculed by the newly taught; it gets into disgrace; it is heard in holes and corners only; it dies; and, worst of all, it leaves no synonym." To render a dialect word into standard English is the same as translating it into a foreign tongue, and it loses its affective associations. "Such paraphrases," he adds, "are but a sorry substitute for the full significance the original words bear to those who read them without translation, and know their delicate ability to express the doings, joys and jests, troubles, sorrows, needs and sicknesses of life in the rural world or elsewhere." That may all be true. But what of the reader unfamiliar with those words? They will communicate little or nothing to him, whereas a word with possibly less nuance for the poet might.

One expects to find dialect words in Hardy because of the subject matter of the poems. As the poet himself said, however, the actual number is relatively small and they occur almost exclusively in the poems which are meant to be dialect poems. Only a few like garth (yard), leaze (a grass field), moils (drudgery), treen (trees) occur many times.[1]

The poet's sensitive use of archaic words frequently heightens the poetic thought of a passage. In the last stanza of "Julie-Jane," for example, he speaks of her as

> Bubbling and brightsome eyed!
> But now— O never again.

"Laughing" might be a substitute if one needed only to maintain the rhythm. In "brightsome," however, he found a word accurate in connotation, satisfactory rhythmically, and one which also satisfied

[1] Further interesting examples found in isolated cases are caddle (quandary), capple (white, pale), drongs (narrow land, steep rocks rising out of the sea), eweleaze (grass field stocked with sheep), fulth (fullness, repletion), gallied (frightened), grinterns (compartments in a granary), laitered (searched), peckled (speckled), shrammed (numbered), snocks (a knock, a smart blow), tallet (loft), tardle (entanglement), vlankers (fire-flakes), wonning (dwelling), wych (wych-elm) and Kentish and southern words substituting initial z for s—zell, zilver, zummer and Zundays.

his desire for a heightening of the effect by alliteration. "Intermell" in "Rake-Hell Muses" is chosen for the sake of rhyme; "unshent" for the same reason; "phasm" not only because the short *a* sound is desirable, but for a greater suggestiveness than phantom, image, or another substitute—"One thin as a phasm on a lantern-slide" ("A Plaint to Man"); "weeted" because it expressed most accurately what he desired to say in a trochaic rhythm—"Weeted not the songs they sung" ("The Faded Face").

The obsolete words occur more frequently than the archaic and as frequently as the dialect. Because many of the words still survive in his speech vocabularies, if not in his written ones, an American will not be as conscious of many of Hardy's departures from accepted standard as would an Englishman. On the other hand, he is apt to confuse certain common words, such, for example, as "picotee"—the name of a flower—with those now considered archaic, obsolete, or dialect. In many instances Hardy has retained words that are ill-lost in our speech. In "A Sunday Morning Tragedy," for example, the mother says:

> I kissed her colding face and hair,
> I kissed her corpse—the bride to be!—

"Colding" to indicate that the body still had traces of warmth is a happy choice. Coll (embrace), demilune (half moon), dorp (village), gaingiving (to gain), gallanting (flirting), wanzing (diminishing), to whim (to act in a whimsical manner), and yieldance (yielding) are but a few others. None carries the rich connotation of the slangy "dewbeating" to describe the young man getting the start on the other man:

> What will you do when Charley's seen
> Dewbeating down this way?
> —You'll turn your back as now, you mean?
> Nay, Carrey Clavel, nay!
> —"To Carrey Clavel"

The same may be said of these words as of the dialect and archaic words. They bolster the poetic structure of the poems. "Demilune," rhyming with "moon" and "soon" gives a more accurate image than possible with any other word; "embowment," rhyming with "moment" has a similar effect; and similarly "gallanting." "Gaingivings," a word used several times by Hardy, is not more accurate than other possible words, but satisfies the rhyme. "Wych" for "wych-elm" is easier for the sake of rhyme. "Dorp" and "wanzing," on the other hand, are preferred by the poet because of the enhanced poetic communication which he finds in alliteration: "All find in dorp or dell"; "Come weal, come wanzing, come what may." Occasionally, however, the concentration of an archaic word gives it desirability. "Whimmed" is a good instance. In the line "But she's whimmed her once too often, she'll see!" the poet markedly intensifies the communication through condensation.

Among the words classified by the *Oxford Dictionary* as rare, many are common to nineteenth century poetry. A few, however, are interesting: dolesome, griff, lacune, palinody, ratheness (earliness), stillicide, and welterings (twistings). Again we see that their choice depends on exigencies of rhyme, alliteration, or condensation without sacrifice of accuracy of meaning. There is little real reason in "The Revisitation" for the use of "dolesome" instead of "doleful." "Griff" (a small ravine) rhyming with "if" ("The Clock of the Years"), "lacune" (emptiness) rhyming with "commune" ("In a Whispering Gallery"), and "palinody" rhyming with "Lodi" ("The Bridge of Lodi") are clear examples of the use of the rare word instead of the common "lacuna" and "palinode" for the exigencies of rhyme. A fine example of the use of a rare word to satisfy the demands of rhyme and to intensify the mood is "stillicide" rhyming with "who yet abide" ("Friends Beyond"). In "A lone cave's stilli-cide" one can hear the water dripping from the roof of the cave like rain water from the eaves of a house. "Ratheness" is chosen not only for the sake of alliteration, but for its vowel quality of long "a" in the progression of vowel sounds, a progression comparable to those found in Hopkins.

> Yea, to such rashness, ratheness, rareness, ripeness, richness,
> Love lures life on.
>
> —"Lines"

"Welterings" satisfies the demands of alliteration as well as rhyme:

> Is it that you are yet in this world of welterings
> And unease . . .
>
> —"Why Do I?"

Hardy makes scant use of "poetic" words. A few of the less familiar are cerule, illume, largened, obliterate, tinct, vill, vanned, and yestreen. Examined in their context we can understand the reason for their selection. The first three—cerule (cerulean), illume (illumine), largened (enlarged)—are clearly chosen because of their rhythmic fitness lacking in their modern forms.

> "Earth is a cerule mystery";
> "Illume this fane";
> "My largened love and truth to you."

"Obliterate" (obliterated) as an adjective occurs only in the title, and was probably chosen because it is not only the form of the verb appearing in the poem, but also because of its emotional connotation for the poet. "Tinct" carries an associative context denied to the word "color" or other substitutes. The word not only means the elixir used for transmuting metals into gold, in which sense Hardy has used the word, but may also recall the darker meaning of the word as used by Shakespeare to describe the effect of Hamlet's words on his mother in the closet scene:

> That mirror
> Works well in these night hours of ache;
> Why in that mirror
> Are *tincts* we never see ourselves once take
> When the world is awake.
> —"Moments of Vision"

"Vill" (village) is twice used because of the exigencies of rhyme —with Heath-Plantation Hill and with "thrill" and "still"—and once for the sake of rhythm and internal rhyme—"Till here on the hill, betwixt vill and vill." "Vanned" (winged) is chosen in "Waved by mighty-vanned flies" for a different and subtler reason. It carries over from the previous stanza the effect of the rhymes "strand" and "land." "Yestreen" likewise serves a double purpose. It satisfies the demands of rhyme and at the same time evokes the associative memories from Coleridge and the much earlier ballad of Sir Patrick Spens.

Larger than any of these classes of words and one important to an understanding of Hardy's art is that of the coined words. An examination of even a few of Hardy's coinages merits the same deductions possible from the other groups. Coinage of words is, of course, warranted by the nature of the language. Rhyme dictates a few of them. "Abrim" in "with hearts abrim" rhymes with "to him"; "claytime" (death) with "Maytime"; and "cohue" with "two." This last instance is of doubtful value, however, because of the difficulty of meaning. Alliteration inspires "clamoured" in "Fulfilled its clamoured code" and "aethered" in "we breathe an aethered air." Rhythm accounts for many like "artfeat" for "feat of art" and "birthtime" for "time of birth."

Most of the coinages, however, are definitely attributable to Hardy's insistence on accuracy of communication; although a few such as "acheful" and "acrosswise" lack any particular vitality. "Beglimpsed" in "beglimpsed through the quaint quarried glass"; "bespat" in "now in a mud-bespat city"; "dampered" in "Thuswise a harpsichord, as 'twere from dampered lips"; "afar" in "I'd have afar ones near me still"; "aforedays" in "Over this green aforedays she/ On light treads went and came"; and "bedwise" in "without a word/ Bedwise he fares" are examples of this device for accurate communication. He occasionally uses verbs as adjectives and nouns, or nouns for adjectives.

Although I have chosen my examples at random, they reveal as clearly as would a more detailed examination Hardy's concern for accuracy of communication of idea, as well as his concern over the artistic aspects of his problem. He is always a conscious artist in his poetry, but he does everything in his power to conceal the art in the general impression of the whole.

Certain weaknesses persist, however, in spite of his care for their eradication. Latinisms in close conjunction with colloquial words are frequent, and the reason is obvious. Hardy was largely self-educated. Like every young person eager to advance himself, he placed a value on the unusual word that a person of greater sophistication would avoid. In time he, too, realized that a heavily Latinized vocabulary was not the characteristic of cultured speech, and he sought to avoid it. Many of the words had become so much a part of him that he unconsciously retained them. His syntax does not, however, betray a Latin influence. That, like his phrasing, is direct. In spite, too, of his care, he lacked a sense of the power a word can have in itself. It is this plus the unusual patterns of much of his verse that leads some critics to accuse him of disguising prose rather than transmuting it, a charge from which in hundreds of instances he can by no means be exonerated. His lines frequently betray an ineptitude in the choice of words that one cannot excuse. I am inclined to believe, however, that this shortcoming in Hardy is almost a virtue. The presence of inkhorn terms with coined, rare, archaic, colloquial, and obsolete words makes a style out of what, were it more rare, would be stylelessness. It bolsters the provincialism after which he sought. One might almost say that his style is his provincialism. William Archer said of this quality of Hardy that he sometimes seemed "to lose all sense of local and historical perspective in language, seeing all the words in the dictionary on one plane, so to speak, and regarding them all as equally available and appropriate for any and every literary purpose."

Hardy's consciousness in the matter of details further reveals itself in his formation of alliterative compounds which number in the hundreds. Alliteration is important in his poetry—possibly on account of the influence of Swinburne whom he greatly admired—and demands somewhat extensive examination. His use of these alliterative compounds is but one phase of this problem. They show an active imagination working to achieve a desired emotional effect. We not only have "blast-beruffled" birds, also referred to as "casement comers"; but we have such evocative compounds as conscience-capped, fog-fleece, grace-beguiled, history-haunted, languid-lipped, mother-ministry, poesy-paven, rote-restricted, sanguine-souled, and so forth. We also have many compounds with heart: heart-halt, heart-harm, heart-heaves, heart-hydromels; with love: love-leaf, love-light, love-line, love-looks, love-lore; with self: self-centered, self-slaughter, self-smiting, self-struck; with soul: soul-smart, soul-stifling, soul-subliming, soul-swoon; with time: time-torn, time-touched, time-trail, time-trenched; and with world: world-weaver, world-webs, world-welters, world-wide, world-wise, world-work. That this was conscious on the poet's part is evident from his poem to Shakespeare. For one word impossible completely to decipher in the manuscript he substituted "bright-baffling."

In addition to the numerous alliterative compounds Hardy makes extensive use of alliteration with no noticeable sacrifice of accuracy. He does not confine alliteration to the images. The alliterating letters vary from two to five in one line. He captures the carefree quality in an image from the age of romance and chivalry:

> A Troubadour youth I rambled
> With life for lyre,
> The beats of being raging
> In me like fire . . .
> —"The Dead Man Walking"

The significance of "beats of being" is apt to be overlooked because of the more obvious "life for lyre" in the preceding line. The emotive connotation of the successive p's in an interesting vowel combination in "the passing preciousness of dreams" is more strongly haunting than had he substituted any synonym for "preciousness," a word in itself rich in associations.

Hardy could easily have written a more forceful line in "A Plaint to Man" than "And now I dwindle day by day . . ." without recourse to alliteration. He chose this, however, because of the force he wished the d's to carry to the next line: "Beneath the deicide eyes of seers." "Deicide," a good word in itself and one which Hardy transfers from the category of nouns to adjectives, receives greater emphasis because of the preceding line.

That this was not accidental with Hardy is evident from the following examples in which the alliteration is too conscious:

> Under the sure, unhasting, steady stress
> Of Reason's movement, making meaningless
> The coded creeds of old-time godliness.
> —"A Cathedral Façade at Midnight"

> Where bristled fennish fungi, fruiting nought
> —"The Graveyard of Dead Creeds"

"Fruiting" is a clear case of a selection for alliteration.

> The sun and shadows wheel,
> Season and season sereward steal.
> —"A Spot"

> Each wills to work in ancient style
> With seedlip, sickle, share and flail,
> Though modes have since moved many a mile!
> —"The Jubilee of a Magazine"

Who feels that delight is a delicate growth
  cramped by crookedness, custom, and fear,
Get him up and begone as one shaped awry;
            —"In Tenebris, II"

Rose the peewits, just as all those years back,
    wailing soft and loud,
And revealing the pale pinions like a fitful
    phosphorescence
Up against the cope of cloud.
            —"The Revisitation"

An examination of the manuscript of *Past and Present* throws additional light on this aspect of his poetry. This "fair copy" is anything but such. There are over three hundred alterations varying from alterations of single words to that of whole stanzas, and an occasional addition. The poet's critical activity did not cease when the manuscript was in the hands of the printer; he made several significant alterations on the proof-sheets. In "Shelley's Skylark," for example, he quite obviously changed "speck" to "pinch" for the sake of an alliteration—"That tiny pinch of priceless dust"—that intensifies the emotional control over the reader.

For a similar reason he altered "night-birds" to "night-moths" in "Or by night-moths of measureless size." More obvious is his choice of "Sanct-shape" via "godhead" from the original "God-shape" in "No more sees my sun as a Sanct-shape." It is interesting to notice, however, that Hardy sometimes wisely rejected alliteration for greater power. He altered "And what in modern maidens match" to "And what in newer maidens" and finally to "And what in recent maidens match," just as he substituted "bends" for the alliterating "gives" in "She bends a glance of pain" because he realized the inappropriateness of alliteration in such instances.

He sometimes cast his lot with alliteration unwisely. In "The Tramp-woman's Tragedy," for example, a poem which he considered one of his best, he originally wrote in stanza 11, "Thereaft I traipsed the world alone." He altered the effective "traipsed" to the unemotive "walked," for the obvious purpose of alliteration, and by so doing weakened the original force of the line. The blank verse passages of *The Dynasts* yield many instances that are deplorable.

On the whole, however, his revisions show his concern for accuracy. In the last line of "Before Marching, and After" he alters "glory" to "brightness":

> Where Death stood to win; though his name was to borrow
> A brightness therefrom not to fade on the morrow.

"Glory" was extravagant for what he wished to say. So, too, was "marvelled" in line 7 which he altered to "wondered." Line 2 illustrates a similar quality plus his concern for force. Originally the line read:

> Where the old Egdon pines starved and thinned.

"Old" lacked the desired force in the word preceding Egdon. "Starved" was the emotion he wished to stress. He rewrote the line enforcing this idea, and adding "trees" to maintain the basic rhythm:

> Where the starved Egdon pine-trees had thinned.

A better example occurs in "The Supplanter." Originally the line was weak—"He turns as one whose mind is lost." He altered this in the "fair copy" to "He turns remorseless-passion tossed." In the proofs he gave it its final form which is a great improvement— "He turns—unpitying, passion-tossed." We may take another illustration from "Catullus: XXXI." He altered line 13 from "We press the kindly couch at last" to "We press the pined for couch at last." "Pined for" is much more affective than "kindly."

Whatever the mood of the piece Hardy generally achieves his best effects by means of a diction that is strongly monosyllabic. Exceptions occur and frequently spoil the unity of a poem; these exceptions are most frequently dictated, as we have seen, by the necessity of the rhyme, rhythm, or alliteration. One can afford to overlook the occasional verbal infelicities for the sake of the concept underlying the poems in which they occur.

The outstanding quality of Hardy's diction, however, is its economy and accuracy. Few poets are able to limn a scene with his clarity and precision. The result came from careful revision. Often he made three or four attempts before achieving perfect lucidity. An instance in a well-known poem, "New Year's Eve," is the manner in which he indicates the four seasons by four color words:

> "I have finished another year," said God,
> "In grey, green, white, and brown."

This economy enhances, too, the sense of dryness in a poem which Miss Millay might possibly have seen before she wrote her poem "To Jesus on His Birthday":

> "Peace upon earth!" was said. We sing it,
> And pay a million priests to bring it.
> After two thousand years of mass
> We've got as far as poison-gas.
> —"Christmas: 1924"

It also intensifies the sense of laboriousness in "Doom and She." Accuracy of meaning, together with sounds that impart sadness and hopelessness to the burdened movement of what is obviously a lullaby, heightens the tragedy of "To an Unborn Pauper Child." The opening lines of "No Buyers" catch the sense of labor as the man and woman trudge along with their cart.

Hardy's achievement in diction is perhaps more clearly revealed in a poem reflecting a change of mood within its narrow confines. Examples are numerous in that class of poems dealing with death, where one stanza reflects the mood while the beloved was yet alive, the second the mood after her death. "The Church Builder" affords an interesting example of another kind. The tone of the poem changes from ecstasy, complete confidence, and faith in the first four stanzas to a mood of let-down and doubt in the last six stanzas.

Liking economy in the use of his materials, he does not over-ornament his poems. He is content to impart his effect by a few well-chosen details rather than to attempt an achievement by an endless piling of detail on detail. He selects such as suggest the picture to the imagination and then lets imagination do the rest. "Her Dilemma," "Weathers," and "In Time of 'The Breaking of Nations'" are interesting from this point of view, particularly the latter two. This economy of means is more manifest in his later poems than in his earlier ones.

But let us return to Hardy's revisions in *Poems of the Past and the Present*. We have no way of knowing the extent of the reworking of the poems before they reached this "fair copy." Of the changes, more than a hundred and twenty are clearly for the intensification and greater lucidity of meaning, about thirty-five for the sake of rhythm, about twenty for alliteration, and fewer because the whole passage needed reworking. Several of these latter passages remain unsatisfactory.

Let us examine a few of the intensifications. There is a single instance of a change from the passive to the active voice. A few aim at greater simplicity. Line 11 of "At a Lunar Eclipse," originally "Be hemmed in what that puny arc implies," became "Be girded by the coasts yon arc implies" and finally "Be hemmed within the coasts yon arc implies." A more obvious example is in line 14 of "The Lacking Sense." "Distilling cramps" became "inweaving cramps," and then the simpler "admitting cramps." The vowels of "admitting" are better suited to their context. A third instance reveals Hardy's attempt to delete words with a more learned tone. "Commix" in line 5 of "The Sleep-Worker" becomes "have place" in the final version: "Wherein have place, unrealized by thee." The substitution for "No man can move the stony gods to spare" of "No man can change the common lot to rare" in line 30 of "To an Unborn Pauper Child" reduces the violence. The majority of changes, however, tend to heighten the affective connotation of the passage. These may be simple changes like the mere alteration of "years" to "days" or "thirty" to "twenty" in "The Colonel's Soliloquy." In general, however, it is such a heightening as we find in the substitution for the unaffective "the Power predominant" of the much stronger "the lurid Deity," or of "throbs" for "tingles," of "frail" for "gay," or "peoples" for "nations," of "tragedy" for "agony," and of "hovers" for "neighbors" (as a verb) via "tokens" and "borders" in "When trouble hovers nigh." At times the change completely reverses the sense, as "transport tossed" for "trouble tossed" in "Two sat here, transport-tossed" or "wilted" for "weltering" via "frigid."

A few changes result from a desire for more fitting consonant and vowel sounds. "Chart" is clearly an improvement over "page" in "Ere their terrestrial chart unrolls," just as "on sleepy noontides" catches the mood of relaxation more effectively than "at eves of murmurings," or even the later "on warm still noontides." The poet quite obviously substituted "gibbet" for "gallows" in "He wived the gibbet-tree" because of the vowels. The most significant changes, however, were those dictated by the exigencies of rhythm.

It is readily apparent from the alterations made in the "fair copy" of *Moments of Vision*, that Hardy was conscious of the available techniques for heightening his communication, more conscious than some of his critics have been willing to admit. His comment on the technical practices of William Barnes throws light on his own.

His ingenious internal rhymes [Hardy wrote], his subtle juxtaposition of kindred lippings and vowel-sounds, show a fastidiousness in word-selection that is surprising in verse which professes to represent habitual modes of language among the western peasantry. We do not find in the dialect balladists of the seventeenth century, or in Burns, . . . such careful finish, such verbal dexterities, such searchings for the most cunning syllables, such satisfaction with the best phrase.

The aforementioned "field, flock, and lonely tree" is an excellent example. We not only have the long *e* sound in "field" and the long *o* sound in "lonely" separated by the short *o* of flock, but the position of *l* in each word is deftly handled to secure a gently falling quality. The sound moves forward in each succeeding word until in "lonely" it holds the initial position. In the refrain of "Lines —To a Moment in Mozart's E flat Symphony" the position of *l* is stationary, and the musical effect results from the forward movement of the vowels—"love lures life." He combines many devices in vowel gradation, alliteration, repetition, and so forth, in two lines from "At the Royal Academy":

> There summer landscapes—clump, and copse, and croft—
> Woodland and Meadowland . . .

"New Year's Eve" furnishes interesting examples of the poet's care in manipulating the vowels for emotional effect. The arrangement of the already mentioned use of "grey, green, white and brown" to indicate the seasons is no accident; the progress of the seasons is not the determining factor. The determining factors are alliteration in "grey" and "green," and the rhythm afforded by the vowel progressions: long *a*, long *e*, long *i*, short *a* and the diphthong *ow*. With similar care he conveys the emotion of plodding, unthinking creativeness in the last stanza, by the frequency of the long *a*'s and long *o*'s abetted by the alliterating *w*'s.

> He sank to raptness as of yore,
> And opening New Year's Day

> Wove it by rote as theretofore,
> And went on working evermore
> In his unweeting way.

He manipulates the vowel sounds in "A Sign Seller" in such a way as to impart a sense of load, and in "The Robin" to effect a change of mood. In stanza 1 the long *i*'s predominate and heighten the sense of joyfulness in living; the quality of the sound subtly changes from stanza to stanza until in the fourth, one feels the robin's depression. More important, however, is the effect of the consonants: stanza 2 has frequent stopped consonants, *d* and *k*. In the last stanza the frequency of the liquid *l* in conjunction with the fricative *f* heightens the melancholy of the thought.

> When up aloft
> I fly and fly,
> I see in pools
> The shining sky
> And a happy bird
> Am I, am I!
>
> But when it lasts
> And snows still fall,
> I get to feel
> No grief at all,
> For I turn to a cold stiff
> Feathery ball!

Similarly, "Silences" affords an interesting combination of sounds, particularly in line 3 of the third stanza. In the first two lines the vowels vary in interesting combinations with the *t*'s and *s*'s; then in line 3, when two adjacent words are similarly stressed the vowel is the same:

> But the rapt silence of an empty house
> Where oneself was born
> Dwelt, held carouse
> With friends, is of all silences most forlorn.

"A Wife In London," "Weathers," "The Well-Beloved" with its "Thou lovest what thou dreamest her;/I am thy very dream," "Regret Not Me," "To The Moon," and "Standing by the Mantel Piece" with its "Tonight, to me twice night" are only a few additional examples from many that illustrate the care Hardy exercised in this phase of his art often neglected by the tyro. Many of the lyrics written in 1912 and 1913 after his wife's death are further illustrations.

Closely bound up with the problem of rhyme and yet fitting for present discussion is his use of internal rhyme in "The Last Signal," a laureate poem suggesting Whitman's "When Lilacs Last in the Dooryard Bloomed." The end of line 1 is repeated in the middle of line 2. It better illustrates, however, the defect of not sufficiently varying the relative position of certain sounds and of crowding the stanza pattern to hold more than it rightfully can.

Better, and more interesting, is the sound pattern of "On One Who Lived and Died Where He Was Born." The stanza form, in anapestic dimeter, save for the final line, although interesting in the manner in which the exigencies of rhyme force a weaving of end-sounds, does not account for the poem's appeal any more than does his use of anapests, third paeons, alliteration, and so forth. It is a combination of many factors; but the manner in which the poet weaves a delicate tracery of repeating sounds throughout all parts of the stanza is important:

> When a night in November
> Blew forth its bleared airs
> An infant descended
> His birth-chamber stairs
> For the very first time,
> At the still, midnight chime;
> All unapprehended
> His mission, his aim.—
> Thus, first, one November,
> An infant descended
> The stairs.

Important as the foregoing aspects are, they are subtle details that reveal themselves only after careful reading. Perhaps even the poet was not always conscious of how much he was achieving. A phase of his art that more readily confronts the reader is the matter of imagery.

7

IMAGERY

HARDY'S IMAGES are an interesting and valuable mirror
for the man; his use of them a Kleig-light for the artist anxious to
understand him. To wrench them from their setting does them vio-
lence, yet not the violence that a similar operation would effect in
the poetry of John Donne. This is not to say that Hardy's images
are mere extraneous ornaments and those of Donne the very essence
of his poetry; yet there would be some truth in the implication. If
Hardy's images failed to bolster and vivify his communication, they
would diminish his stature as a poet. If they were not fused into
the structural pattern of the poem, if their color did not blend with
the other colors, they would mar its form. And form, we have
already seen, was important to him, as important as melody and
story:

> "Today my soul clasps Form; but where is my troth
> Of yesternight with Tune: can one cleave to both?"
> —"Rome—the Vatican: Sala delle Muse"

In his best work he managed to keep his troth with all three. But
we must effect the separation.

Time, for example, a frequently recurring ingredient in the
poems, has inspired the poet to a wealth of images for the sake of
vivifying that aspect of the subject that is for the moment para-
mount in his mind. These images, ranging as they do over so many
phases of life, frequently *are the thought* and should keep us alert
to the objection of attempting a logical philosophy from the poems.

A jotting made by Hardy early in November, 1905, throws sig-
nificant light on the quality of his images that we might expect to
find, and do. "The order in which the leaves fall this year is: Chest-

nuts; Sycamores; Limes; Hornbeams; Elm; Birch; Beech." How many professed nature lovers could enumerate the order of the fall of the leaves? The merit of his images lies not only in their appropriateness, but in the accuracy of his observations of the minutiae as well as of the larger aspects of nature. He sees the microcosm in the macrocosm and vice versa. It is this that excites the reader.

A superficial examination reveals images from literary sources and from the worlds of art and music, as well as from the world about him. Shakespeare and the Bible inspire more than any other literature, but Bacon, Keats, and the literature of romance, in addition to stock images common to all poetry, contribute their share. A glance at his reading is enough to indicate that literature would naturally be a fecund source. In 1887, for example, the "books read or pieces looked at" included:

Milton, Dante, Calderon, Goethe.
Homer, Virgil, Molière, Scott.
The Cid, Nibelungen, Crusoe, Don Quixote.
Aristophanes, Theocritus, Boccaccio.
Canterbury Tales, Shakespeare's Sonnets, Lycidas.
Malory, Vicar of Wakefield, Ode to West Wind, Ode to Grecian Urn.
Christabel, Wye above Tintern [Tintern Abbey?].
Chapman's Iliad, Lord Derby's ditto, Worsley's Odyssey.

After finishing *Tess* in 1890 he seems, says Mrs. Hardy, "to have dipped into a good many books—mostly the satirists: including Horace, Martial, Lucian, 'the Voltaire of Paganism,' Voltaire himself, Cervantes, LeSage, Molière, Dryden, Fielding, Smollett, Swift, Byron, Heine, Carlyle, Thackeray, *Satires and Profanities* by James Thomson, and Weisman's *Essays on Heredity*." We could easily expand the list to include Schopenhauer, Nietzsche, Comte, James, and others. Directly or indirectly his poetry shows the effect of this catholic reading.

It makes little difference, however, whether his images stem from literary sources or from his own observation, so long as they do not degenerate into poetic formulae. From whatever sources, they throw valuable light on his inward thought and feeling. When borrowing from previous authors he has been careful to make the images his own and to weld them into the pattern of the poem with no visible joints. The finished piece has greater strength than one forged from a single piece of metal. Many readers will recognize that some of our younger poets have read Hardy's images with profit and have exercised squatters' rights.

Before considering the appropriateness of the image as a bolstering force in the poem, an examination of the nature of his borrowings and the quality of his observations of the world about him is necessary. The most traditional borrowings, as might be expected, are connected with life, death, God, fate, time, and the universe; the fresher images with youth, love, and the natural world. Time as a gambler, a tyrant, a sculptor, as toothless, and as a dream are common to Shakespeare as well as to a number of earlier and later writers. So, too, is the concept of time running like the sand in an hour glass. These are common to poets of all ages. The medieval traces in death likened to a headsman, fate imaged with his masked face, and in the philosopher's stone effecting no alchemy are patent. Bacon fathers an image which Hardy intensifies with "frightful" and attempts to disguise by substituting "hazardry" for "fortune":

> . . . He who goes fathering
> Gives frightful hostages to hazardry!
> —"Panthera"

From Sophocles to Matthew Arnold and beyond, the ebb and flow of the tide has inspired poets. Hardy characteristically connects it with Chance:

> The tide of Chance may bring
> Its offer; but nought avails it.
> —"The Opportunity"

The idea of Fortune bearing gifts, of turning her wheel, or riding on a wheel has been similarly provocative. Hardy uses them all and, moreover, does not hesitate to invent mythology to suit his purposes. Change, for example, is the "strongest son of Life." Traditional images cling naturally to death and to God. He speaks of Death's sudden finger, Death's door, the Apocalyptic concept of Death the horseman, and of God the potter. The concepts of the wings of evening, the thick lids of Night, New Year the child or "calm comely Youth, untasked, untired" are commonplace and throw little commendable light on the poet.

He shows more originality in his use of images from Biblical sources, images, however, which he could have drawn from his own observations. A strong suggestion of the parable of the tares permeates its transference in

> Till dangerous ones drew near and daily sowed
> These choking tares within your fecund brain.
> —*The Dynasts,* 201

as well as in the "corn-chaff under the breath of the winnowing fan." More obvious in its Biblical origin is the comparison of the caged nightingale which soon dies to "those in Babylon/ Captive they sung," and indirectly through Keats, that the bird he hears

> . . . sings the selfsame song,
> With never a fault in its flow,
> That we listened to hear those long
> Long years ago.
> —"The Selfsame Song"

We must be careful not to let the melody of Keats prevent our enjoyment of Hardy's melody because of the evocative power of an image.

Numerous poems reveal an intimate knowledge of the Old and New Testaments. Hardy likens the suffering of the protagonists in "The Stranger's Song" and "The Flirt's Tragedy" to the sufferings of Cain, the happy man's expression to that on Moses' face after Sinai, and the specters that danced at the Argyle to the sparks within Satan's smoky halls. He describes his youth as a time when the radiance of life fell about him like manna. The rain clouds over Pokeswell Hill are like "the sweetest image outside Paradise," a hymn lingers "like the notes afar/ Of banded seraphim," and the new organist evokes a psalm tune for the poet as did the witch of Endor for Saul. The use of "bond-servants" to characterize mankind, and the image of shouldering the cross for life which appeared to the young girl as "vinegar and gall" are definitely New Testament.

The Dynasts, too, contains many images obviously Biblical in origin. In the scene at Trafalgar, Nelson is telling Burke to go to his place below deck. "Ah, yes," he says, "like David you would see the battle." Later, in looking over some despatches, Napoleon remarks: "The ominous contents are like the threats/ The ancient prophets dealt rebellious Judah!" When Berthier is commenting to Napoleon on his campaign, he remarks:

> . . . the enormous tale
> Of your campaign, like Aaron's serpent-rod,
> Has swallowed up the smaller of its kind.
> —*The Dynasts*, 254

Of the conference between Napoleon and his generals the Ironic Spirit likens it to the "sad Last-Supper talk/ 'Twixt his disciples and this Christ of war!"

The foregoing images recall but do not prove Mrs. Hardy's statement that her husband could fittingly have been called churchy; not, she said, "in an intellectual sense, but insofar as instincts and emotions ruled." Churchiness certainly inspires the image of the waves that

> . . . supplicate now—like a congregation there
> Who murmurs confession . . .
> —"The Voice of Things"

His "churchiness" is apparent not only in the titles to numerous poems—"The Chapel-Organist," "The Christening," "The Church and the Wedding," "The Church-Builder," "The Young Church-warden," and so forth—but also in his frequent reference to church bells, particularly their tolling, and to prayers, and even to the "psalmodies" roared by the wind.

Hardy frequently speaks of worms in connection with the grave and death, but with no particular freshness.

His images on Life show a strong traditional literary influence. Life is a mad spinner; a pilgrimage; an hour glass; and man is chained to the wheel of life. To speak of man as "but Fortune's sport" echoes Shakespeare, just as does likening man to a puppet, although this latter could as easily have originated from Hardy's observation of puppet-shows at a fair. Much more apparent is the Shakespeare reference when the Spirit of the Years calls the Sinister Spirit "thou Iago of the Incorporeal World." But to speak of great men as "meteors that consume themselves/ To light the earth" or to compare a soul-image to a "far colossus on a plain" are quite clearly literary, just as when he speaks of an "Iliad of woes" or of a "Cly-temnaestra spirit" of a girl.

It is obvious, too, that Hardy recalls his reading of the medieval joust in the "rain-shafts" which "splintered" on him. He makes use of a similar image in "A January Night" in which the rain "smites" the protagonist. Unfortunately, however, for the sake of alliteration he weakens the stanza by overemotionalizing it, a tendency which he carries over into the second stanza in the image of the writhing ivy shoot. From literary sources also comes the bared sword lying between lovers. The idea of sanguine conflict is more fully developed in "The Tree," evoking the recollection of a legendary fight between the hero and a demonic creature:

> Its roots are bristling in the air
> Like some mad Earth-god's spiny hair
> The loud south-wester's *swell and yell*
> *Smote* it at midnight, and it fell.

Hardy draws upon archery for his characterization of swallows, which range themselves on the roof "in wistful waiting rows/ Till they arrow off and drop like stones." In flight they move "in the curves of an eight/ Like little crossbows animate."

One could indefinitely multiply the images from literary sources. Certainly we cannot censure Hardy for their use as long as they are appropriate and are not a substitute for accurate thinking. The train of thought and sensation which such images evoke is a rich and pleasurable experience. Our enjoyment of the immediate poem is not only great, but we reexperience at the same time the emotion connected with the original contact with the image and thereby intensify in ourselves the author's communication. This is, of course, a constant source of enjoyment in reading poetry. Other poets than Hardy have made extensive use of this device.

More interesting than the images from literary sources, however, are those resulting from the poet's own observations. To distinguish one class from the other is often impossible. Nor is it necessary to make a sharp cleavage, because both give us insight into the poet's mind. Images drawn from everyday life frequently reduce in importance a concept of large proportions. The actions of the Immanent Will, for example, are likened to "a knitter drowsed,/ Whose fingers play in skilled unmindfulness"; the moon "to the lustre-lacking face/ Of a brass dial gone green"; and the stars to a dog:

> They wag as though they were panting for joy where
> they shine, above all care.
> —"The Wanderer"

Hardy draws enough images from the ordinary life of a small English market town and the near-by gentry to be called a poet of the village. This selection better reveals his close affinity with the least changing aspect of English life than does the subject matter itself. He is so integral to the scene that he naturally draws on it to illustrate less provincial concepts. He likens, for example, the swaying of the yew-plumes to the movement of "mockers' beards," and the crowded sails of warships "bulge like blown bladders in a tripe-man's shop/ The market-morning after slaughterday." He thinks of success as the village flirt who would willingly jilt "her anxious lover for some careless blade."

He draws from the village carpenter and builder his description of the waning moon by speaking of "the curve hewn off her cheek as by an adze," and thinks of "never-napping Time" using his little chisel. The action of Napoleon and his cavalry and the reflections of the town lights bore like augers. The island of Labau stands "like a knot in the gnarled grain represented by the running river." The thatcher's craft gives point to death; and he elsewhere adds a touch of superstition to this same image by referring to Death as having

> . . . won that storm-tight roof of hers
> Which earth grants all her kind.
> —"A Wet Night"

The beggar is a familiar sight passing through the village. Life is such a person:

> O Life with the sad seared face,
> I weary of seeing thee,
> And thy draggled cloak, and thy hobbling pace,
> And thy too-forced pleasantry.
> —"To Life"

The beggar's rags vivify, too, a bit of nature; the late hollyhocks being "rags of bloom." Watching the vagrant as he passed through the village but paying little heed to him were some chatting villagers. Trees are like these men who frequently turn aside from their pipes and conversation to spit—"And the trees went on with their spitting amid the icicled haze." Hardy probably had these same villagers' wives in mind when he described the effect of the heavy rain:

> . . . Each gutter and spout
> Babbled unchecked in the busy way
> Of witless things.
> —"We Sat at the Window"

More startling, however, is the manner in which in "The Darkling Thrush" the poet achieves a human touch by comparing day to the village drunkard and the refuse found at the close of winter to the dregs of the empty bottle: "And Winter's dregs made desolate the weakening eye of day."

From weaving and knitting come several images which reveal Hardy's characteristic minimization of larger aspects of the world. I have already mentioned that his observations of the world led him to think of the creator not as a cognizant power but as the work of a "knitter drowsed." The figures of military aides "move to and fro like shuttle-cocks," and Napoleon's words, says Queen Louisa, "darn the tearings" of his sword. Rain descends like silken strings and gathers along the fence rails "like silver buttons ranged in a row,/ And as evenly spaced as if measured." The rays of the sun thread through the smoke "like woof lines in a loom," and the "leaf-wove awning of gree." The Danube appears from the distance like a "crinkled satin ribbon." The waves beating against the rocky cliffs, when seen from above, are "white selvaged and empurpled," a waterfall is a "gauze of descending waters," the flapping leaves of May are "delicate filmed as new spun silk," and England's gold forms "the weft of the armies marshalled at Ulm."

Other domestic minutiae assist the poet in communicating his ideas. Mankind is likened to a clock which the Will winds up "to click-clack off Its preadjusted laws," and Nature to a sundial. The best image of clocks occurs in his description of the bats:

> Swart bats, whose wings, be-webbed and tanned,
> Whirred like the wheels of ancient clocks.
> —"The Musical Box"

The coming of night or morning does not exalt the poet to a mystic mood. Those phenomena remind him of homely things—an ill-fitting potlid or shutters. At the close of day, for example,

> The sky at its rim leaves a chink of light,
> Like the lid of a pot that will not close tight.
> —"Suspense"

and at the coming of dawn the "stars close their shutters."

The sun is like an open furnace door "whose round revealed retort confines the roar/Of fires beyond terrene." The use of "terrene" tends to counteract the industrial quality of the image. Time is no more than a gentleman maintaining a rabbit warren who "but rears his brood to kill," and generations of his ancestors than the reflection of a candle flame in a mirror which "shows images of itself, each frailer as it recedes." Certainly he had a laundress in mind when he chose "flapped" to alliterate with "float" in describing the apparent action of the wind in the following vignette:

> And the wind flapped the moon in its float on the pool,
> And stretched it to oval form;
> Then corkscrewed it like a wriggling worm.
> —"At Rushy Pond"

The roar of the tides from beyond the lofty coastlands are only "smitings like the slam of doors,/Or hammerings on hollow floors." "Smitings" as applied to doors is an interesting example of his choice for the sake of alliteration. Like his choice of "terrene" it neutralizes the image. In another image he substitutes "tombs" for "floors"—like "hammering in a hollow tomb"—heightening the mood. Canning's speech was grave, Sheridan is reported having said, with bits of shiny ornament stuck on—like the brass nails on a coffin. Even when describing an ordinary thing, however, Hardy can manage to reduce it and capture a listless quality that is the very nadir of enthusiasm. The open fireplace, he says, "spread/Like a vast weary yawn above his head." The images drawn from the everyday life of his Wessex are infinite.

The barnyard also yields its quota. A grave is likened to a grain bin, and even Shakespeare to the

> . . . strange bird we sometime find
> To mingle with the barn-door brood awhile,

Then vanish from their homely domicile—
—"To Shakespeare"

He pushes matters to an extreme, however, when he puns by say-
ing that "the nightmares neighed from their stalls."

We know that Hardy was fond of dumb pets; his poems to "Wes-
sex" amply attest to that. It is not surprising, therefore, to find dogs
furnishing images. That stars wag from joy I have already pointed
out. Similarly "the Pleiads aloft seemed to pant/ With the heather
that twitched in the wind." The east wind "snarls and sneezes" and
dawn when "night was lifting" was a dog that "had crept under
its shade." Less precise is the dawn that was "close lurking by." [1]

To anyone who has been an intimate witness of any of the innu-
merable fairs that make the pulse of the English villagers beat more
quickly for a two or three days' stretch, Hardy's images are a vivid
reminder of that experience. Marketing and bargaining there are,
of course, as there are at our country fairs, but the principal attrac-
tions for the younger persons there, as here, are the "midway," the
sports, and the games. By the fair's activities Hardy illuminates
many of his ideas. The successful lover is the winner at a lottery,
because Hardy realizes that the average full-blooded young man
does not choose his mate with mathematical precision. It is prob-
ably the joy of the young couples that he has in mind when he
describes water as "rife with revelry." The young stalwart, stand-
ing with the sledge hammer to see if he can ring the bell by the

[1] Hardy has written several poems about domestic animals. Nowhere, however, do his
sentiment and sentimentality so nearly fuse as in those poems dealing with his dumb
friends. Bird-catching and cruelty to dogs stirred his imagination and aroused his in-
dignation. The sentimental approach of "The Bird Catcher's Boy" in which the son
prefers death to following his father's occupation and of "The Mound" with the mon-
grel's cursing of mankind when he realizes that his master intends his death throw
much light on Hardy and his general philosophy of life although as poems they are of
little worth. In fact, the majority of the poems on this subject are of little general
interest. They possess a "laureate" quality, are limited in their appeal, and do no more
than scratch the surface of profound emotion. Whether it be an ode in commemoration
of the centenary of the S.P.C.A., or verses to one of his own pets—a favorite cat or his
beloved dog—Wessex in particular, or verses evoked by the sight of a stranger burying
his pet cat, the result is the same. ("Compassion," "Last Words to a Dumb Friend,"
"The Roman Gravemounds," "Dead Wessex, the Dog to the Household," "A Popular
Personage at Home.")
    But of more than laureate quality are "The Milestone by the Rabbit Barrow," "Wag-
tail and Baby," and "The Boy's Dream"; and the reason is that the animals are merely
incidental to the main theme of the poems—the problems of life.

force of his blow, an unfailing sight at a fair or carnival, vivifies
Time as "the Fair's hard-hitter." The irony of Joseph's progress to
Madrid, "glorious as a sodden rocket's fizz" is obvious. Puppet
shows, pantomimes, and mummings seen both at fairs, in the thea-
ter, and at various seasons about the countryside are used over forty
times to intensify his ideas of change, life, the world, love, time,
death, trees, the Immanent Will, and so forth. Nor does he over-
look the sharpers. Napoleon's "three years' ostentatious scheme . . .
was . . . scarce other than a trick of thimble-rig," the old shell
game; and Pitt regards the foreign despatches as "trustless as cheap
Jack/ Dumfounding yokel at a country fair."

The moors and the surrounding country are more than back-
ground. The endless days separating the lover from the beloved
"seemed hopeless hills [his] strength must faint to climb." He com-
municates his feeling about the hills and barrows, however, by a
figure from womankind, her breasts in particular. Rainbarrow, for
example, "bulged like a supine negress' breast." He intensifies his
attitude toward barrows by comparing them to a figure of fertility
he might well have seen in the Vatican:

> Where barrows, bulging as they bosoms were
> Of Multimammia stretched supinely there.
> —"By the Barrows"

The more gradual slope of hills is caught in their comparison to
"awakened sleepers on one elbow lifted,/ Who gaze around to learn
if things during the night have shifted." The trees assume a volup-
tuous quality when he likens them to a disrobing woman:

> The trees are undressing and fling in many places
> Their radiant robes and ribbons and yellow laces.
> —"Last Week in October"

On the other hand, he intensifies the starkness of the tragedy by
speaking of the regiments crashing "like trees at felling-time."

I have already suggested the manner in which Hardy sees the
macrocosm in the microcosm and I think the chosen images sup-
port the statement. The effect on the reader of such a selection of
images is to rob the poem of any sense of ecstasy. To turn from one
of his images to any image taken at random from Shelley illus-
trates the essential difference in their natures. Hardy is matter-of-

fact. Shelley always the aspirant, the reacher after an ecstatic moment of perfect fulfillment, to whom a treasured spell is "like veiled lightning asleep" or "like the spark nursed in embers." This inability or reluctance to soar in his images, and I think it is probably both, gives Hardy's poetry a quality of the earth that never lets us forget the realist. Some of his images drawn from flowers are appealingly beautiful. Even these, however, never transcend the immediate world about him, never fire him with an exaltation of spirit, never give the impression of having been struck off at white heat. They are accurate, calm, and deliberate. Such, for example, is the figure of the evening-star "hanging like a jonquil blossom" or, again, the "marge of his hair like morning frost," or her curls like "fir-cones—piled up, brown—/ Or rather like tight-tied sheaves." Life is "an unfenced flower, benumbed and nipped at unawares," infant shapes are like "mushroom balls on grassy ground," poor children are "frail human flowerets, sicklied by the shade," and a maiden's lips are "peony lips." Men are "but thistle-globes on Heaven's high gales,/ And whither blown, or when, or how, or why/ Can choose us not at all," and dancers are "weightless as thistle-ball." He admirably catches the silvery quality of lamps at dusk by comparing them to "dandelion globes." Soldiers are like "a thicket of reeds in which every seed should be a man," or they "sway like sedges in a gale" and "spin like leaves." It is interesting to observe, however, that he also draws from the military to illustrate such widely differing concepts as time and the sea:

> . . . . the unslumbering sea,
> That sentrys up and down all night, all day,
> From cave to promontory, from ness to bay.
> —"A Singer Asleep"

He frequently captures in his images of nature graciousness and humor without a sacrifice of accuracy. One unconsciously wonders if Miss Millay had not read "A Backward Spring" before writing her "Spring Song." Birds and insects aid the poet. Delicacy is inherent in the whispering "soft as the fan of a turtledove" and in the description of his early vision "delicate as a lamp-worm's lucency." Music, water, art, the military—all serve Hardy's purpose.

The Dynasts is a storehouse for images belittling mankind. Soldiers fall "like sedge before the scythe" or like melting wax. The marching columns look like no more than "a file of ants crawling along a strip of garden matting," or an "insect-creep" or "slow worms through grass." The busy soldiers look like "cheese-mites," or they "glide" on "like water from a burst reservoir." The accoutrements of the cavalry flash in the sun "like a school of mackerel." The stage directions, particularly, contain numerous of these views of mankind as if seen from an eagle's aerie.

A mere enumeration of images is not sufficient. More important is the manner in which they are woven into the fabric of the poem. They have an emotive quality, it is true, even when suspended in alcohol for all to see. Their true measure is apparent, however, only when we see them as an integral part of the whole. Only then can we have some concept of Hardy's stature.

The aesthetic aspect of his images per se is not enough. When Hardy is at his best he achieves his effects with admirable economy. In the two stanzas of "Weathers" he vivifies the pleasant and the unpleasant scenes by the selection of telling details. Apart from the value of this poem as an example of the poet's evocation of a mood with the aid of vowel sounds—the front vowels and the voiceless sibilants of the first stanza, the back vowels and voiced sibilants of the second—the details intensify the mood. Happiness and joy are inherent in the showers that "betumble the chestnut spikes," the "little brown nightingale" singing at the top of his voice, the cronies before the inn, the girls with their light dresses, and those dreaming of that part of England where summer has already arrived. "Betumble" is the inevitable verb. But "drip," "thresh" and "ply" as epithets for the beeches, "throb" for the hillsides, with the rivulets that "overflow," the dripping gates, and the rooks intensify the dismalness of the second stanza. The same economy and simplicity are characteristic, too, of "In Time of 'The Breaking of Nations.'" The word "stalk," however, raises a question in the reader's mind. It is good enough, but whether or not it is exactly the picture the poet had in mind is debatable. It satisfies the need of rhyme and of alliteration on *s,* but does it not overintensify the scene?

We recognize a similar accuracy in the selection of details in the almost unbearable heat of the hot summer day in "The Five Students." Particularly effective is the sparrow who "dips in his wheel-rut bath" as a prelude to the increasing heat of the sun which, boiling "the dew to smoke by the paddock path," later, standing overhead, is responsible for the following vignette, the rhythm of the final line suspending all movement:

> The air is shaken, the high-road hot,
> Shadowless swoons the day,
> The greens are sobered and cattle at rest . . .

Better known are those poems in which Hardy evokes the mood of the moors even more forcefully than in his novels. He is a master at painting nature in revolt as well as presenting her in her most gracious aspects. He loves each by turns, but it is the rougher nature that most strongly appeals to the romance in his make-up. Absorbed in his thoughts of the woman as is the man in "The Wind's Prophecy" he is conscious of the details of the landscape. He travels on

> . . . by barren farms,
> And gulls glint out like silver flecks
> Against a cloud that speaks of wrecks,
> And bellies down with black alarms.

"Bellies down" gives to the cloud characteristics of a lumbering animal settling itself. The distant prospect for this traveler is bleak:

> A distant verge morosely gray
> Appears, while clots of flying foam
> Break from its muddy monochrome,
> And a light blinks up far away.

The strong iambic beat of the first two lines with the relaxation in the third and fourth and the alliteration enhance the dryness of the movement. Carefully selected details and the same dry beat give a similar movement to "A Meeting with Despair." His choice of "harden" in "while I saw morning harden upon the wall" conveys a similar effect.

An outstanding example of Hardy's portraiture of a desolate scene is one familiar to most of his readers—"The Darkling Thrush." Line after line adds details pertaining to death that make a depressing total. If it is not death directly, it is death by implication and symbol as

The tangled bine-stems scored the sky
Like strings of broken lyres . . .

The contrast is the greater, therefore, when after a multiplicity of
images concentrated on the single idea the verse suddenly sweeps
through four lines without a caesura to the overpowering "of joy
illimited." The greater sweep occurs in the fourth stanza. So little
cause for such carolings, says the poet,

That I could think there trembled through
His happy good-night air
Some blessed Hope, whereof he knew
And I was unaware.

The placing of the caesura after Hope, followed by a gradual
relaxation throughout the rest of the stanza is an enviable artistic
achievement. The endowment of the storm and wind in "Night-
Time in Mid-Fall" with human characteristics, the storm striding
over the night and the "winds footing swift" and the leaves that
"totter down still green" is effective.

We have already noticed in the image of the bine-stem scoring
the sky the poet's use of the sky as a silhouetting background for
plant life. In a similar genre is the opening image in "The Prospect":

The twigs of the birch imprint the December sky
Like branching veins upon a thin old hand . . .

But how different the tone imparted by "score" and "imprint"; one
is destructive and forceful, the other gentle. Human, too, is his
description of the iced airs that "wheeze" and "snore." "The Har-
bour Bridge" is a further development. Against "the day's-end sky,
fair-green in glow" he paints the bridge over which pass several
couples, and finally one particular couple who play out their drama
in this setting. The most striking image in this poem is undoubtedly
that of the burghers gliding by

As cut black-paper portraits hastening on
In conversation none knows what upon:
Their sharp-edged lips move quickly word by word
To speech that is not heard.

An artist likes an overcast sky because the colors of the landscape
are at such times more interesting, the contrasts greater, the colors

richer. Hardy, sharing their preference, as we have already seen, is frequently at his best in his descriptions of fog and rime.

Rain and archery fuse in "On the Doorstep":

> . . . imprinted on the step's wet shine
> With target-circles that quivered and crossed

Very different is the mood of the storm in "The Division." The wind is here compared to a person with a broom, probably someone akin to a witch.

> Rain on the windows, creaking doors
> With blasts that besom the green.

The transition to the barnyard from the green is not difficult, and every fork of the snow-covered tree is "like a white web-foot" ("Snow in the Suburbs").

Nature intensifies the bitterness and hatred of the father in "A Daughter Returns." Having recognized his daughter's profession by her dress, he drives her from home, shouting:

> When the cold sneer of dawn follows night-shadows
>   black as a hearse,
> And the rain filters down the fruit tree,
> And the tempest mouths into the flue-top a word
>   like a curse,
> Then, then I shall think, think of thee!

It is vivid description, but is it possible to imagine a father indulging in elaborate nature description when at white heat? From a realistic or psychological point of view it has little right in the poem, but I do not think we would have it away.

At times he speaks of the sour spring wind which "blurting boisterous-wise, . . . bears on it dirty clouds across the skies," to heighten the shepherd's imperviousness to his surroundings as he counts his flock. The alliterating explosives "blurting boisterous" intensify the emotion by onomatopoeic means but would be far less affective without "sour." The wind is also likened to a bassoon to which the cypresses croon in a poem in which a man wishes to recall his friends by playing the old melodies to which they formerly danced. The carpenter's trade contributes "planing up shavings of crystal spray" to describe the darting moor hen. The poet's use of human injuries to vivify the setting sun which lay like a "crimson wound" is in the same category as Housman's "the sun bleeds on the road to Wales" and, indirectly, Eliot's description of evening "like a patient etherized upon the table."

In numerous ways Hardy vivifies his thought by images from music. Metaphors are frequent. In youth, for example, life courted him with soft symphonies and sweet color; the song of the universe is "full-fugued," troubles are "strange orchestras of victim-shriek and song." Similes from music abound, many of them likened to a song. He speaks, however, of the sea roaring its "psalmodies," of the gargoyles "mouthing a tune," of the moon's light "falling like a friendly tune," of the corn-blade's "husky note." For additional similes we have those dealing with musical instruments: lyres, 'cellos, viols, flutes, lutes, and so forth. If we had only the images we would know Hardy's great interest in music, chiefly homely music, to be that of the amateur, and primarily the village amateur. Nothing in his images is incompatible with the earlier statement in Chapter I on his musical taste—that his interest is essentially in folk melodies and hymn tunes because of the essentially human referent. Abstract music held little appeal for him.

He also employs many images from childhood. Small boys typify the pollard willows which stand "like shock-headed urchins, spiny haired." "The field, flock, and lonely trees" in "Nature's Questioning" look to the poet "like chastened children sitting silent in a school." He robs the graves of the children in the cemetery of their dignity when he speaks of their having been laid therein at different times, "like sprats in a tin." Life, too, is minimized when he compares it to a "senseless school" which made him "grimace, and foot and prance,/ As cats on hot bricks have to dance."

He does not always minimize objects or ideas by seeing in them resemblance to commonplace materials of everyday life. He also sees in the minutiae a resemblance to the greater things. A thistle seed born along by the breeze is like a comet with its tail streaming along behind. Stars may remind him of eyes, just as eyes will remind him of stars. He moves easily among the great as among the small, among the abstract as well as among the concrete, and in this ability lies the key to his sanity. He has liberated himself from suffering by suffering. He persisted in his strenuous humility of self-knowing, and by that persistence he achieved a liberation in his own immediate life as well as into the greater reality, into the freedom of the universe. He persisted in living in the environment of his early years even after fame came to him. He realized the eternal truth of the statement that a prophet is not without honor save in his own country, and realized that perhaps in the long run it was salutary. It helped him keep his balance in a world in which many lesser persons with greater public reputations had lost theirs.

He can look at the stars as they wear west and see in their movement a likeness to a "slow tide flowing." He can look at the waning moon and catch its color in the epithet "watery light," or he can look at the "hazy mazy moonlight at one in the morning" and see it "spread out as a sea across the frozen main." The frail light of the new moon may strike the earth "like a friendly tune . . . like a liquid ditty." In other words, he moves easily from the realm of sight to that of sound and touch.

An appreciation of Hardy's imagery does not rise from the study of such obvious examples as I have presented here. It is best seen in a detailed study of those less obvious metaphors enclosed in single words, many examples of which have already been given and many more will inevitably follow.

An interesting facet of Hardy's diction is his use of color words for their connotative value: white, gray, pink, rose, red, scarlet, purple, russet, brown, green and black. Rose and pink typify joy and happiness; green, youth; gray, dullness; red, war and conflict. The most recurring color of all is gray. We have, to name but a few, "the drizzling gray/ Of an English May," "a distant verge morosely gray," the hills that "grayly gazed," "frets" that "freeze gray your face and hair." Closely bound up with the emotional connotation of "gray" is his frequent use of the words implying coldness: arctic, chill, clammy, cold, freeze, bleak, frost, ice, and shivering, often used in conjunction with the coldness of a corpse. Rumors come like a "chilling breath," fear falls "like frost," an object has a "cold white look," dawn wears a "cold sneer," Time's "fierce frost" kills memories, the heath-hemmed pond has "a frigid face," and the house is "bleak and cold." Much of the depressing effect that persons often associate with Hardy's poems arises from his choice of such color and tactile words.

He best reveals himself the poet in the admirable way in which his diction bolsters his thought, in his use of rare, archaic, obsolete, learned, and other image words to fix the impression of the poem in the reader's mind—in other words, in his successful communication of his ideas. Few poets are able in a few words so to vivify a landscape as to harmonize or contrast with the mood of the protagonists of the poem. He has written some pure nature poems, it is true, but his usual use of natural setting is as a background against which the dramatic action of the poem shapes itself. The background is definitely localized. Dull would be the reader indeed who could not visualize the following:

> That day when oats were reaped, and wheat was ripe,
> and barley ripening,
> The road-dust hot, and the bleaching grasses dry.
> —"When Oats Were Reaped"

Just as a person who has made an extensive study of mathematics can never wholly discard his tendency to approach every problem from a strictly logical point of view, beginning at the beginning and moving steadily forward, so can a person trained in architecture, as was Hardy, never approach a poem without a keen sense of its architectural unity, nor without a searching sense for the materials appropriate to the task in hand. Hardy is essentially functional. He shows, true enough, as in his use of the refrain, the same love of Gothic ornament that he admired in architecture, but his basic design is generally sound; so sound, in fact, that he can frequently give value to a commonplace thought by the clothing with which he envelops it. His least significant poems, except for many of these which I have called "laureate," show the carefulness of a conscientious craftsman.

Instances of his felicitous diction are already apparent in some of the passages quoted to illustrate his stanzaic structure. Further ones will give a more detailed picture. But any selection must be inadequate. At most it can but stimulate the reader to find others for himself, and perhaps better ones. He is not an imagist in the sense that H. D. and Amy Lowell are; his aim was otherwise. Nor do his images give more than an insight into one phase of his diction which, generally speaking, is straightforward, the result of an intense observation of his subject, and at times almost classical in its finish. In his few best poems he is of the school of Ben, and nowhere more than in his deeply moving and direct "Let Me Enjoy" or "The Rambler" in which word follows word with inevitability. The music, serious and stately, conceals the art which undoubtedly went into the composition of these pieces. Directness is not always an asset in keying the tone of a poem, however, as he was aware in "Something Tapped." The indefiniteness of the opening word "something" enhances the mysteriousness after which the poet sought.

⁂ 8 ⁂

PROSODY

So FAR WE HAVE PAID little attention to a phase of
Hardy's poetic technique that is important to any just understand-
ing of his achievement. We have looked at isolated words and
images, but we have not examined the rhythmical use of those
words; and it was rhythmical demands that frequently dictated
their final form. It is the manner in which he has fused these details
that contributes to his stature as a poet; fused them, we must re-
member, to fit into the larger unit of the stanza. His care in achiev-
ing this helped him toward his ideal of the intensification of things
in the manner of Crivelli, Bellini, and other painters for the purpose
of making vividly visible, as he said, the heart and inner meaning.

This is important to realize and demands extensive treatment in
any consideration of his subject matter. Few persons, even readers
of poetry, are aware of the extent of his prosodic experiments. Few
know that in the use of the poetic stanza he is one of our most
extensive innovators in the modern, or for that matter, any period
of our poetry. I use the term "extensive" in a numerical sense. I do
not believe that Hardy is a profound experimenter in the way that
Hopkins and Keats were. His ear was not keen enough for him
to be wholeheartedly dissatisfied with all existing prosodic forms
and to struggle to find the most perfect form for his communica-
tions. We find no parallels, for example, of Keats's struggle to avoid
the "chiming" effect of the octave of the Italian sonnet and the too
elegiac quality of the Shakespearian, a struggle which led him to
unsuccessful efforts in a modified sonnet form, in which he at-
tempted to retain the advantages of each type, and through these
to the final solution of his difficulties—tentatively in the "Ode to

Psyche," assuredly in the form of the "Ode to a Nightingale" and "Ode on a Grecian Urn," and supremely in his "Ode to Autumn." Nor do we find the conscious attempt made by Hopkins to lengthen the line of the sonnet by the use of "outriding" feet and other innovations to compensate for the difference of vowel quality in Italian and English. We have no feeling, or only rarely so, that Hardy was forced by his demon as was Beethoven "to search in a hundred variants—the so-called sketches—for the definitive, the valid form for his thoughts." In other words, we feel that he experimented for the sake of experiment rather than from the sense of some deeper need. And yet one must guard against too hasty generalization. In poem after poem he has employed forms which are appropriate and are in close harmony with the subject matter. The iambic dimeter stanza of "Lizbie Browne ($a^2b^2c^2b^2c^2a^2$) catches the timid irresolution of the lover who was always too late, just as the trochaic tetrameter of "The Bullfinches" ($a^4a^4b^4c^4c^4$) reflects a fineness and sadness.[1]

Statistics are sometimes impressive, and seemingly dry tabulations may possess a romantic flavor. This is true in the analysis of Hardy's great diversity of prosodic forms, even though he made little positive contribution to English prosody.

In addition to at least 88 poems in which he employed mixed-stanza forms, he has used over 250 different rhyme schemes in at least 548 different stanza patterns. He employed, for example, 41 different variations of stress in the a-b-a-b rhyme scheme, the most common of all the forms which he uses. The following partial list of the varying stress distribution will give an idea of his treatment of the a-b-a-b pattern. The number in parentheses indicates the number of poems in each form:

2-2-2-2	(1)	3-2-3-2	(8)
2-2-4-2	(1)	3-2-4-3	(1)
2-3-4-5	(1)	3-3-3-2	(6)
2-3-5-6	(1)	3-3-3-3	(19)
2-5-5-2	(1)	3-3-4-2	(2)
3-2-3-1	(1)	3-3-4-3	(6)

[1] Throughout this chapter I shall use the traditional metrical notation. The Arabic exponents indicate the number of stresses in the line; the lower case letters, the rhyme pattern.

3-3-6-3	(1)	4-3-2-5	(1)
3-5-3-5	(1)	4-3-4-2	(2)
3-7-7-3	(1)	4-3-4-3	(42)
4-2-4-2	(3)		

and so on to the last $a^7b^7a^7b^3(1)$. Were we further to divide the stanzas according to the type of metrical feet used, the number would be still greater. The group $a^4b^4a^4b^4$, for example, contains 10 poems that are strongly iambic, one slightly iambic, 5 in which iambs and anapests are about evenly divided, 2 that are strongly anapestic, and 1 that is trochaic. If we also realize that there are over 450 stanza forms which are used only once we have some conception of the problem that confronts the critic anxious to be dispassionate in his appraisal of the poet. He must be careful not to attribute roughness to a poem when the difficulty is with his own ear. That Hardy was always, or even generally, successful, no one could possibly admit. That he succeeded as often as he did considering the extent of his experimentation is surprising. In poem after poem he has fitted the thought to the form without loss of accuracy, has employed images that heighten his communication, and has achieved subtleties of diction that escape the eye of the careless reader. His trouble has been that he has often achieved more than the ordinary reader is prepared for or can easily grasp. In Hardy's, as in all poetry, the words derive a heightened vigor from the pattern into which he has fitted them. Patterns, as I shall point out in the chapter on *The Dynasts,* are absolutely necessary for Hardy if he is to achieve the greater intensity of poetry over prose.

Early in his poetic career he decided that too regular a beat was bad art and he gave importance to stress rather than to too great regularity. By concentrating on stress he hoped to achieve the same subtlety and fluidity of line that is the delight of Gothic architecture, in which he had so deeply steeped himself. He sought to delight by surprise, by seeming accident. Strangely enough, however, the poems that most frequently find their way into the anthologies are those in which the rhythms are most regular, generally most strongly iambic. And yet is this surprising? Actually, Hardy employs only ten stanza forms more than six times. Greater experience in handling one particular form would naturally tend toward greater perfection in that form. The distribution of these ten forms is as follows:

(common meter)	$a^4b^3a^4b^3$	(44)	(ballad meter)	$a^4b^3c^4b^3$	(6)
	$a^4b^4a^4b^4$	(19)		$a^4b^4a^4b^4c^4c^4$	(7)
	$a^3b^3a^3b^3$	(19)		$a^4b^3a^4b^3a^4b^3$	(6)
(long meter)	$a^4a^4b^4b^4$	(11)		$a^4a^4a^4$	(8)
	$a^5b^5a^5b^5$	(9)		$a^3b^3a^3b^3c^3d^3c^3d^3$	(6)

The last form is obviously no more than a double $a^3b^3a^3b^3$. In his anxiety to conceal his art, Hardy sometimes almost conceals the pattern of the poem. In the scansion of the entire poem, however, the pattern generally becomes clear.

Many poems have a very strongly articulated stress, but on the other hand many have an exceedingly delicate one. No metrical notation can possibly convey the richness of these nuances to the reader; nuances which, being sometimes even too much for the poet himself, lead him into engulfing difficulties. Scansion becomes difficult, even perilous. Hardy is careful to maintain the same stanza pattern throughout the poem, except in that group in which for dramatic purposes he mixes his forms. But even there he is consistent. His skill reveals itself in the variation in the type of prosodic feet used from stanza to stanza. Rarely, except of course, in the poems that are strongly iambic ($\smile$ /), anapestic ($\smile \smile$ /), or trochaic (/ $\smile$)—the last type comprising only a small portion of the total— is one stanza of a poem identical with the one immediately preceding or following it. The most usual variations from iambs are anapests, the extent of their uses varying within wide limits from poems containing one or two in a stanza to poems made up almost entirely of them. Without including those in which the anapests are only frequent enough to prevent monotony in a too-regular iambic stanza, say about three in a four-line stanza, there are over 350 poems containing a larger proportion. Of these 38 are strongly anapestic and 161 vary from largely anapestic to mediumly so. In other words, about a third of the poems have more anapests than we should find in a traditional iambic pattern. No generalization about his use of this foot for one particular purpose, however, is possible because the subject matter is extensive in each form: from grave to gay, from tender to bitter and ironic, from youth to age, from joy to disillusionment. We shall only be able to speak of the artistic use Hardy has made of this foot when we compare the subjects in this measure with identical subjects in another measure, a subject for later study, and primarily a problem in tonality.

In the same manner it is interesting to notice that in his use of the trochaic foot (/ ◡) only 30 poems are almost exclusively so, 35 contain frequent trochaics, and 32 two or three per stanza. He uses dactylics much less frequently. Only 5 poems are almost exclusively in this measure, 2 make frequent use of them, and 9 their occasional use. The occasional instances generally occur in combination with trochaics. More interesting, however, is Hardy's use of two types of metrical feet that are frequently neglected in a treatment of modern poetry: the amphibrach (◡ / ◡) and the pae-on.[2] Hardy has used amphibrachs in at least 153 poems generally placing them at the end of the line, most frequently alternating them with lines ending in iambs. The third paeon serves the same purpose in an anapestic line as the amphibrach in an iambic. Hardy has used third paeons in at least 68 poems, but second and fourth paeons less frequently—only in fact, 6 and 8 times, respectively.[3]

I have mentioned that Hardy's versification is not always suc-cessful. His strong lines are apt to be labored. Too frequently, in his endeavor to make clear the intellectual idea behind the poem, he leaves traces of his will forcing the words to do his bidding. The idea may be arresting but the words themselves lack charm and rhythmic domestication and seem to resent being crowded into narrow confines. This is not only characteristic of poems written to celebrate some particular occasion as in the somewhat heavy "Lines" (spoken by Miss Ada Rehan), or the labored lines of "To Shakespeare," or in experiments in foreign meters as the sap-phics of "The Temporary the All," the artificial, awkward, and uncongenial hendecasyllabics of "Aristodemus the Messenian," or in some of his triolets, but is also occasionally true of others in which the form not only does not bolster the thought, but definitely

---

[2] Paeons are of four varieties: 1st (/ ◡ ◡ ◡); 2d (◡ / ◡ ◡); 3d (◡ ◡ / ◡); and 4th (◡ ◡ ◡ /).

[3] Some persons prefer to ignore the paeons and amphibrachs. In my opinion, how-ever, particularly since Hopkins's conscious experiment with these feet, modern poetry practically demands their use in order to avoid an involved terminology.

detracts from the thought's effectiveness. Whether it is a whole poem as "A Poet's Thought," the movement of the verse of which is arbitrary and stiff, or the opening lines of "His Visitor," or the somewhat heavy change in line 4 of "Copying Architecture in an Old Minister"; or the arrangement of lines as in "Near Lanivet, 1872" in which the rhythm is obviously difficult—

> There was a stunted handpost just on the crest,
> > Only a few feet high:
> She tired and we stopped in the twilight-time for her rest,
> > At the crossways close thereby.—

the reader and the poet are at odds. He cannot grasp the emotion the poet wished to communicate.

The greatest obstacle to the poet's successful communication, however, lies in his frequent attempts at enclosing the thought in a predetermined pattern, ill-fitted for the purpose. Whether he was unwilling to make the effort to eradicate the difficulties, or whether his ear was deficient is difficult to say; but in numerous poems one cannot help feeling that a keener musical ear would have prevented many of the jarring notes. Only rarely does one sense in Hardy that delicacy and sensitivity to verbal music always so evident in Hopkins, Yeats, and Keats of the odes. I do not mean to imply or even suggest that Hardy was incapable of achieving beautiful music. He does. But the music is much simpler than that of Hopkins or Yeats and contains little of what we might call their ability at inweaving melodies. His music is that of a simple country song; the reader understands it more readily. But Hardy is not so apt to repeat short groups of words for the sheer exquisiteness of the sound. One feels, for example, that in "Often When Warring" he has made a Procrustes bed of the sonnet form, or as in "The Place on the Map" that he has packed line 2 of each stanza with more than it can rightfully carry. He alternates the rhythm of "In a Wood" from iambic to trochaic in such a way that it is difficult for the reader to make the adjustment necessary to grasp the full force of the thought. Although he frequently successfully employs this device, in this poem of five stanzas it is difficult if not impossible.

The reader, however, must constantly guard against hasty generalizations or snap judgments. The effectiveness of each poem depends to a great extent on the order in which the poems are

read. Hardy rings such a multitude of changes within the course
of a few pages that the fault in communication often lies in the
reader's unconscious permission of the intrusion of mnemonic
irrelevances, and not in any deficiency in the poet. Time after
time, for example, I have made jottings about poems containing
prosy lines, rhythms without subtlety, crowded lines, too faint
stresses, and so forth, only to find upon further reading that I
disagreed with my earlier impressions. Repeated readings make me
increasingly aware of that "art which conceals art" that attracted
Hardy. "On Sturminster Foot-Bridge" is a case in point. It cannot
be scanned with any degree of regularity, and on that account has
puzzled many critics. Hardy warned the reader when he placed
"Onomatopoeic" in parentheses immediately beneath the title.
These lines were intended, wrote Mrs. Hardy, "to convey by their
rhythm the impression of a clucking of ripples into riverside holes
when blown upon by an up-stream wind." "An Anniversary"
presents difficulties of scansion. It contains iambs, anapests, amphi-
brachs, third paeons, and at least one trochee. The pattern is diffi-
cult because it gives no sense of being inevitable, nor is it readily
discernible even after several readings. I think every reader would
scan it differently. The instances in which the pattern is unsuc-
cessful and the thought does not fit the pattern are many. "The
Young Churchwarden" might be a border case, but "St. Launce's
Revisited," "Quid Hic Agis," "On a Midsummer Eve" are perhaps
trivial poems, but the triviality arises from the lack of fusion of
thought and form. "The Re-Enactment" is even a better illustration.
The beat of the stanza is too obvious for the nature of the story;
it is too dog-trotty:

> Between the folding sea-downs,
>   In the gloom
> Of a wailful wintry nightfall,
>   When the boom
> Of the ocean, like a hammering in a hollow tomb,
>
> Throbbed up the copse-clothed valley
>   From the shore
> To the chamber where I darkled
>   Sunk and sore
> With gray ponderings why my loved one had not
>   come before . . .

The poem, true enough, contains some excellent word painting, makes effective use of alliteration (*b, f, w, h,* for example) and of chiming vowels, but contains too much bad Poe or bad Tennyson. "To My Father's Violin" and "News for Her Mother" present the same difficulties. The stanzas, being involved, frequently require a wrenching of the words to fit the obviously artificial patterns. Occasionally a single stanza will detract from the reader's pleasure in a poem, as the third in "The Runic Stone":

> And the die thrown
> By them heedlessly there, the dent
> It was to cut in their encompassment,
> Were, too, unknown.

Hardy has frequently used tail-rhyme stanzas (as a-a-b-c-c-b) effectively. "Transformations," however, is an unsuccessful instance. It pounds too monotonously on the ear. The patterns of "At a Seaside Town" ($a^4b^2b^2b^4$) and "The Musical Box" ($a^2b^4c^4b^4c^4a^2$) with the variations between two and four stresses are likewise difficult.

Actually, however, the instances of wrenched, forced, and artificial rhythms are few and the poems that strike the reader as uninspired, pedestrian, and as employing meters that are merely ingenious rather than flexible belong chiefly to that class which we have called laureate poems, poems celebrating some immediate topical occasion or those crystallising a moment valuable only to the poet. Hardy fully realized that even the best lyrics are not completely lyrical throughout, and that the neutral lines frequently take on a reflected glow from the others.

Interesting treatment of rhythms for bolstering the communication are frequent. In "The Youth Who Carried a Light," for example, the poet wrenches line 3 in stanza 1 in such a way that we see the scene more vividly than would be possible had he continued in the pulsating lyrical measure with which he begins:

> I saw him pass as the new day dawned
> Murmuring some musical phrase
> Horses were drinking and floundering in the pond,
> And the tired stars thinned their gaze.

The sudden wrenching of the rhythm of "Horses were drinking and floundering in the pond," by making it a five-stress line communicates the feeling of floundering to us.

In variation on stresses "The Tree and the Lady" is an interesting experiment. Lines 1 and 4 rise at the end, lines 2 and 3, ending in pyrrhics ($\smile\smile$) fall:

> I have done all I could
> For that lady I knew! Through the heats I have shaded her,
> Drawn to her songsters when summer has jaded her,
> Home from the heath or the wood.[4]

More interesting is the manner in which the poet evokes the distressed mental state of the protagonist in "The Discovery," by the irregularity of the feet and the caesurae.

The consistent use of anapests in lines 8 and 9 of "Reminiscences of a Dancing Man," in a stanza otherwise strongly iambic, intensifies the waltzing movement of the dancers:

> And the gas-jets winked, and the lustres clinked,
> And the platform throbbed as with arms enlinked
> We moved to the minstrelsy;

just as the about equal distribution of iambs and anapests in the five-stressed measure of "In a Museum" hints at the nostalgia of the visitor; or as the similar combination of feet with lines 2 and 4 ending in amphibrachs intensifies the theme of "Aquae Sulis."

The change from strict iambs to trochees and dactyls in lines 4 and 5 of "Beyond the Last Lamp" and then the return in lines 6 and 7 to iambs vivifies for the reader the reluctant pace of the lovers:

> While rain, with eve in partnership,
> Descended darkly, drip, drip, drip,
> Beyond the last lone lamp I passed
> Walking slowly, whispering sadly,
> Two linked loiterers, wan, downcast:
> Some heavy thought constrained each face.
> And blinded them to time and place.

The regular beat of "The Young Glass-Stainer" reflects the boredom of the young man destined to work on Gothic architecture when his heart is in the classic, just as the weakly stressed accent of "In a Whispering Gallery" accords with the hushed awe of the gallery, or the verse of "The Pink Frock" suggests the triviality of the woman.

Hardy's rhythmical effects frequently cost him considerable effort,

---

[4] It is possible, of course, to say that lines 2 and 4 are four-stress ending in 2d paeons.

and even then he did not always succeed. A few examples from *Poems of the Past and Present* give some idea of his care. The alteration of "O it was sad enough, that we were mad enough" to "O it was sad enough, weak enough, mad enough . . ." is a good example. The metrical pattern remains the same, but the texture is much tighter in the revision, probably because of the second caesura. A clearer case, depending solely on rhythm is the alteration of the last half of line 12 in "In Tenebris, II" from the weak "Good God, why should I be here!" to "Why should such an one be here!" Occasionally the change is more subtle, as in line 16 of "In Tenebris, III" with the slight shifting of words from "with no longing or listing to join" to "with no listing or longing to join." The majority of changes are not, however, easily pigeonholed. Vowel sounds, alliteration, rhythm, and greater desire for the accurate word are all reasons for one small alteration.

Typical of Hardy is his use in numerous poems of alternating trochaic and iambic lines ("The House of Hospitalities"), his shift from the heroic couplet to blank verse to set off the speaker from the poet ("Panthera"), and his combinations of iambs and anapests in the "Satires of Circumstance" and other poems to capture a conversational quality.

Hardy's poetry sings much more than the casual reader of his verse realizes; and to make it sing Hardy uses certain technical devices that at least partially explain the effect. To explain them certainly does not explain away the delight one receives from the poems, nor does it give a complete account of his art. The most apparent device is the combination in about equal measure of iambs and anapests, frequently aided by amphibrachs. "The Background and the Figure," "Sitting on the Bridge," and "The Year's Awakening" are good examples. The insertion of a short line or lines frequently intensifies the lilt. "Weathers," "Why Be at Pains?," "The Interloper," and "At Castle Boterel," with their combination of lines of four and two stresses, and "We Field Women," with the first and last lines of one stress in combination with lines of four stresses, are felicitous in their musical appeal. "The Sun on the Bookcase" beginning with iambs, then shifting to anapests in the fourth line, to an initial trochee followed by an iamb and two anapests in the fifth, resolving again into iambs in the short sixth and seventh lines, captures the daydreaming mood of the student:

> Once more the cauldron of the sun
> Smears the bookcase with winey red,
> And here my page is, and there my bed,
> And the apple-tree shadows travel along.
> Soon their intangible track will be run,
> And dusk grow strong
> And they have fled.

Particularly effective in this medium is " 'O I Won't Lead a Homely Life!" in which further to heighten the musical effect the poet employs a great number of liquids (*l, r*) and nasals (*m, n*) in combination with appropriate vowel sounds, as short *i* and long *oo* in the first stanza and long *e* and long *a* in the second. We have already noticed the affective possibilities of well-handled vowel and consonantal sounds, although as I pointed out then, the bearing of sounds on the rhythm is not easily separable from the treatment of rhythm alone. The second stanza of "A Backward Spring" is a case in point. The poem, written in April, 1917, will, as I have already suggested in the preceding chapter, recall to many readers Miss Millay's charming poem on a similar theme; although, to me, Hardy's, being the more subdued in tone, reveals greater artistry. The words describing the actions of the flowers in the first three lines, for example, are so incontrovertibly right the effect of the change in rhythm in lines 4 and 5 might pass unnoticed. "Pants," and "heedless," for example, are the only words for the primrose.

> Yet the snowdrop's face betrays no gloom,
> And the primrose pants in its heedless push,
> Though the myrtle asks if it's worth the fight
> This year with frost and rime
> To venture one more time
> On delicate leaves and buttons of white
> From the selfsame bough as at last year's prime,
> And never to ruminate on or remember
> What happened to it in mid-December.

The poet also achieves a strong lilt with trochees, combined with amphibrachs and an occasional dactyl, as in "Meditation on a Holiday." The mood is not only a joyous one, but can be an optimistic,

courageous one, arising partly from the directness possible with a
metrical foot in which the first element is stressed. The direct
opening of "On a Fine Morning," written in 1899, with its question
"Whence comes Solace?" intensifies the statement of whence its
origins *are not* in strict trochees and whence its origins *are* in
catalectic trochaic tetrameter:

> Whence comes Solace?—Not from seeing
> What is doing, suffering, being,
> Not from noting Life's conditions,
> Nor from heeding Time's monitions;
> But in cleaving to the Dream
> And in gazing at the gleam
> Whereby gray things golden seem.

Trochees are interestingly employed too, in "The Bullfinches,"
" 'If It's Ever Spring Again,' " "Wives in the Sere," "In Childbed,"
and "Ditty." Lines 1, 2, 4 and 5 of "The Bullfinches" are catalectic
trochaic tetrameter, line 3 regularly trochaic with internal rhyme
and the effect is to hurry its reading. Their use with anapests and
iambs in " 'If It's Ever Spring Again' " bolsters the nostalgic mood
of the poem; adds to the charm of the careworn wife in "Wives in
the Sere," suggests the feminine quality of "In Childbed," and
lends exaltation to the lover in "Ditty." Verse movement can also
bolster the sense of premonition as in " 'A Man Was Drawing
Near to Me,' " can capture the matter-of-factness and acceptance by
a couple of their situation ("The Recalcitrants"), can make the
reader react with the masculine force of the protagonist in "The
Wind's Prophecy," can portray forcefully the restraint of masculine
grief ("The Shadow on the Stone"), and can impart the mounting
movement of the spirit, as in "Heiress and Architect" when the
heiress gives her instructions to the architect for the type of building
she desires. In this latter poem the meter not only captures the girl's
mounting spirit but also imparts a sense of its gradual curbing
which is culminated in the dryness of the final stanza. Dryness is
also characteristic of "Your Last Drive." Line 4 in the first stanza
in "At the Wicket-Gate"—"Her father, she, I"—carries weight.
"After Reading Psalms XXXIX, XL, etc." is an interesting *tour
de force,* the final line in each stanza being in Latin. Further in-
teresting rhythmical experiments are the stanzas of "The Marble-

Streeted Town," "Everything Comes," "The Noble Lady's Tale," and the Browning-like "The Collector Cleans His Picture." The use of different rhythms to indicate different speakers is characteristic of "A Sound in the Night" and "Haunting Fingers."

Refrain words, lines, and groups of lines—pointing to the strong and congenial ballad influence in the poems—are of frequent use as a means for achieving a desired tone. A sense of intimate communion, for example, results from the refrain of direct address: the use of "my friend" in "Fetching Her" and "An Experience," of "gentlemen" in each stanza of "An Ancient to Ancients," and "simple shepherds all" in "The Stranger's Song." The position of the refrain is, of course, important, and being so, Hardy is careful to use it to the best advantage. In the humorous "The Sergeant's Song," the "Rollicum-rorum, tol-lol-lorum,/ Rollicum-rorum, tol-lol-lay!" is as meaningless and yet as effective as many of the refrains of Elizabethan song. It personifies the bumptious good humor of the soldier. The other extreme is in "The Homecoming." A purist would even deny its being a refrain, since the lines are not repetitive. They serve much the same purpose as the descriptions of the sea in Virginia Woolf's *The Waves*. They key the tone of the portions of the story which they preface. The roaring of the wind without, caught in these lines—

> Gruffly growled the wind on Toller Down, so bleak and bare,
> And lonesome was the house, and dark; and few came there.—

intensifies the tragedy of disillusionment revealed in the conversation of the elderly groom and the young bride. Between these extremes is extensive experimentation. At the former end is "Voices from Things Growing in a Churchyard" with its double trochaic or falling refrain against the rising feet of the rest of the stanza —"Sir or Madam" of line 2 and "All day cheerily,/ All night eerily!" of lines 7 and 8—or in " 'I Said and Sang Her Excellence' " with its parenthetical refrain in line 3—"(Have your way, my heart, O!)." The three-stressed "Aye, my dear and tender!" of "First or Last" in a poem otherwise two-stressed lends a soothing quality to what is already an interesting prosodic pattern for the evocation of such a mood.[5] Further excellent uses of the refrain

[5] The refrain corresponds in stress to the middle stanza without a refrain.

occur in "Unrealized," "The Respectable Burgher," and "Unknowing." In this last Hardy makes an interesting variation in the final stanza from "We did not know" to "I feel and know."

A more frequent device is the repetition within a stanza of lines almost identical if not actually so. Line 1 in "The Sacrilege" and "The War-Wife of Catknoll" is repeated or nearly so, by line 3; in "Family Portraits" and "The Fallow Deer at the Lonely House," by line 4; in " 'As 'Twere To-Night,' " "By Henstridge Cross at the Year's End," and "The Coming of the End," by line 5; "To Lizbie Brown" and "She Did Not Turn," by line 6; in "The Blinded Bird," by line 7; in "An Appeal to America on Behalf of the Belgian Destitute," and " 'If You Had Known,' " by line 8; and in "A Two-Years' Idyll," by line 9. In a similar way line 2 is repeated by line 6 in "In the Seventies" and "Autumn in King's Hintock Park"; by line 7, in "To the Moon"; by line 9, in "Read by Moonlight." Line 3 is repeated by line 4 in "The Garden Seat"; and so on through many other combinations, The repetition is naturally more successful in some poems than in others. At times it adds nothing; at others it detracts. More involved, but scarcely more successful because the reader senses the artificiality, is the repetition within a stanza of the opening two lines of the stanza as in "Overlooking the River Stour," "When I Set Out for Lyonesse," " 'I Rose and Went to Rou'tor Town,' " and "Her Love-birds." Repetition of line is, as in "The Spell of the Rose," occasionally irregular. Its success is doubtful.

More interesting, however, is a type of repetition which Hardy might have adapted from one or other of the French forms with which he frequently experimented, although English models exist and derive ultimately from the characteristic of an echo in nature, one of the best being found in Shelley's *Prometheus Unbound*. I refer to his use as a refrain of half a preceding line. Occurring early in the stanza, as in "Summer Schemes," it can lend a buoyant note, or, as in "A Trampwoman's Tragedy," it can convey the mood of reminiscence in the speaker:

> Now as we trudged—O deadly day,
> 　　　O deadly day!—
> I teased my fancy-man in play
> 　　　And wanton idleness.

I walked alongside jeering John,
I laid his hand my waist upon;
I would not bend my glances on
My lover's dark distress.
—"A Trampwoman's Tragedy"

He inweaves the music and theme to capture the essential quality of the wanderer of the road.

A similar effect is possible at the end of a stanza, as in "The Man with a Past," in which the refrain intensifies the reminiscence as would a drawn-out sigh. The movement of the lines preceding the refrain has an important bearing, of course, on the effect of the refrain itself. The lyrical optimism of "Song of Hope" is carried forward by the upswing of the refrain, the impetus of which is given by the movement of the stanza itself with the frequent trochaics and amphibrachs modifying the basic iambic structure. The refrain in "The Broken Appointment" intensifies the disillusionment and resentment of the neglected woman. A slight modification of the refrain can often arouse the reader to a heightened interest in the poem. In "A Trampwoman's Tragedy," for example, just as we think we are accustomed to the refrain the poet introduces a variation that pleases us by surprise:

Inside the settle all a-row—
All four a-row
We sat. . . .

Even more effective is the variation in stanza 2 of "The Ghost of the Past" with the change in direction:

As daily I went up the stair
And down the stair . . .

Hardy achieves a hesitant quality in "The Sea Fight" by his repetition in the first half of line 5 of line 4 in its entirety:

And he died
And he died, as heroes do.

Similarly the use of the last two words of line 2 for line 3 in "The Echo Elf Answers" is an interesting exercise. On a more extensive scale is his repetition of the word in lines 2 and 4 of every stanza in "The Weary Walker" to catch the spirit of almost unbearable fatigue.

The refrain is not always confined to the limits of a stanza. "Wearily waiting" as the refrain for stanzas 1 and 3 of "Postponement," and "Cheerily mating" for 2 and 4 afford an interesting contrast. In "Autumn Rain Scene" line 3 of each stanza is identical, with no repetition within the stanza. The effect is of a continuous, deadening downpour unrestricted in locality. The refrain can even be a song, as in the moving " 'The Curtains Now Are Drawn' " with the sharp contrast of gladness and sadness between the stanzas; can be the repetition of the same rhyme words from stanza to stanza as in "Burning the Holly," a typical song rhythm with its frequent internal rhymes; or can even be a masculine rhyme at the end of each stanza, as in "The Mother Mourns," with the final words being lane-unchain-pain-refrain-disdain-brain, and so on; as in "My Cicely" with the masculine rhyme on long *e;* or as in "Rake-Hell Muses" with the rhyme on *-el.* A more conscious effect is that in "The Nettles" with the stressed syllable of the second foot of line 2 rhyming with the final syllable of line 1, that in "The Last Signal," or that in " 'I Worked No Wile to Meet You' " with the alternate lines of each stanza ending with the same personal pronoun you, me, or us; or the repetition of "mirror" in "Moments of Vision." Greater success lies in "On One Who Lived and Died Where He Was Born" because of the subtle manner in which the poet weaves a tracery of words and phrases within each stanza and in the modulation of these words and phrases from stanza to stanza.

A casual glance at the rhyme schemes of Hardy's poems is proof of his interest in rhyme, but such a glance does not tell the whole story, nor does any account of the frequency of internal rhymes. "The Sun on the Letter" is a case in point. As the stanza is a-b-c, it would seem that rhyme might be absent; an examination of the poem as a whole reveals, however, that each line of each stanza rhymes with the corresponding line of every other stanza. A similar stanza is employed in "A New Year's Eve in War Time" with the exception that stanzas 1 and 7 have one more line than the others. "Mismet" is also an interesting experiment in that the rhyme words of the three-stressed section of the stanza are identical with the one-stressed section immediately following. The poet attempts to bind the stanzas of "Vagg Hollow" together by making the last line of one stanza rhyme with the first line of the stanza immediately following. In "A Sheep Fair," line 9 of every stanza rhymes with line 9 of every other stanza. Even a casual reading of many of the preceding poems indicates that Hardy's experiments were not always successful; that is, the technical devices do not enhance the value of the poem. A further glance at other poems will throw additional light on the more obvious qualities of Hardy the technician: "The Country Wedding"; his *tour de force* through 36 lines on a single rhyme in "The Respectable Burgher," which does, however, heighten the satiric import of the poem; his use of feminine rhymes; and so forth.

Hardy attempted to find the best metrical scheme for the idea of which he was capable. Find, I think, rather than evolve. The rewriting of "From Victor Hugo" in a five-stress stanza instead of his original four-stress stanza is a case in point. Originally the stanzas read as follows:

> Child, were I King, I'd yield my rule,
> Crown, sceptre, vassal-service due,
> My chariot, my porphyried basins cool
> My fleets, that make the sea a pool,
>   For a glance from you!
>
> Love, were I God, the earth and airs
> Angels, the demons under me
> Vast chaos with its womby lairs,
> Time, space, I'd give—aye, upper spheres
>   For a kiss from thee!

He made the revision in the "fair copy" as follows:

> Child, were I king, I'd yield my royal rule,
>   My chariot, sceptre, vassal-service due,
> My crown, my porphyry-basined waters cool,
> My fleets, whereto the sea is but a pool,
>   For a glance from you!
>
> Love, were I God, the earth and its heaving airs,
>   Angels, the demons abject under me,
> Vast chaos with its teeming womby—lairs
> Time, space, all would I give—aye, upper spheres,
>   For a kiss from thee!

But in this tendency to take a stanza pattern where he might find it and not evolve it according to his innermost needs does there not lie a great weakness? Is it not true of Hardy as it is true of a minor poet that the choice of meter almost determines the quality of the work? Everywhere in his work we find evidences of potential genius that only occasionally becomes actual when he finds or makes the form which is necessary to him.

Hardy reveals his artistry, too, in the manner in which he uses the caesura. He knew that in poetry, just as every good composer recognizes in music, significant pauses between tones intensify the effect of the tones or series of tones they separate. Occasionally one hears an oversimplification of this in the epigrammatic statement that the most important parts of music are the moments of silence. They are, if the sounds they separate are themselves cogent; otherwise they are as meaningless as the sounds themselves. In "You Were the Sort That Men Forget," for example, the movement of each stanza differs from the others. Hesitancy, the attempt of the man to express himself accurately, is the keynote of the opening lines of stanzas 1 and 2. Once he is under way his words come unhaltingly. A similar situation exists in "Four Footprints," particularly in the third and fourth stanzas when the bride is trying to explain to her lover that she had taken the other man as her husband out of a sense of duty to her parents. Again in stanza 3 of "To a Lady Playing and Singing in the Morning," the poet catches the apologetic note of the young man reluctant to leave her. The appeal of the young man to the lady is heightened by casting the first line of the first two stanzas into trochaic catalectic trimeter, thereby giving a greater air of directness to his pleading:

> Joyful lady, sing!
> And I will lurk here listening
> Though nought be done, and nought begun,
> And work-hours swift are scurrying.

The absence of a caesura in stanza 3 of " 'The Wind Blew Words' " after its irregular use in stanzas 1 and 2 heightens the emotional upsweep of the protagonist. Further good examples of the poet's ability at enhancing the effect of his thought by manipulating the caesura are "In the Servants' Quarters," "By Her Aunt's Grave," "Her Death and After" (which reflects the starts and stops of conversation in spite of its complicated nature), and "The Slow Nature." Others reveal how he powerfully heightens the emotional tone through this technical device. Perhaps the most familiar example of its effective use is in "The Man He Killed." The young soldier, troubled by the thought of the man he had killed in the enemy ranks, attempts to justify the act against a young person like himself, a potential friend. He ineffectually tries rationalization. The poet captures the puzzled mind of the speaker by his use of the caesura:

> "I shot him dead because——
> Because he was my foe,
> Just so: my foe of course he was;
> That's clear enough; although
>
> "He thought he'd 'list, perhaps;
> Off-hand like—just as I——
> Was out of work—had sold his traps——
> No other reason why.
>
> "Yes; quaint and curious war is!
> You shoot a fellow down
> You'd treat if met where any bar is,
> Or help to half a crown."

The perplexity is heightened, too, not only by the repetition of words, but by the repetition of vowel sounds like the long *o* in the first stanza—foe, so, foe, although—appearing at irregular intervals in the lines. The tempo seems to quicken in lines 2 and 3 of the last stanza, because of the absence of a caesura. Its use in the strongly iambic rhythm of "In the Servants' Quarters" offsets any tendency to monotony in the beat, and by so doing gives a greater conversational quality to the movement of the verse than would otherwise be possible. More deeply moving are the instances in "After the Last Breath." In stanza 1 these impart to the reader the protagonist's sense of resignation now that death has finally come.

> There's no more to be done, or feared, or hoped;
> None now need watch, speak low, and list, and tire;
> No irksome crease outsmoothed, no pillow sloped
> Does she require.

Many persons have praised the last pages of Mr. Hemingway's *Farewell to Arms,* pages which I feel Mr. Hemingway would never have written had he experienced what he attempts to describe. His hero would never have ranted nor cursed at the death of his beloved. Hardy's "Just the Same" presents a much more authoritative picture of the bereaved husband or lover. The finality of the incident is clinched by the sustained pause after "sat," by a strong one after "past," and by one of like intensity after "again." Notice particularly the three groups: one stress in the first, two in the second, and three in the third. From that point the movement is freer and the pauses much lighter:

> I sat. It all was past;
> Hope never would hail again;
> Fair days had ceased at a blast,
> The world was a darkened den.
>
> The beauty and dream were gone
> And the halo in which I had hied
> So gaily gallantly on
> Had suffered blot and died!
>
> I went forth, heedless whither,
> In a cloud too black for name:
> —People frisked hither and thither;
> The world was just the same.

It is also apparent that the poet's desire for alliteration determined the choice of "den" and "hied."

In a different mood are the first three stanzas of "Julie-Jane." The strong caesura after the first monosyllable in the first line of each stanza imparts a sense of unbounded joy that is heightened by the poet's use of the dialectal "a" for "she."

> Sing; how 'a would sing!
>
> Dance; how 'a would dance!
>
> Laugh; how 'a would laugh!

The tone shifts in the fourth stanza to one less vibrant and hearty and appreciably slows down in the last. At least one other poem shows the importance to the poet of the unity of the inner burden with the outer movement of the stanza. In "I Said to Love," the first three stanzas move along convincingly enough. The final stanza is extended by two lines, and their addition interprets the fierceness of the lover in his denunciatory mood.

Every reader will find his own examples of Hardy's skill in

handling rhythms and caesurae. I have made no attempt at being exhaustive; I have wished merely to give enough varied examples of his failures as well as of his successes to show that easy generalizations are dangerous.

We cannot leave the discussion of Hardy's prosody without some consideration of the influence on it of music. Here, rather than in his use of music as subject matter, Hardy reveals his greatest interest. Without attaching too much significance to the possible sources, it is interesting to notice that more than twenty-five poems carry the parenthetic "song" beneath their titles, one group of poems is called "A Set of Country Songs," more than ten have a reference to "song" or "singing" in their titles, and others to "music" and "musical." Frequently he has placed beneath the title informatives like "written to an old folk tune," "echo of an old song," "a new theme on an old folk measure," "to an old air," "with an old Wessex refrain," "Medieval Latin sequence meter," or has keyed the poem with a musical term like "scherzando," "minor mode," and "nocturne." That *Psalms and Hymns, 1858* was a favorite book of Hardy's, and that he was fundamentally "churchy" probably accounts for his frequent use of the long, short, and common meters. When he has a good tune on which to build, his results, as in "A Maiden's Pledge" and "Burning the Holly," are excellent. Quite obviously the latter is set to a popular dance tune. The rhythm of "Music in a Snowy Street" catches the triple-time beat of the old strain that he loved; so, too, does line 5 of "Song to an Old Burden" the movement of the dancers with its iteration of "around"— 'Shall I then foot around around around.' The more purely lyrical measures suggest that Hardy, like Burns, when given a good tune can write a good song; rarely can he both write the words and compose the melody. He can adapt a visual melody almost as effectively as a heard one: the movement of the ballet, for example, dictates the movement of the verse in "The Ballet":

> They part, enmesh,
> And crush together again,
> Like the pink petals of a too sanguine rose
> Frightened shut just when it blows.

I have often wondered just why Hardy enclosed in quotation marks the titles to about seventy poems. From a cursory glance at

the poems thus titled I think one receives the impression that these
are almost all in a more purely lyrical measure than others, and yet
I can detect no real consistency. Were these by chance more directly
inspired by familiar melodies than others? I ask the question but
immediately admit that I am not the answerer. Perhaps his practice
is so obvious that it passed me by without my seeing it.

❯❯❯ 9 ❮❮❮

ARCHITECTONICS

Hardy's Reputation as a poet will depend neither on his thought nor on one or several of the characteristics of his technical achievement. This is, of course, a truism; but like most truisms, too frequently overlooked. His stature will be determined by the success of his fusion of all his various characteristics in the completed poem, in his skill and success as an architect of poetry. It is this phase of his work that we must now examine. In his best poems not one detail is superfluous. It will be obviously impossible to dissect the architectonic quality of more than a very few poems, but the reader can examine more for himself, and the greater the care he devotes to such an analysis the greater will be the reward.

It is relatively simple to analyze the manner in which the poet breaks the subject matter of any one poem into its segments—simple and valuable. From such an analysis we can observe the poet's economy. A poem is, of course, no haphazard affair; but an inevitable relationship exists between each stanza and the one immediately preceding it, as well as among all the stanzas. The pattern of "John and Jane," to choose a simple illustration, is typical of Hardy's care. The poem depicts four phases of John's attitude toward life: stanza 1, the carefree period of his bachelorhood; 2, the "ecstasy and grace" of his early marriage to Jane; 3, the joy in and hope for the "baby-child"; and 4, the disappointment of John and his wife years later "with their worthless son." In sixteen lines an all too frequent drama unfolds itself. The fourth line of each stanza helps greatly to tighten the organic unity of the poem. Each, in fact, clinches the subject of the stanza. "Does John," "Do John and

Jane," "Do John and Jane with a baby-child," and "Do John and Jane with their worthless son" heighten the communication.

Although many details in the poems elude the layman, Hardy is not an architect's architect. We have seen in "John and Jane" that the blocks look similar from a distance and they fit well together. Careful scrutiny of the separate blocks indicates that each is cunningly contrived. How does he blend and fuse the materials used in these blocks? Here is stanza 1:

> He sees the world as a boisterous place
> Where all things bear a laughing face,
> And humorous scenes go hourly on,
> Does John.

"Boisterous" captures the gusto of youth, just as "laughing" reflects the unbounded optimism of a strong, healthy young animal. The arrangement of the vowels in "humorous" and "hourly" followed immediately by "on" reflects the same swaggering joy. The rhythm is strong, additional impetus being given by the short fourth line —"Does John."

Stanza 2 moves more slowly:

> They find the world a pleasant place
> Where all is ecstasy and grace,
> Where a light has risen that cannot wane,
> Do John and Jane.

Several things contribute to this slower pace. The long *a* sound in "they," and the long *i* sound in "find"; "pleasant" instead of "boisterous," the alliterating *p*'s; the liquid *l* and *r* frequently occurring; the affective associations of the words "ecstasy" and "grace"; and, finally, the longer fourth line—all assist in this more leisurely tempo. In a similar way we could analyze the remaining stanzas.

The poet employs a geographical plan in "Epeisodia." Again the poem tells of three episodes in the lives of a couple, summarized in the final lines of each stanza: "There caressed we," "There pressed we!," and "There shall rest we." The idyllic aspect of their courtship is reflected in a pastoral scene of rolling grazing land dotted with wood clumps. The consummation and the ensuing matter-of-factness harmonize with the dullness of the city. The third stanza is pitched on a still lower key against the desolate landscape so frequent in Hardy.

The weather determines the stanzaic division in "The Weathers" and "We Field Women" with the closing lines of each stanza: "How it rained!," "How it snowed!," "How it shone!" In "The Colour," as the title suggests, color determines the obvious pattern. Most frequently, however, Death or Time are the determining factors. "Looking Across" and "The Five Students" employ both, and are valuable to the person interested in seeing how the same subject differently garbed can create widely divergent effects. A curl of hair, the memory of an old song, or an old tune on the chimes are other devices used by the poet to give compactness to his structure.[1]

More pertinent, however, will be a detailed examination of a few poems, and these are the better ones. "Weathers" will serve as well as any, and I have already quoted parts of it elsewhere. Here is stanza 1:

> This is the weather the cuckoo likes,
>   And so do I;
> When showers betumble the chestnut spikes,
>   And nestlings fly:
> And the little brown nightingale bills his best,
> And they sit outside at "The Traveller's Rest,"
> And maids come forth sprig-muslin drest,
> And citizens dream of the south and west,
>   And so do I.

The time is late spring. The poet carefully selects details to make a full and joyous picture. Nothing disturbs the mood, not even the showers which only "betumble." And after the shower how fresh, clean, and bright will be the air! How blue the sky! The cuckoo, that "wandering voice," enchants in the daytime and the low warble of the nightingale in the evening. Young men gather at the "pub" to flirt with the girls who saunter by. The pleasantest touch, however, is that the more staid members of the community begin to dream of their summer holiday at the seaside—in Devon, Cornwall, or elsewhere along the south or west coast. The poet bolsters the mood by the facility of the rhythms. Liquids abound; the vowels

---

[1] "On a Discovered Curl of Hair," " 'The Curtains Now Are Drawn,' " "The Chimes Play 'Life's a Bumper.' "

are practically all front and predominantly short; the sibilants, explosives, and stops are unvoiced. The rhythm is tripping because of the ten anapests that are intermingled with the iambs.

The mood of the second stanza is depressing; and for obvious reasons:

> This is the weather the shepherd shuns,
> And so do I;
> When beeches drip in browns and duns,
> And thresh, and ply,
> And hill-hid tides throb, throe on throe,
> And meadow rivulets overflow,
> And drops on gate-bars hang in a row,
> And rooks in families homeward go,
> And so do I.

Frequently, as in "The Lake Isle of Innisfree," a poet uses numerous "ands" to slow the pace of the verse. Since there are the same number in each stanza of "Weathers," Hardy used them merely for the sake of pattern rather than mood. Instead of ten anapests, there are only four in stanza 2. The pace is less tripping, more pronounced. The time is late autumn, probably about the time of the equinoctial storms when there is little chance of clouds breaking. Rain, in fact, has been long and continuous, and has made sodden the meadows. The wind is strong and lashing—"thresh" and "ply" attest to that. The sound of the heavy sea from beyond the hill, the pounding on the cliffs is admirably caught in "throb, throe on throe." "Hill-hid tides" is itself difficult with the repeating aspirates *d*'s and short *i*'s. The image of the rooks, birds traditionally associated with ill omens, intensifies the desolateness of the scene. The entire picture is bolstered by the predominance of long back vowels in "throe," "row," "go," and so forth, the voiced sibilants in "browns," "duns," "tides," the voiced stops, and in the contracting effect of such words as "shepherd shuns," but particularly "thresh." Other readers will find additional qualities to enjoy.

"Snow in the Suburbs" is less obvious but no less accurate than "Weathers." The movement of the stanza is, in fact, more accurately keyed to the subject matter than is that of "Weathers." The mood of the poem is implicit in the movement of the verse. Two stanzas of eight lines each give, respectively, the undisturbed scene and the first intrusion of life. The four-line third stanza gives point, intensification, and a final homely touch characteristic of Hardy the animal lover. He is economical in the use of his materials. What an abundant snowfall!

> Every branch big with it,
> Bent every twig with it;
> Every fork like a white web-foot;
> Every street and pavement mute:

Then, lengthening the rhythm in lines 5 and 6, he presents an image that is both accurate and humorous:

> Some flakes have lost their way, and grope back upward, when
> Meeting those meandering down they turn and descend again.

The choice of "grope" indicates the sense of labor, and the slightly accented "when"—like a person stopping—is a focal point. Line 7 returns to a more pedestrian pace although "glued" prevents the actual intrusion of such a quality. The softness of the quiet is caught in the "fleecy fall" of the last line and the alliterating *w*'s:

> And there is no waft of wind with the fleecy fall.

The second stanza pleases the reader more than the incident pleased the sparrow:

> A sparrow enters the tree,
> Whereupon immediately
> A snow-lump thrice his own slight size
> Descends on him and showers his head and eyes,
> And overturns him,
> And near inurns him,
> And lights on a nether twig, when its brush
> Starts off a volley of other lodging lumps with a rush.

The short fifth and sixth lines between the longer pairs on either side catch the dramatic suddenness and near catastrophe for the bird, a catastrophe which amuses us.

The third stanza completes the picture with the arrival of the stray cat and his struggle up the steps made difficult by the snow:

> The steps are a blanched slope,
> Up which, with feeble hope,
> A black cat comes, wide-eyed and thin;
> And we take him in.

The final line is really a triumph. With epigrammatic terseness it brings the poem to an effective close, and we leave the snowscape and enter the house.

In a different mood is "Former Beauties," a variation on the "ubi sunt" poems. The poet looks incredulously at the market women who although only "mid-aged" are old and withered from hard work and asks if these were the ones that he and his friends had known in their budding maidenhood. If they are, then they must have forgotten those earlier moments, else the memory would light their faces. The short second and fourth lines of the stanza heighten his questioning mood and give point to the several vignettes.

> These market-dames, mid-aged, with lips thin-drawn,
>   And tissues sere,
> Are they the ones we loved in years agone,
>   And courted here?
>
> Are these the muslined pink young things to whom
>   We vowed and swore
> In nooks on summer Sundays by the Froom,
>   Or Budmouth shore?
>
> Do they remember those gay times we trod
>   Clasped on the green;
> Aye; trod till moonlight set on the beaten sod
>   A satin sheen?
>
> They must forget, forget! They cannot know
>   What once they were,
> Or memory would transfigure them, and show
>   Them always fair.

Hardy selects only the fewest details, but with such care that the reader's imagination fills in the balance. "Mid-aged," "thin-drawn" lips, and dried skins are ample basis for a sketch. To intensify the contrast he recalls varying episodes from their former days: flirtings and courtings at the markets, sentimental trysts, and village dancing —moments of relaxation when their femininity was most apparent; not at work in the fields, in the dairy or kitchen where the heat and toil parched their skins. The romance of the dancing is heightened by the image of moonlight:

> till moonlight set on the beaten sod
> A satin sheen?

Hardy stresses the contrast by the movement of stanza 4 and the repetition of "forget." The scansion does not differ from the preceding stanzas—strongly iambic—but the diction itself lends a greater emphasis. "Must" and "cannot" are positive. The final lines are important to an understanding of Hardy. As long as the soul is alive and the spirit free beauty remains.

"The Fallow Deer at the Lonely House" will impress many readers of Hardy as an uncharacteristic poem. That we must be wary of what we call "uncharacteristic" is, of course, already evident. This poem, however, bears repeated readings and like most of Hardy, in fact, makes one hesitate to attempt a final judgment of his work. In two short stanzas he creates a mood; one might hazard the opinion that it is the mood of a domestic tragedy:

> One without looks in to-night
> Through the curtain chink
> From the sheet of glistening white;
> One without looks in to-night
> As we sit and think
> By the fender-brink.

> We do not discern those eyes
> Watching in the snow;
> Lit by lamps of rosy dyes
> We do not discern those eyes
> Wondering, aglow,
> Fourfooted, tiptoe.

A first possible reaction to this poem is that it has somewhat the quality of a poem by Robert Frost, a reaction, however, which is quickly dispelled with rereading. In fact, our final impression is one of the intense loneliness of the couple who no longer have anything to say to one another. They live under the same roof, but there is no longer any communication between them. We do not know the nature of the wall that separates them, but it may be the one most frequently found in a household without children. The persons have advanced at different paces and there is no longer any common meeting ground. One need not ask which is the lonelier—the fallow deer or those by the fire. The extreme simplicity of the diction with the repetition in each stanza of the line that intensifies the setting, the effective use of the caesura, the crispness of the rhyme words in the first stanza contrasted with the slower moving ones in the second are well handled. The outstanding feature to me is the last four lines. The apparent cheerfulness of the room does not reflect the feeling of the two sitting by the fire.

An examination of the Hardy manuscripts gives additional proof of his structural care; his concern for clarity and balance. "The Widow Betrothed," for example, contains one such instance. In the original draft the following stanza was omitted:

> Yet in my haste I overlooked
> When secondly I sued,
> That then, as not at first, she had learnt
> The call of motherhood . . .

He did not include it, in fact, until he saw the proofs. He then realized that the force of the preceding stanza might easily be missed without some further word of explanation. He achieves an even more significant tightening of the texture by the changes in stanza 6. Originally it was rather weak:

> To-morrow—could you—could you come?
> I hardly now can stay
> My child has sickened and I would
> Fain not leave him today!

The rhythm of line 4 is awkward, and the rhyme on long *a*, stay-today, unconvincing. The movement of the whole lacks driving power. He altered the stanza in the manuscript to the following:

> To-morrow—could you—would you call?
> Make brief your present stay?
> My child is ill—my one, my all—
> And can't be left today.

The change of rhythm in line 3 is a much more accurate communication of the mother's anxiety, and together with line 4 makes for a simple directness lacking in the original version. "Make brief," however, does not accurately reflect her attitude toward her lover. It is too abrupt, too harsh. In the proofs he altered "make brief" to "abridge" which dispels any sense of harshness or coldness. The substitution for the two long vowels *a* and *e* and the terse *k* and voiceless *f* for the shorter vowels and lengthened consonant sounds of "abridge" effects the desired change.

The poet's trials with the next to the last line of the poem further shows his concern over the unity of emotion for which he seeks. Before he finally arrived at "But a new love-claim shares her since" he experimented with and rejected in turn "But she has found new interests since," "But she has caught fresh love-calls since," and "But she has caught new love-calls since."

An examination of "Tess's Lament" illustrates the manner in which the poet uses repetition, vowel and consonantal sounds to convey the haunting sadness of the forlorn woman. One can see the abandoned creature rocking back and forth in the movement of the stanzas which alternate in subject matter between her present misery and her idyllic past. Stanzas 2 and 5 are less desolate than the others because they are tenderly recollected moments of happiness. "My Cicely" mirrors the impatience of the man when he discovers that a girl he thought dead still lives; "Friends Beyond" with its unnaturally lengthened lines captures the drawling voice of the old speaker.

"The Darkling Thrush," written in December, 1900, well exemplifies Hardy's fusion of the various elements of a poem. A just favorite with anthologists and meriting, if any one poem does, the epithet "typical," it enables us to see the artist at work. Here is the poem:

> I leant upon a coppice gate
>   When Frost was specter-gray,
> And Winter's dregs made desolate
>   The weakening eye of day.
> The tangled bine-stems scored the sky
>   Like strings of broken lyres,
> And all mankind that haunted nigh
>   Had sought their household fires.
>
> The land's sharp features seemed to be
>   The Century's corpse outleant,
> His crypt the cloudy canopy,
>   The wind his death-lament.
> The ancient pulse of germ and birth
>   Was shrunken hard and dry,

And every spirit upon earth
  Seemed fervorless as I.

At once a voice arose among
  The bleak twigs overhead
In a full-hearted evensong
  Of joy illimited;
An aged thrush, frail, gaunt, and small,
  In blast-beruffled plume,
Had chosen thus to fling his soul
  Upon the growing gloom.

So little cause for carolings
  Of such ecstatic sound
Was written on terrestrial things
  Afar or nigh around,
That I could think there trembled through
  His happy good-night air
Some blessed Hope, whereof he knew
  And I was unaware.

The undoubted crystallizing force was quite obviously, I think, the song of the aged thrush. When Hardy's own mood harmonized with the desolateness of the setting—"fervorless" is his term for it —the contrast of a joyous note would stimulate his imagination. He knew he could give greater significance to the incident by relating it to a greater idea, call it cosmic if you wish. He related it to a problem that beset him early and late, a problem the satisfactory solution to which he could never reach, although he was wise enough to know that his approach was nearer than that of the ordinary person and as near as that reached by many advanced thinkers of his day. Once he seized the "idea" of the poem, the rest was an aesthetic matter. He must not only fit the idea into a logical frame but must infuse the content with emotion. He knew that he had to be emotional "in" his poetry but not emotional "about" it. He recognized, too, that certain technical means give architectural unity and create emotional reactions, and he attempted to find those that fitted the idea. He sought, therefore, an appropriate introduction, the most suitable stanza for the mood he wished to create, supporting images, and a bolstering diction. As I shall elsewhere point out, it was his delay in devoting himself to the acquisition of a technique by which to externalize his ideas that partially prevented his supreme success. The value of the opening stanzas, then, with their many technical details plus these same details in the last two stanzas lies in their contribution to what I have already called the quality, atmosphere, and flavor upon the imaginative palate of the basic idea.

The stanza form is virtually a double common meter—a^4 b^3 a^4 b^3-c^4 d^3 c^4 d^3—which he had encountered many times in hymns and ballads. His contribution is the broader emotional tone that he makes possible for this stanza.

Stanzas 1 and 2 provide the setting. The poet is standing with his back to the wood lot looking out over the desolate scene. The day has been short; already the frost has reformed and is now ghostlike —"specter-gray." He is completely alone. Lines 7 and 8 enhance the sense of desolation in the manner of "Snow in the Suburbs." Outside all is cold, gloomy, and desolate; inside there is warmth, cheer, and companionship. Notice, however, that even when men were outside they "haunted near." Stanza 2, continuing the description, is important for its picture of the mental state of the poet. The intensely dismal scene "seemed fervorless as I." His depression is deep. When the reader is in the mood of the scene and the poet, then the song begins—"a full-hearted evensong/ Of joy illimited." Only after we are surprised by the suddenness of the song does the poet stop to explain the source. Could this aged, weak, small, storm-beset bird thus sing because he saw that there are things which lie beyond the range of observed phenomena? Momently the poet thinks so. But chained by reason he cannot sustain his belief in the gleam. "Evensong" not only describes the bird's song as well as satisfying the rhythm, but is a strong link with the later idea of God. "Full-hearted evensong" conveys the idea of an active belief. Other words are interesting. The adverb "darkling" in the title prepares us for the detailed setting of stanzas 1 and 2, as well as carrying an emotive association with Keats's "Ode to the Nightingale" with its "darkling I listen." The suffix "-ling" stirs me as the starker "in the dark" could never do.

Hardy has used both "coppice" and "copse." "Coppice" is the more common term and satisfies the iambic rhythm of the stanza. The somewhat learned "terrestrial" in stanza 4, in a poem strongly monosyllabic, likewise satisfies a rhythmical demand. "Outleant," a nonce word, was coined to rhyme with "death-lament." Alliteration dictates many choices. I think, for example, that alliteration inspired the image of "Winter's dregs" making "desolate the weakening eye of day" rather than the image the alliteration. A better fusion of alliterating elements with the image occurs in lines 5 and 6 on *s*—stems-scored-sky-strings; and on *k*—scored-sky-like-broken. Nor must we overlook that on *h* in lines 7 and 8. Although the image in lines 10 and 11 is clear, I sense that the desire for alliteration on *k* dictated "crypt"—corpse-crypt-cloudy-canopy, and similarly that the *k*'s in "ecstatic" inspired cause-carolings. The alliterating *b*'s in the nonce word "blast-beruffled" probably led to the earlier "bleak." In spite of the demands thus made on language, Hardy has managed to secure enough variation in the vowel gradations to offset the tendency to overconscious consonantal manipulation.

The images in stanzas 1 and 2 deal with death either directly or by implication. Strings of broken lyres are a traditional symbol of death. (Mourning cards and funeral monuments are abundant proof of this.) Rather, one should say broken strings of lyres; and I think that is what Hardy meant. Had he said just that, however, the rhythm would have been distorted. The likening of the "land's sharp features" to the "Century's corpse" was a residuum of his thinking on the significance of the end of the century. What had been accomplished in the nineteenth? what did the twentieth hold in store? The rest of the images in stanza 2 depend on the conception of the corpse idea.

His varying use of the caesura, as I have also noted elsewhere, gives interest and variety to his verse movement. Two passages are important. The absence of caesurae in the first four lines of stanza 3 gives a tremendous upswing to the verse, an upswing, however, that receives a sharp impulse from following close upon the paralyzing effect of line 10—"was shrunken hard and dry." "Shrunken" is powerful. Following the upswing to "joy illimited," the poet suddenly begins again at a low emotional level, not only using epithets with a falling quality in their vowels, but perceptibly slowing the line with caesurae—"an aged thrush, frail, gaunt, and small." Then he begins a new upsweep in stanza 4, rises continuously to the end, pausing only long enough for the reader to catch his breath after "around" and "blessed Hope."

But there is a fly in the ointment. Everything is not as well as it seems, and the trouble lies in the apparently innocent "that I could think," similar in significance to the last line of "The Oxen"—"hoping it might be so." The effect is only momentary and lasts only so long as reason is suspended.

The scope of Hardy's architectonic power can best be seen in *The Dynasts,* material, however, for another chapter. It can be well seen, too, by the comparison in his early and late volumes of poems identical in subject. The chapters on Hardy's subject matter will enable the interested reader to make his own examination. It is surprising, for example, to realize the number of instances in which Hardy has repeated in his late poems material found in his earlier work. When read in juxtaposition the reader becomes increasingly conscious of Hardy's artistic development up to and including the volume *Human Shows. Winter Words* adds little to his artistic stature; if anything, it detracts, and that in spite of additional touches it gives us of his character both as man and poet. The basic differences in his earlier and later works lie in his tendency to tighten the structure of his verse by the choice of a less learned diction, by his tendency toward more monosyllables, by his willingness to eliminate ornament, and by a surer sense of the fitness of his prosody to his thought. In other words, he became more of an artist.[2] This is not, of course, invariably the case; nor is it as apparent as in Yeats or in almost any of our older poets of first rank. He was moving in the right direction and had age not overtaken him and relaxed his powers he might have gone farther than he did. Hardy's difficulty was that although he early enough made up his mind as to what he wanted to do, he was not convinced that it was worth the necessary effort. When he finally realized where true satisfaction lay it was too late to accomplish what he desired. I think he understood himself well enough not to complain.

[2] The best examples of his nature painting in Chapter 10 are all from the later work.

✺IO✺

NATURE

ANY ADEQUATE discussion of nature in Hardy's poetry in brief compass is manifestly impossible. It is not only a dramatic agent in many poems on the subject of woman, love, God, and mutability, but it is important to a thorough understanding of his diction, rhythm, imagery, and architectonics. Nature plays a much greater role, however, than merely to help swell a scene or two. Nature was the sounding board for his own soul. In his youth, for example, the waves sang to him of an all including joy; twenty years later they reverberated a "long ironic laughter at the lot of men"; in his later years they supplicated like a congregation murmuring confession—but with him outside deprived of prayer.

Three passages from his notebooks—May 30, 1877, January, 1881, and January, 1887—chart the course by which he arrived at that understanding of nature, the source of much of his power. The first provides the clue to his drenching of external things with what we might call the personal or dramatic essence. He is objective and subjective at the same time, a thing in itself which should make us hold the words in suspect. After a walk to Marnhull he recorded his discriminating observations:

The prime of birdsinging. The thrushes and blackbirds are the most prominent,—pleading earnestly rather than singing, and with such modulation that you see their little tongues curl inside their bills in this emphasis. A bullfinch sings from a tree with a metallic sweetness piercing as a fife. Further on I come to a hideous carcase of a house in a green landscape, like a skull on the table of dessert.

The second stresses the necessity for the "personal essence."

Consider the Wordsworthian dictum (the more perfectly the natural object is reproduced, the more truly poetic the picture). This reproduction is achieved by seeing into the *heart of a thing* (as rain, wind, for instance), and is realism, in fact, though through being pursued by means of the imagination it is confounded with invention, which is pursued by the same means. It is, in short, reached by what M. Arnold calls "the imaginative reason."

The manner in which the "confounding" takes place reveals itself in his statement about the music of Wagner being "weather" and "ghost" music, which he felt "like any other, may be made to express emotion of various kinds; but it cannot express the subject or reason of that emotion."

The third explains the source of much of Hardy's power.

After looking at the landscape ascribed to Bonington in our drawing-room, I feel that Nature is played out as a Beauty, but not as a Mystery. I don't want to see landscapes, i.e., scenic paintings of them, because I don't want to see the original realities—as optical effects, that is. I want to see the deeper reality underlying the scenic, the expression of what are sometimes called the abstract imaginings.

The "simply natural" is interesting no longer. The much decried, mad, late-Turner rendering is now necessary to create my interest. The exact truth as to material fact ceases to be of importance in art—it is a student's style—the style of a period when the mind is serene and unawakened to the tragical mysteries of life; when it does not bring anything to the object that coalesces with and translates the qualities that are already there, —half hidden, it may be—and the two united are depicted as All.

Now that, it seems to me, is vitally important to an understanding of Hardy's entire achievement. The mystery of which he speaks, rather than the beauty, is inherent in his famous description of Egdon Heath, just as it is inherent throughout his poems. It gives point to what I have elsewhere stressed, that too many persons forget that Hardy's poetry differs from most poetry in that it is not the poetry of a young man. It is the poetry of a person who has been awakened to the "deeper realities" of a landscape and the "magical mysteries of life." Less confusion about Hardy would exist were one to compare his poetry with other poetry written in middle and late age—Shakespeare of *Antony and Cleopatra,* the elder Milton, the elder Dryden, or the elder Yeats.

Two years later, he wrote a detailed footnote to this earlier observation. He was speaking chiefly of the Turners painted after 1832.

Turner's water-colours: each is a landscape plus a man's soul. . . . What he paints chiefly is *light as modified by objects.* He first recognizes the impossibility of really reproducing on canvas all that is in a landscape; then gives for that which cannot be reproduced a something else which shall have upon the spectator an approximate effect to that of the real. He said, in his maddest and greatest days: "What pictorial drug can I dose man with, which shall affect his eyes somewhat in the manner of this reality which I cannot carry to him?"—and set to make such strange mixtures as he was tending towards in "Rain, Steam, and Speed," "The Burial of Wilkie," "Agrippina Landing with the Ashes of Germanicus," "Approach to Venice," "Snowstorm and Steamboat," etc. Hence, one may say, Art is the secret of how to produce by a false thing the effect of the true.

Bearing the foregoing statements in mind, and at the same time paying due attention to his genius for observed fact as they reveal themselves in the following three entries, we have a basis for approaching Hardy's nature painting.

April 1, 1893. I note that a clever thrush and a stupid nightingale sing very much alike.

Spring, 1898. Scene at the Imperial Institute this afternoon. Rain floating down in wayward drops. Not a soul except myself having tea in the gardens. The west sky begins to brighten. The red, blue, and white fairy lamps are like rubies, sapphires, turquoises, and pearls in the wet. The leaves of the trees, not yet of full size, are dripping, and the waiting-maids stand in a group with nothing to do.

June 9, 1917. It is now the time of long days, when the sun seems reluctant to take leave of the trees at evening—the shine climbing up the trunks, reappearing higher, and still fondly grasping the tree-tops till long after.

In Hardy's application of "clever" and "stupid" to the thrush and nightingale, in his use of the "waiting-maids" as a dramatic referent, and in the sentience with which he endows the sun, the chief characteristics become more noticeable.

The technique by which he achieves his purpose is not always easily discernible at first glance. Examine, for example, his manner of capturing the mystery of a moment in nature. "Afterwards" illustrates one method. He vivifies the moment of the moth-hour of evening by a few well-chosen details. Will those who survive him, he asks, remember what "to him . . . must have been a familiar sight?"

> If it be at dusk when, like an eyelid's soundless blink,
>   The dewfall-hawk comes crossing the shades to alight
> Upon the wind-warped upland thorn . . .

A more effective symbol for the hushed half-light than the simile of the "eyelid's soundless blink" would be difficult to find; or a more suggestive description of the hawk's flight than "comes crossing the shades." The loneliness of the setting is caught in "the wind-warped upland thorn," a phrase rich in connotation because of the alliteration, vowel progression, which rises until "thorn," and to abundant use of the liquids (*l, r*) and nasal (*n*). The remaining stanzas are as rich in their evocative quality. To employ "nocturnal blackness, mothy and warm" in conjunction with the hedgehog traveling "furtively over the lawn" also suggests the mysterious. In a different manner, almost with a sense of the mystical, he captures the same quality in stanza 4.

> If, when hearing that I have been stilled at last, they stand at the door,
>   Watching the full-starred heavens that winter sees . . .

"Full-starred heavens" and "winter" give the necessary details, at the same time spurring the imagination to an exalted flight. The leisurely pace of the verse throughout the poem further enhances the mood. An equal keenness of observation of homely natural phenomena, but without capturing the same quality of mystery, invests "I Am the One." The difference arises from two causes—the more matter-of-fact, brisker stanza-movement, and the daylight setting—a difference made even more manifest in "I Watched a Blackbird." The quality of observation in this poem is that of a trained naturalist.

The mystery of nature, free, however, from a sense of brooding, forces itself into the final stanza of "The Sheep Boy" with its picture of the headstrong flight of the bees in the presence of the oncoming fog swirling up the vale and folding the landmarks "into those creeping scrolls of white." "Night-Time in Mid-Fall," a picture of a wild night, the details of which, says the poet, he knows

from their sound, is another illustration. The first stanza is accurate
reporting; the second permits the intrusion of rumor, folklore, and
superstition, and, attending them, strangeness and mystery.

> The streams are muddy and swollen; eels migrate
>   To a new abode;
> Even cross, 'tis said, the turnpike road;
> (Men's feet have felt their crawl, home-coming late):
> The westward fronts of towers are saturate,
> Church-timbers crack, and witches ride abroad.

" 'Tis said," cracking Church-timbers, and witches give an eerie
note. Similar are the "spirit astray" of "A January Night," and the
sound of the telegraph wire in "Nobody Comes," which

> Intones to travellers like a spectral lyre
> Swept by a spectral hand.

To insist too much on the quality of "mystery" in Hardy's na-
ture descriptions, however, is to do him an injustice. Such poems as
"Overlooking the River Stour," "Growth in May," and "Lying
Awake" are full of the brightness and joy of life and convey no
sense of brooding. Even in poems describing drenching rains Hardy
shies clear of anything suggestive of the mystical if the subject mat-
ter does not warrant it. The first stanza of "A Sheep Fair" well
illustrates this point:

> The day arrives of the autumn fair,
>   And torrents fall,
> Though sheep in throngs are gathered there,
>   Ten thousand all,
> Sodden, with hurdles round them reared:
> And, lot by lot, the pens are cleared,
> And the auctioneer wrings out his beard,
> And wipes his book, bedrenched and smeared,
> And rakes the rain from his face with the edge of his hand,
>   As torrents fall.

"An Unkindly May" is equally unemotive. Hardy has purposely
kept it on the level of factual reporting because of the prosaic na-
ture of the shepherd who stands by the gate "unnoting all things
save the counting his flock."

Hardy, like Keats, recognized that every season has its own
beauty, and he is partial to none. Although the two poems are dis-

similar in mood, in both "The Best She Could" and "Last Week in October" falling leaves in autumn remind him of a woman undressing. The latter poem, particularly, suggests a healthy sensuality and abandon which, however, is curbed in the second stanza by the comparison of a leaf caught in a cabinet to a hanged criminal. "The Later Autumn" is another personification of the season as a woman, but the poem has none of the graciousness which infuses Keats's *Ode to Autumn*. But we need not criticize it because the lines have a drier movement.

A detailed discussion of the many poems on nature is unnecessary. It is important, however, to point out the presence of a human referent in all of them. Only in his later years was nature painting almost sufficient in itself. We remember, of course, that Hardy cared little for nature as unrelated to man. "A Light Snow-Fall after Frost" gives point to what I mean. The four-stanza poem falls into two distinct parts. Stanzas 1 and 3 contain the human element; stanzas 2 and 4 are pure description of a snowscape. The "at last" in line 1 indicates that for some time before the appearance of any human being the poet has been watching the scene from the window. The rest of the stanza whets the reader's imagination. Here is the stanza:

> On the flat road a man at last appears:
> How much his whitening hairs
> Owe to the settling snow's mute anchorage
> And how much to life's rough pilgrimage,
> One cannot certify.

"Mute anchorage" is perfect. The only detail of the man we have is that he is aged and gray. Together with the landscape he forms a monotone which is carried over to stanza 2. The poet here presents a moment of observation that heightens our admiration for him. Lines 4 and 5 indicate the almost imperceptible change in the temperature and force into our consciousness a detail that but for the poet would have remained unobserved.

> The frost is on the wane,
> And cobwebs hanging close outside the pane
> Pose as festoons of thick white worsted there,
> Of their pale presence no eye being aware
> Till the rime made them plain.

"Thick white worsted" admirably catches the quality of wet snow.

A second man appears in stanza 3. This time, however, as a contrast to the whiteness of the snow, we have a "ruddy beard," a "faded green" coat, and his face red as the "berried holm-trees" (holly). Notice the poet's inference in lines 4 and 5:

> A second man comes by;
> His ruddy beard brings fire to the pallid scene:
> His coat is faded green;
> Hence seems it that his mien
> Wears something of the dye
> Of the berried holm-trees that he passes nigh.

Stanza 4, although free of such mystery as pervades "Afterwards" or "Night-Time in Mid-Fall," has a mystery of a different, even, perhaps, of a greater kind—the mystery of the indefinable moment when one thing ceases to be what it has been.

> The snow-feathers so gently swoop that though
> But half an hour ago
> The road was brown, and now is starkly white,
> A watcher would have failed defining quite
> When it transformed it so.

"Once at Swanage" is a further instance of Hardy's use of the human element. Throughout the first nine lines the poet concentrates all his effort at limning a moment supernatural in its aspect to give an affective connotation to the final line:

> And there we two stood, hands clasped; I and she!

In a different manner he catches the spirit of the hour in "Winter Night in Woodland." Each of the four stanzas depicts a different but simultaneous activity: the howling fox disliked by man; the bird-baiters and poachers; the smugglers, and the choir making their annual round at midnight singing carols.

Late Lyrics and Earlier and *Human Shows* are rich in poems that throw light on nature in Hardy. Every reader will and should find his own favorites. Each poem reveals in some measure the fidelity of his observation. He has carried to nature the capacity for minute detail that his training in copying from old churches and aiding in their restoration developed in him. Even more important was the lesson he learned from the great masters of painting. They taught him how, by a few essential details, to abstract from a scene its spirit. His quick and penetrating mind synthesized the apparently diverse elements into what in the seventeenth century would have been called wit. The reader becomes reluctant to admit that "by a false thing" Hardy produced "the effect of the true"—reluctant, because he refuses to believe that what he reads in the poems is not the very essence of truth. It is the truth.

PART III

THE ACHIEVEMENT

For I esteem those names of men so poor
Who could do mighty things, and could contemn
Riches though offer'd from the hand of Kings.
And what in me seems wanting, but that I
May also in this poverty as soon
Accomplish what they did, perhaps and more?
Extol not Riches then, the toyl of Fools,
The wise mans cumbrance if not snare, more apt
To slacken Virtue, and abate her edge,
Then prompt her to do aught may merit praise.

JOHN MILTON

»» I I ««

THE DYNASTS

THE STORY OF *The Dynasts* has been told many times
and told well. I shall repeat, therefore, only those portions necessary
for my immediate purpose—the evaluation of Hardy, the poet. The
story is one of a many years' struggle with intractable material, the
struggle of every creative artist determined to win through to his
goal. The story contains much quiet heroism and plenty of dogged
perseverance. If, to change the metaphor, Hardy failed to gain com-
plete control over the Leviathan and to subdue it to his will he must
not be too severely censured; on the other hand, the mere size of his
undertaking does not merit his being given the victor's crown for
only partial success.

Mr. Chakravarty in his *The Dynasts and the Post-War Age in
Poetry* has given the best as well as the most exhaustive treatment
of *The Dynasts*. I differ from him, however, in one important mat-
ter. He recognizes the imperfections of the work but is willing to
pass over them for the sake of its philosophical scope. To me they
are of such import as seriously to mar the work's effectiveness.
Since I am concerned with Hardy's aesthetic achievement in poetry
—which, of course, cannot neglect the significance of the content,
as even most of the writers who once held the opposite opinion have
come to realize—the present chapter will be in some measure an
elaboration of those characteristics which Mr. Chakravarty mentions
but leaves undeveloped. In due course I shall refer to some of his
specific statements.

Hardy was familiar from childhood with certain aspects of the
Napoleonic wars, particularly with the story of the emperor's threat-
ened invasion of England as current among village legends. This

gradually assumed an importance in his imagination that would not permit its being cast aside. He treated it in *The Trumpet Major,* but only barely touched the material he had collected. It demanded treatment; but years passed before he could in any way adequately cope with the solution of the aesthetic problem of the presentation of the subject on the scale that it warranted, an aesthetic problem which he failed to solve. He was not clear in his mind either as to the scope of his material or at what point or points to focus his attention. He was anxious, however, to correct an historical injustice arising from "the slight regard paid to English influence and action throughout the struggle by those Continental writers who had dealt imaginatively with Napoleon's career." His first thought had been that a ballad or ballad sequence might be the mold into which he could cast the subject matter, but by June, 1877, this form had given way to the idea of a "grand drama."

Consider a grand drama, based on the wars with Napoleon, or some one campaign, (but not as Shakespeare's historical dramas). It might be called "Napoleon," or "Josephine," or by some other person's name.

In March, 1881, he had still not completely given over the idea of the ballad form. He thought of it as a "Homeric Ballad, in which Napoleon is a sort of Achilles," although a few days later he jotted down another plan:

Mode for a historical Drama. Action mostly automatic; reflex movement, etc. Not the result of what is called motive, though always ostensibly so, even to the actor's own consciousness. Apply an enlargement of these theories to, say, "The Hundred Days!"

This is apparently his first idea of a philosophical scheme or framework such as he later adopted. This gave him something tangible to work on as well as something congenial to his increasing conviction that human life more nearly accorded with this concept than with any other. Almost a year later (February 16, 1882) he expressed the idea more pithily but without reference to the Napoleonic story:

Write a history of human automatism, or impulsion—viz., an account of human action in spite of human knowledge, showing how far conduct lags behind knowledge that should really guide it.

For several years he wrote no more about the matter, although he was constantly mulling over the subject. He was seeking a satisfactory form for the expression of his ideas. The canvas must be large, but something must act as a focus for the reader's attention. The work could be, as he was earlier aware, no mere chronicle play or series of chronicles. In September, 1888, a new possibility suggested itself to him "for carrying out that idea of Napoleon, the Empress, Pitt, Fox, etc. A spectral tone must be adopted . . . Royal ghosts . . . 'A Drama of Kings.' "

From this point on, then, the material begins to shape itself in his mind more rapidly and more concretely. "View the Prime Cause or Invariable Antecedent as 'It,' " he wrote on April 26, 1890, "and recount its doings." Eleven months later the plan had become sufficiently definite for him to speak of it as "A Bird's-Eye View of Europe at the beginning of the Nineteenth Century. . . . It may be called 'A Drama of the Times of the First Napoleon.' " By June 26, 1892, the various ideas had fused themselves in his mind: "Considered methods for the Napoleon drama. Forces, emotions, tendencies. The characters do not act under the influence of reason." From a general consideration of his aesthetic problem he proceeded to the active collection of his material. By 1896 he had given his drama the provisional name of "Europe in Throes" and had conceived it in three parts, with five acts in each. With this plan in mind he not only took notes in Brussels, at Waterloo, and other places, but began his reading in the British Museum, finally finishing the first part in September, 1903, part two in 1905, and part three in 1907.

Such, briefly, is the story of the evolution of *The Dynasts* into its final form. The structural problem with which Hardy wrestled for over a quarter of a century still presents problems for the critic. And it is to this that we must first direct our attention if we are to arrive at any just evaluation of the work. By calling *The Dynasts* an epic-drama it would seem that he would preclude the evaluation on the basis of any accepted set of criteria. We must not apply the criteria of any one form, nor do we need to do so. In scope *The Dynasts* is probably as vast as that of any literary work. Even *Para-*

dise Lost with its Ptolemaic concept of the universe seems small in comparison with the extent of the Napoleonic territory. But it seems small because it is such a well-coordinated whole. *The Dynasts,* on the other hand, remains when all is said but a "bird's-eye view." It lacks the close-knit structure that results from a unifying imagination working at white heat on tractable material. I cannot agree with the critic (*Nation,* April 16, 1908) who saw it as "a colossal unity and a staggering significance" and who believed that we should not permit "infelicities of detail" to disturb us any more "than swallow nests should disturb us . . . on the façade of the 'awful past.'" The narrative has balance, breadth, and sweep, but it lacks organic unity; and that simply because he attempted to pack into one work more diverse elements than one work could possibly hold, or than he should expect it to hold. Long as *The Dynasts* is, it is not long enough to be a successful work, because, even had Hardy the ability, there was not space enough for him to fuse these unrelated episodes into a correlated whole.

It is not enough to say that Napoleon is a sufficient focal point. Because the Napoleon we see is not one Napoleon but many facets of one Napoleon. Hardy did not possess the psychologic insight needed to see the qualities that fused those many facets into a single whole including all of them, without blurring the outline. Perhaps I should not use the term "did not possess," but rather "would not." Or, as Mr. Chakravarty says: "It seems he was determined not to give Hardy the novelist some supreme chances of his life." This also recalls a tendency of the English novelists and playwrights in general: their predilection for the novels and plays of manners rather than, like many of their continental brethren, novels and plays of character, works that seem to probe subsurface qualities rather than brilliantly to display surface ones. I can better explain what I mean by comparing *The Dynasts* with another work that unconsciously springs to mind—Tolstoy's *War and Peace.* Strangely enough, a week after reading *The Dynasts* many of the historical personages have slipped from memory, but years after reading *War and Peace* the characters remain as vivid as when their acquaintance was first made. The answer is not far to seek. Tolstoy's subject is also vast in scope, but it has much greater unity than Hardy's. The Russian does not attempt to show us 130 scenes; he shows us only a few, but those few he develops at such length and plumbs so far beneath the surface that they are indelibly impressed on our memories. He takes time, in other words, to arouse us to an emotional pitch and maintain us at that pitch long enough for the experience to become unforgettable. None of the scenes of *The Dynasts,* on the other hand, ever really exploits the material to the full. They remain sketches for scenes rather than scenes, and they shift their background so rapidly that we never have time really to fix the characters against that background.

A novelist, it is true, can take time to build up his scene in the manner of Dostoievsky in *The Brothers Karamazov,* in which the description of the famous night of revelry covers over a hundred pages. A dramatist cannot work so leisurely; but he must seem to do so. One never feels in Shakespeare's tragedies that he is hurrying any of the scenes leading up to the climax. He gives detail after detail of all the characters important to an action so that when the crisis is reached he can concentrate all of his powers on the behavior of those characters at this moment of intensest action. We must remember, however, that never once has he taken his attention from that moment toward which he was striving. *The Dynasts* has none of this. It is all preparatory action for crises that do not materialize.

The effect is the same as when being shown a series of portraits. One is not given time to study the composition, the details of the subject, interesting aspects of background which highlight the subject, and so forth. Instead he must look on John aged 2, John aged 17, John aged 9, John aged 36, John aged 24 in rapid succession. They are like photographs of Junior scattered around his mother's room. In other words, Hardy neglects one of the fundamental tenets for the treatment of character laid down by Aristotle in the *Poetics.* Compare, for example, the portraits of Alexander II in *War and Peace* and in *The Dynasts.* In the former he is a pulsating human being; in the latter he is no more than an automaton. It is not that *The Dynasts* does not have its high moments of characterization. It does. Sheridan's speech is witty; Nelson's are moving; Pitt's communicate a sense of dryness, to name but a few; and there are moments when one character's impact upon another gives flashes of dramatic brilliance, but it is only a flash. The longest single scene —that of the Battle of Waterloo—is also the best. It is, in fact, as Mr. Chakravarty says, a complete drama in itself: "It is rich in pathos, swift in its march of events; brilliant dialogue and description alternate with exquisitely tender pictures of Nature and animal life." It has all those things; but it has what much of the rest of the work lacks: significant form. It is not, then, that Hardy was incapable, but that his material was too extensive for the time he allotted himself. And lacking time his characters remain two-dimensional, bloodless representations rather than becoming vibrant personalities. Many are little more than names. Mr. Chakravarty sees that

in spite of its discursiveness and panoramic scope, [it] reveals an unmistakable poetic principle, a unity of vision and of interpretation of life and nature. The themes touched upon are multitudinous, leading to theories of state, social history, military manoeuvres, reflection on human character, psychological conflicts of well-known figures of history (p. 21).

To a great extent the foregoing is all true. The difficulty lies in "touched upon" and even more in the absence of passion underlying the "unity of vision."

The scope of his materials necessitated his maintaining the bird's-eye attitude, which, from the point of view of artistic achievement, is frequently fatal to the artist. He must seem, perhaps, to maintain such a point of vantage, but actually he must impregnate each of those tiny segments with that intensity of vision and depth of passion which make them glow. This cannot be done from a bird's-eye point of vantage. We need only remember that in just a few more than three hundred lines Shakespeare revealed to us Cordelia, one of his most beautiful heroines. Josephine has more space allotted to her, but she never quite comes to life. Maria Louisa gives signs of becoming a sympathetically projected woman, but the charming touches in the scene of her first appearance never develop. We await with interest the outcome of her marriage, but nothing is presented to us except a lovely automaton quietly accepting her fate. Hardy has read her story in history books, and there she remains. She simply does not quicken. So, too, could we mention other characters in this epic-drama. He has conceived his characters through his mind and not with his heart.

The question naturally arises as to the cause of this. I have already suggested that the poet's lack of a passionate unifying imagination was one reason; another is his failure to experience those flashes of insight that illuminates a character so that its subtlety can be read by anyone who is attentive; a third is that although he possesses a dramatic sense, he is no dramatist. These are the basic reasons which lead us to an examination of lesser but more apparent ones, the first of which is that of diction.

The quality of the appeal of the shorter poems becomes more understandable after a reading of the historical parts of *The Dynasts*. Their appeal is the result not of a warmth that springs from the heart, but of an incisiveness springing from the head. The blank verse of *The Dynasts* has a similar appeal. It is a competent medium for communicating an idea, but little emotion accompanies that idea. The verse is stark and hard. The poet's lack of flexibility and dexterity in handling this particular medium prevents his achieving the range or the ease demanded by the magnitude of his task. Critics violently disagree with one another on the blank verse of *The Dynasts*. To one group it is "so free that it practically disregards convention"; it is verse "of marvelous blankness"; it is "of the facile dog-trot sort" (*Athenaeum,* Jan. 4, 1902, Jan. 23, 1904, April 16, 1908). The most devastating critic of the work was Wilfred Scawen Blunt, who wrote to Sir Sydney Cockerell:

On your recommendation I sent for *The Dynasts* and read it conscientiously through, without finding anything at all in it which has any business to be called poetry except the little piece of the battle of Talfalgar imitated from Kipling. The subject is of course interesting as a resume of a great epoch. But it is nothing more than that—Alison's *History of Europe* done into very poor blank verse, eked out with prose where the writer gets into difficulty with his lines. I really do not think it is a bit better than Doughty's verse.[1]

To another group it is to be ranked with the finest of Shakespeare and Milton. Certainly it is extremely prosaic in such remarks as Lord Wellington's:

> Now I must also go,
> And snatch a little snooze ere harnessing;

---

[1] *Friends of a Lifetime,* pp. 183, 184. About Doughty's poetry Blunt has remarked that it was "the worst of the XIX Century."

and it can likewise rise to a plane of more passionate movement in speeches like that of the dying Josephine:

> Yes . . . Glad am I
> I saw that child of theirs, though only once,
> But—there was not full truth—not quite, I fear—
> In what I told the Emperor that day
> He led him in to me at Bagatelle.
> That 'twas the happiest moment of my life.
>
> *The Dynasts*, III, 3

But even here there is a certain pomposity arising from the lack of flexible rhythms. It is essentially cold and rhetorical.

On the whole, the blank verse never stirs the reader to a sympathetic response. The verse is correct, perhaps too correct; but it remains prosaic and uninspired. The frequent injection of learned words in place of the homely ones is a contributing factor. The poet's partiality for dactylic endings may be another. The greatest, however, is that the earthly sections of the poem never grip the poet's imagination as does the supernatural framework.

The images, as I have already pointed out in Chapter 7, are not at fault. They have the same quality of accuracy and propriety as those of the shorter poems. They do not, however, tend to ennoble man. If anything, they tend to reduce him in importance. Hardy needed the restraining influence of rhyme and definite stanzaic patterns to heighten the effectiveness of his communication. The supernatural framework, cast into a stanzaic mold strongly reminiscent of the choruses of Shelley's *Prometheus Unbound,* is proof of that. The choruses of the Spirits are better poetry than the blank verse. But neither one contains Hardy's best poetry.

Before speaking of the choruses, a word is necessary about the prose passages—the stage directions and descriptions of the Dumb Shows. Discussed in connection with Hardy's prose, these would be an antidote to some of his too highly wrought passages. Strangely enough, it is these prose passages, however, that furnish not only the finest images in the entire work, but the finest poetry. They account for much of that unusual quality of *The Dynasts* which results from the point of distance and elevation from which the poet and we view the human struggle. It is these passages, too, that make understandable the dramatic skeleton of the terrestrial puppet-show.

Hardy shows a mastery over his prose medium that he only rarely shows over his poetic one. This is the result of the long arduous earlier years devoted to its perfecting. These passages possess a concentration which they share only with the choruses of supernatural spirits. The heightened quality of these choruses derives also from the fact that in these passages where the poet's nature was not hampered by the necessity for accuracy of historical facts his imagination had freer rein.

Much has been written of the philosophy imbedded in this portion of the poem. Mr. Chakravarty has given, as I have suggested, the best and clearest statement of it. In his Preface Hardy himself made a clear enough statement about these "Intelligences, called Spirits."

They are intended to be taken by the reader for what they may be worth as contrivances of the fancy merely. Their doctrines are but tentative, and are advanced with little eye to a systematized philosophy warranted to lift "the burthen of the mystery" of this unintelligible world.

Hardy actually took a more positive attitude than that statement would seem to imply. To a letter written by a Mr. Edward Wright on the "philosophy" of *The Dynasts,* he replied (June 2, 1907) in part as follows:

In a dramatic epic—which I may perhaps assume *The Dynasts* to be—some philosophy of life was necessary, and I went on using that which I had denoted in my previous volumes of verse (and to some extent prose) as being a generalized form of what the thinking world had gradually come to adopt, myself included. That the Unconscious Will of the Universe is growing aware of Itself I believe I may claim as my own idea solely —at which I arrived by reflecting that what has already taken place in a fraction of the whole (i.e., so much of the world as has become conscious) is likely to take place in the mass; and there being no Will outside the mass—that is, the Universe—the whole Will becomes conscious thereby: and ultimately, it is to be hoped, sympathetic.

I believe, too, that the Prime Cause, this Will, has never before been called "It" in any poetical literature, English or foreign.

This theory, too, seems to me to settle the question of Free-will vs. Necessity. The will of a man is, according to it, neither wholly free nor wholly unfree. When swayed by the Universal Will (which he mostly must be as a subservient part of it) he is not individually free; but whenever it happens that all the rest of the Great Will is in equilibrium the minute portion called one person's will is free, just as a performer's fingers are free to go on playing the pianoforte of themselves when he talks or thinks of something else and the head does not rule them.

A careful analysis of the choruses of the various spirits will reveal that this is a correct statement of the basic ideas underlying the poem. The Spirit of the Years, representing the insight of the ages, is a passionless phantasm from which we elicit our information of the "loveless, hateless" It. The chief motivating forces are the Pities who approximate to the universal sympathy of human nature. Other spirits, such as the Spirit Sinister, Spirit Ironic, Rumours, and so forth, give richness to the exposition of the ideas. The general nature of the Immanent Will is clear enough from the Fore Scene, a general nature which is identical with that expressed in *New Year's Eve*. The spirit of the Years is speaking:

> It works unconsciously, as heretofore,
> Eternal artistries in Circumstance,
> Whose patterns, wrought by rapt aesthetic rote,
> Seem in themselves Its single listless aim,
> And not their consequence.

To which the Chorus of the Pities replies:

> Still thus? Still thus?
> Ever unconscious!
> An automatic sense
> Unweeting why or whence?
> Be, then, the inevitable, as of old,
> Although that So it be we dare not hold!

The idea of the Immanent Will's emergence into consciousness becomes clear in the final choruses of the After Scene. It is not enough that the Pities should expect the growing consciousness because they represent human nature; the idea must receive more positive statement, and does.

Semichorus I of the Pities

> Nay;—shall not Its blindness break?
> Yea, must not Its heart awake,
> Promptly tending
> To Its mending
> In a genial germing purpose, and for loving-kindness' sake?

Semichorus II

> Should It never
> Curb or cure

Aught whatever
Those endure
Whom It quickens, let them darkle to extinction swift and sure.

Chorus

But—a stirring thrills the air
Like to sounds of joyance there
That the rages
Of the ages
Shall be cancelled, and deliverance offered from the darts that were,
Consciousness the Will informing, till It fashion all things fair!

The lack of freewill of Napoleon and others is clearly enunciated by the Spirit of the Years:

Thus do the mindless minions of the spell
In mechanized enchantment sway and show
A Will that wills above the will of each,
Yet but the will of all conjunctively;
A fabric of excitement, web of rage,
That permeates as one stuff the weltering whole.

The Spirits serve, however, a greater artistic purpose than that of a mere philosophy. Mention has already been made of their unifying power in the epic drama. An elaboration of this function is necessary if we are to appreciate their full significance. They do not remain aloof in their sphere content only to deal with abstractions. They play a much more intimate role with the human actor than that. They frequently help motivate the action. The Spirit of Rumour, for example, walks into an assembly or a ballroom and talks with the persons there; but for the most part they are content to comment.

The prosodic content of these choruses reveals many of the characteristics observed in connection with the shorter poems: rhyme and abundant alliteration, although with less variation in metrical feet. They are strongly iambic. Hardy was wise in adhering to a strongly stressed iambic foot in these sections because the laxity of the blank verse needs a more rigid pattern to counterbalance the disintegrating effect. The poet's imagination works with much greater intensity and a much lessened sense of laboriousness than in the dramatic sections where, as we know well enough, the material frequently bogged him down. The Battle of Leipzig caused him great difficulty because he was unable "to synchronize with any certainty its episodes from descriptions by historians," and he was under the constant necessity of telescoping events, and hence, he wrote, "it was sometimes necessary to see round corners, down crooked streets, and to shift buildings nearer to each other than in reality."

Particularly successful is the rondeau, "The skies fling flame" (III, ii, 2). The verse of these supernatural passages sometimes shows strange origins, particularly the choruses of the Ironic Spirits. "A pertinent query, in truth!" (I, vi, 5) has a strong Gilbertian flavor, and "First 'twas a finished coquette" (II, v, 6) smacks strongly of the music hall. Others are too ponderous and too heavily brocaded. For the finest lyrics in *The Dynasts,* we must turn to the songs of more popular nature: the Boatman's song, "In the wild October night-time" (I, v, 7); that of the Budmouth Dears, "When we lay where Budmouth beach is" (III, i, 1); the Wessex girl's song, "My love's gone a-fighting" (III, v, 6); and "We be the King's men" (I, i, 1) are the most outstanding of many.

Although one cannot help admiring the scope of *The Dynasts* and appreciating the poet's accomplishment, one nevertheless feels that Hardy does not succeed. Reread today, it helps us to a better perspective of the conflict which dwarfs the exploits of Napoleon, and in any time of trouble and conflict it would probably do the same. We must not, however, let our dispassionate appraisal of it be colored by that. The work stands with its stark, grim, hardness as a powerful frame; but for me at least, it is only a frame. It does not have the unity that, as one reads, gradually catches him in its grip and carries him to a great emotional experience which abides. He is quickened by starts and stops, but the effect is not continuous nor related. The reader's temperature is little more than normal when he finishes the last page. He is not left with that sense of which he is invariably aware when he has shared in a great aesthetic experience.

It is possible, of course, that this vast work of "mixed magic and clumsiness," as Rebecca West has called it, has greater interest for Englishmen than it has for Americans. It undeniably has a greater interest for everyone in a time of international conflict than in a time of peace, as I have discovered in my own reading and reread-ing of it. It is a large "vision of the lot of man," and it may be true, as Mr. Blunden suggests in his valuable study of Hardy, that it has no rival "in the way of a chronicle giving us, as in life, as at our window this very morning or midnight, the cities, government, the personages, speeches, marketplace or downland or shipboard episodes, ghost stories, terrors, humours, small and great turns of fortune of the Napoleonic wars." All those things are part and parcel of the work, but I for one do not feel that these incompatibles are fused with impelling and absorbing art. But when, in fact, does any pure chronicle achieve a strong aesthetic reaction? Shakespeare's certainly do not; nor does Marlowe's one effort; nor do any of the modern attempts. Bulk and scope are not enough.

The failure of *The Dynasts* lies deeper in the nature of Hardy than in any of the foregoing causes, and about this I shall say more in the next chapter. Again, Mr. Chakravarty is fully aware of these characteristics. I differ from him only in point of emphasis. I shall quote two passages: one from page 24, the other from pages 32 and 33:

Hardy launched the modern Age in poetry by applying the principle of human consciousness as far as possible to all experiences, and sensitized it to an entire range of phenomena in a pyschological manner not used in poetry before him. No facts of life, evil, hurtful, baffling, or wholesome, were seen as unrelated to each other; a poet's vision had to take in the whole of history . . . in a manner that would satisfy *rational imagination*.

Reason does not claim to be able to explain the meaning of the process; it is neither fatalistic as to the future, nor can it offer any hope; in that sense *Hardy's drama itself is concerned to represent all sides and not to draw a moral conclusion*. It is neither an elaboration of a dark doctrine of despair, nor is it a beatific story with evil and its triumphs left out of the picture.[2]

The italicized passages give an understanding of Hardy's whole approach to poetry. I can say, with Shelley, that didactic poetry is my abhorrence. Poetry must not deliberately set out to preach. But the vivifying power of an imagination working at white heat must necessarily make a choice: it must select and from this selection a moral conclusion must be possible. When it is so working it cannot be limited to what is rational. It must see farther than that. All great poetry that has survived from whatever age reveals an imag-

[2] The italics are mine.

ination that has achieved those two things. The same is true, as Mr. Maxwell Anderson has shown, of any great drama that has survived. To confine an artist to the realm of reason is to confine him to the realm of shadows. One of the most hopeful signs at the present time in an age of seeming but not real chaos is the growing realization by men in all walks of life that only through the operation of an imagination transcending reason can we let go the shadows and grasp the substance.

⁂ 1 2 ⁂

AN EVALUATION

In PARTS I AND II, I have attempted a disinterested exposition of the thought and diction of Hardy's shorter poems with only occasional illustrations from *The Dynasts*. In the foregoing chapter I have sought to fill in the picture by a necessarily incomplete account of *The Dynasts*—incomplete because Mr. Chakravarty has already made a valuable exposition of its thought and supererogation is not my wish.

All this was necessary in order to clear away much of the deadwood that has obscured Hardy's stature as a poet. But we must not stop here. Judgments of isolated ideas or of uncorrelated phases of his technique, although valuable in themselves, are not enough. They are merely the tools for a more intelligent approach to his work and to an appreciation possible only after the last line had been written; when, in fact, a different age could see his age in perspective and him in relation to his age. We are still too close for a final evaluation of his poetic achievement; but some generalizations are possible. I believe that posterity will place him somewhere between the limits set by his contemporary idolators and detractors.

In order to understand Hardy we must realize, as I have already pointed out in Chapter I, that he is both Victorian and Modern. Prosodically we might call him the last of the Victorians. His difficulty is that technically he came too late to perfect any of the traditional forms of poetry. He has made no real contribution to English prosody in spite of his experimentation, which to me is half-hearted experimentation. This does not mean that there are not times when the force of his thought is sufficiently great to give new and almost unexpected life to old forms. In his few best poems this happens. Taken as a whole, however, Hardy is too fragmentary. Individual poems may satisfy the canons of criticism, may fuse thought and form to create a forceful aesthetic reaction, but the effect of the poems taken as a whole is unsatisfactory. He is a modern in his ideas. That is, as Mr. Chakravarty remarks, he "launched the modern Age in poetry by applying the principle of human consciousness as far as possible to all his experiences, and sensitized it to an entire range of phenomena in a psychological manner not used in poetry before him." These ideas, ideas which I think the elder Browning was more prepared to accept, or at least was less shocked than was Hardy, are those of the scientists of the Victorian Age, the ideas of Mill, Huxley, Darwin, and others. The ideas that impregnate his poetry are still too inexpertly grasped to be fused into workable materials. He did not fully comprehend their manifold implications. This accounts both for the tentative and the nostalgic qualities in his work. His successors, building on his foundations, will be able to improve upon his experiments. This failure fully to grasp the significance of ideas deprives his poetry of the cohesiveness that results from conviction, and because of this the reader is left with no unified impression. He senses a struggle, at times an intense one, to evolve a faith, but the struggle never resolves into the exaltation of achievement. The reader never moves steadily forward with the poet sensing that he is being led upward as he is with Dante, Milton, Shakespeare, and Goethe, nor as he is with Donne, Wordsworth, Keats, Hopkins, or Yeats. Nor has he done as did Browning, whose problem, as Sir Leslie Stephen has justly remarked, was "always to show what are the really noble elements which are eternally valuable in spite of failure to achieve tangible results." Consequently the reader is left with a sense of frustration and indecision. He sees beauty, occasionally great and carefully wrought beauty, in the individual fragments, but they lie scattered on the ground and form no edifice in a realm where there are many mansions.

The critic's problem is a perplexing one. Can he examine minutely these fragments and give them the praise that only the finished work merits? When praising this or that fragment he runs the risk of being understood as praising the whole achievement, of being inconsistent in his point of view when a consistent one is impossible.

Hardy does not take his place among the great poets, although greatnesses are in him. If by greatness we mean "the construction of an inner world and the communication of this inner world to the physical world of humanity" I think we could say that he is great in a few of his shorter poems in which he struggles with his faith—his desire to believe and his slavery to reason. In these he is never conciliatory, he is not self-conscious, and his feelings reveal nobility of soul, although a frustrated one. These poems are soul-searching. Because of these qualities we find in them his best although not his most obvious music. Music that issues from the mystical depths of human inwardness and spiritual absorption is not the most easily grasped.

But what is true of Hardy is also true of the majority of his contemporaries. Scarcely one from his age is among the few lofty souls who inhabit Parnassus, because his age was one of transitions; one would like to say development, rather than of great culmination. Some writers refused to recognize that only the shell of a great age still stood, and that new plans were shaping themselves. Browning, for example, maintained to the end his belief that the building was intact. His stout refusal to accept any other view gives a rugged vitality to his best works that still captures the reader. Arnold recognized that the main structure, faith, had fallen, but believed a wing of the structure, love, remained. Morris, Rossetti, and Ruskin would exchange the building for one of pseudo-medieval architecture, and Swinburne, too often one for a garden by the sea with houris and the music of dulcimers. Hardy would have none of it. He did not belong to their social order. He had none of the advantages of birth that they enjoyed and he was precluded from the education that their social stratum and the financial condition of their parents assured them. Nor was a person of his social rank in the mid-nineteenth century permitted to forget that he was of a different breed. How different, the description of his subject matter has already made amply evident. He realized that he must build a place for himself on a solid foundation of understanding and observation. He chose the site on the south side of the main street of a Wessex village, gathered native materials, but never finished the structure. The site offered many views. To the south loomed hills and barrows; and the woods dipped into the valleys. On stormy days the boom of the sea was clearly audible, and on clear nights when he walked to the cliff's edge he could gaze at the stars. But never for one moment did he think he heard the music of the spheres, although he wished that he might.

He preferred, however, to observe the village life from a comfortable chair and occasionally to saunter into the market-square to talk with some of his acquaintances of long standing. He was amused and interested in young romance, and he often recalled his own early days of love-making. He loved the village and its people and the surrounding countryside, and their little homely acts reminded him of similar acts on a larger scale that he had seen in the world. Everything about Wessex, even the superstition, fatalism, and paganism that many who know that part of England feel to be a characteristic of its people found a sympathetic response in him. He was content, for the most part, to remain local. He could revel in the natural beauty of the countryside, but he sufficiently understood and valued the truth of Darwin's ideas about the survival of the fittest not to be able to accept the idea of the sympathy and goodness of Nature. In this, however, he was inclined to lose sight of the forest for the trees. He could appreciate, too, the inherent nobility of many of the Wessex characters, but he realized that in such a community nobility is not the dominant note. His extraordinary insight into the actions of the common man enabled him to do what Burns, on a more purely lyrical note and with a more direct outpouring of feeling, did for Scotland. He spoke for the inarticulate inhabitants of his country. This is not to say that there is not much in common between him and other late-Victorian poets. The spirit of the age simply manifested itself in a different way with him.

Fortunately we are far enough away from the Victorians in point of time and experience to refrain from easy generalizations that tell nothing. The poetry of each reflects his individual reactions to the leaven that was working. Each will be of inestimable value to an

understanding of an age great in many ways and yet petty and in-
hibited in others. Each was a revolutionary in the way that any
person of imagination and vision must be a revolutionary. One poet
will voice his own deep despair, another will find joy in his inter-
pretation of the same phenomena; one will lose his faith, another
will find it, a third will tenaciously cling to the one he has. He will
refuse to face certain problems and by his refusal will reveal the
torment caused by those problems. We all need some center of ex-
perience from which to utter our aspirations or from which to argue
if the world beyond our experience is to have any meaning for us.
The artist transforms and multiplies his experiences by imagina-
tion. He may come, as I think Hardy did, to think that what is true
of his art will also be true of the world it mirrors. The value of
Hardy's poetry, in fact, lies in his observation of the world colored
by his own spirit. I do not think Hardy lacked the courage neces-
sary for the attainment of true greatness—the courage to say the
ultimate. He could not see the ultimate.

His poetry is in one respect not intensely personal. In another,
it is. He is not primarily concerned with the joys or sorrows that
he himself had experienced. He is not, in other words, essentially a
subjective poet in the usually accepted meaning of the term. He
more nearly resembles Browning in this than any other poet; but
as I have already suggested, Browning with a difference. From ob-
serving carefully what he says of others we are able to form an
accurate picture of the poet in his least self-conscious moods. This
does not mean that his work is not drawn from his own experi-
ence; but it does mean that it was only rarely drawn from his own
deepest inner experience, an experience which defies analysis in
workaday terms. He was deeply penetrated by natural objects which
he valued for themselves and for their part in the larger scheme of
human life. He has what Mr. Blunden has happily called "an ampli-
tude of observed fact," and he used it with a dramatic referent. In
all but a few cases, his poems tell or suggest stories frequently melo-
dramatic. Even some of the more purely lyrical poems have what
Mr. Van Doren has called a "narrative reference." They refer to the
drama "running throughout the man's poetry, of his successive ad-
justment to the universe." We find little exasperation or resentment

in his verse that life is as it is rather than as he would have it be. He saw life clearly enough to realize that such an attitude was futile and unavailing. Instance after instance had convinced him of the constant presence of ironies in life and that few things happen as we wish they might happen. A misunderstood word, an insignificant gesture, or a trivial accident is frequently enough to alter one's life. He expected and fortified himself against the disillusionment or disappointment which might follow such a slight circumstance.

Although Hardy's sympathies were broad and his tolerance was all embracing, the final effect of his poetry is not warm and pulsating. His poetry is of the head rather than of the heart. His preoccupation with form rather than color reveals the dominance of the intellectual over the emotional. One never experiences a nostalgic sadness when reading him in spite of the nostalgic quality in the work itself. Although he wrote some poetry early in life, the vast corpus of his work was the result of middle and old age when our spirits, as he himself said, "are less subject to steep gradients than in youth." It is the importance of this that many persons are inclined to miss when they speak of him as a pessimist. As William Dean Howells has pointed out, it is easier for a man past fifty to see the stark realities of life than it is for a young person filled with the hope of accomplishment. The person who does not see that everything happens in the world for the best can commonly give plenty of reasons for such a point of view; he who maintains that everything is as it should be is hard put to it to find adequate evidence. Certainly, Hardy has such a ruthless honesty and sincerity when presenting his observations on life in general, and the people of Wessex in particular, that the worst that can be said of him is that he is a realist with a realist's limitations. He does not distort facts nor gloss over truths. Hardy's work as a restorer of old churches brought him into direct contact with real and concrete things. This quality invests his poetry. We must not think, however, that the stark realities of life necessarily depressed him. Mrs. Hardy dispells any such fiction. She once wrote to Sir Sydney Cockerell about her husband: "He is now—this afternoon—writing a poem with great spirit; always a sign of well-being with him. Needless to say it is an intensely dismal poem." He himself attests the great pleasure writing verse gave him, although he cared little about its publication.

The pitch of his verse is more measured than that of a poet in early youth, and this general tone is contemplative rather than passionate, nostalgic; one might even say elegiac. This does not mean that he lacked vitality. That was continuous, and, Antaeus-like, resulted from his contact with the earth. At times, however, the lyric impulse of his verse becomes definitely more pronounced than in the major corpus of his work; such, for example, as in those poems after the death of his first wife. Occasionally, too, he captures a Shelleyan quality which, could it soar higher, would burst into song; but this is rare rather than frequent. He was artist enough to realize that were he to attempt to capture in his middle and late years the ecstatic exuberance of youth, his work would have the ring of insincerity, a quality he vigorously fought against.

Elsewhere I have dwelt in detail on the strength and shortcomings of his diction. His general inability to realize the concealed power of words in themselves and not only the power resulting from a strict pattern is another cause for his failure to achieve a place among the greatest. He waited too long before devoting his best efforts to poetry. There was too much of the hard, practical countryman in his make-up for him to be willing to sacrifice economic security for the sake of an uncertain artistic achievement. I am not blaming him for his choice. It is one that most persons would make unless some great emotional crisis shows that the dividends of economic security are in themselves of little satisfaction. Even then we wish a modicum of security. None of our great English poets was without this security. From the point of view of the artist, however, he cannot lay aside his pursuit until he has achieved this security. He must work unceasingly at perfecting his art. He cannot lay it aside in his early years, resume it as a serious interest only in his later years, and hope to achieve greatness. Poetry is a jealous mistress. She will bestow her greatest favors, and then but rarely, only on her passionate devotees.

Had Hardy worked unremittingly at poetry during the years when his creative energy was at its best he might well have forged an instrument that would have been worthy his maturest deliberations. He might have been able to fuse his images into his thought until they were indistinguishable from the thought—until they were a part of it and from this fusion greater strength would have sprung. He might have accomplished this, but he did not. Evocative as his images often are, they remain in all but his best work—a small corpus—things of ornament and void of inner passion. He might, too, have arrived at a sense of the inevitability of words in association. And this he only rarely achieved.

To say this is not to say that he gained nothing from his choice. His economic independence enabled him to broaden his horizon, more deliberately to observe the workings of the forces of life, to follow trails that otherwise might have remained closed to him. But his choice did prevent a conscientious experimentation with the tools of his craft at a time when it could have exerted a profound influence. Certain periods of life are best fitted for certain occupations. In youth one should devote himself to developing the techniques which he will later put into productive use. Hardy had to forge his tools for poetry and learn to use them at a period when new techniques are difficult to acquire.

We must not overlook the importance of scientific thought in his work. Science was rapidly pushing back the limits of the universe, was uprooting traditional beliefs in the methods of the world's motivation, and was uncovering the secret springs of men's thoughts and the taboos which govern men's conduct. He lost his faith in the traditional illogical concept of a benign god and of a personal immortality, and he accepted with stoicism a monistic concept in which God, the Immanent Will or It, as he preferred to think of it, was neither loveless nor hateless but was a blind power creating without concept of what it was doing. With these ideas, he had formulated a personal philosophy which permitted him to accept life as it came. He believed too implicitly in his own statement:

> "Little in their lives cessation
> Moderns see for surge of sighs;
> That have been schooled by lengthier vision,
> View life's lottery with misprision
> And its dice that fling no prize!"

Hardy's difficulty, which resulted in a serious defect in his poetry, was that he did not see high enough. He could not accept the truth of an inspiration lying beyond reason. He rid himself, it is true, of the familiar half-truths that satisfied many of his contemporaries, but the truth he uncovered was still not enough. His bent robbed him of a profoundly moving conviction of an ideal, the adherence to which would have immeasurably tightened the poetic texture of his verse. His early verse, we have seen, expressed his conviction that this was necessary, but he did not follow his own conviction. I do not mean to suggest that he did not himself live a rigidly self-disciplined life, or that he did not believe that an ideal was necessary. But the necessity is not implicit in the texture of his verse, and it is his poetry with which we are solely concerned. In other words, the necessity for cleaving to the dream was not a passionate conviction with him which inspired much of his writing.

He failed to grasp that what he had found true for himself was, in fact, a universal truth, broader in scope than the many smaller truths he so clearly enunciated. The relaxation which we feel in much of his poetry may be due to age, but I am inclined to believe that it arises from this lack of ideal. A person need not believe in an anthropomorphic god, nor even in a god within himself; but he does need—and we find it to be a fundamental quality in all great poets—the inspired conviction of the majesty and dignity of which the human spirit is capable. If he can grasp the reality of a God which it would be futile for the finite mind to attempt to confine in a definition, so much the better. He must believe with Shakespeare in what a noble thing is man; he must believe with Milton in the sublimity to which mankind may attain if he looks upon the spirit as responsible for itself; and he must believe, it seems to me, in spite of the conception of life's being a series of satires of circumstance or a chain of chance causations, that man's spirit is capable of walking upright with nobility and dignity. This is not to deny the importance of heredity and environment, but it is to believe that man has some measure of control over his mind as well as over his external being.

In youth, belief in love is frequently a great enough ideal; later and particularly with age, a different ideal is necessary. In an age when a traditional faith is impossible to many, the nature of what that ideal is to be is the problem which every thoughtful person must continuously struggle more clearly to define. It is ridiculous to think, as many persons seem to do, that the circumstances of modern life are such as to deprive us of something in which to believe.

Hardy's weakness, as I have elsewhere observed, lies in his insistence on thought on the horizontal level: thought arising from the interaction of the ego with observed phenomena. He moved in the wrong direction. He should have struggled upward. His failure to reach any goal in the direction he moved toward was not his fault. There simply was no goal there, and because of this, he gradually relaxed in his struggle and assumed that he had found all there was to find. No man could maintain his ideals, no man could help becoming indifferent, who had concentrated over a long period of years on observing the ugliness in life and the reverse side of the human emotions of love and faith. It is worth noting that the poems that have most interested his readers are those in which he struggles to apprehend through reason what is only possible to grasp through an active faith. He had lost, perhaps had never entertained, the conviction of the existence of the absolutes of Good and Evil. In this he reflects the tendency of his age. By his too great dependence on the inviolability of reason as a means for the attaining unto final truths he put a limitation on his ability to grasp the whole truth. I think, too, he partially realized this. He was dissatisfied with the conclusions at which he could arrive—the mental struggle that much of his poetry reveals attests that—but he could not free himself from the shackles that bound him. The fret of thinking never passed those barriers to the region that permitted the sheer ecstasy of contemplating. His lark never lost itself in the light.

By attempting to arrive at the total pattern of experience, Hardy weighted the scale in favor of a negative aspect of the pattern. So anxious was he to be unbiased and to withhold moral judgment, which, I suppose, proceeds out of the isolation of experience, that he was unwilling to say "*this* thing is more important or valuable than *that*." He was most frequently concerned with the primitive instincts of the soul. He attempts to find a relationship between man and the whole universe, but he finds too few things in the relationship that ennoble. But if he is to attain the highest reaches he must find that nobility. His lack of conviction and his indifference are in themselves enough to loosen the fiber of his verse. He was prouder of his tolerance than of anything else, but a passive tolerance is not enough. He had lost his conviction that fighting was worth while, because he was not convinced that the world was progressing.

Yet, is this the whole picture? Is there not another point of view from which we can get a more favorable light on his seeming indifference? Did he not possess a generosity of spirit and an instinct for compassion which gave translucence rather than sharp clarity to his mind and forbade him the rhetoric of judgment which we are too inclined to mistake for indifference? Poems could be brought forward as evidence for either position. We cannot take a single view when two are possible. Whether or not one predominates over the other is a matter each careful reader must decide for himself. Since he wrote largely of the reverse side of human emotions the absence of condemnatory judgments is a virtue. By restricting himself to the negative aspects, however, he robbed himself of what the late Sir Walter Raleigh called the poet's most effective instrument: "his moral reflections, his saws, and his sentences." And of these Hardy makes no use whatever. Hardy did not regard poetry as a medicine to purge the soul's illnesses. It was wine, beer, or water, a thing of the earth and sun, and often the taste was bitter.

All this is not to say that Hardy failed; because he did not. He only failed to find a resting place on Parnassus. He achieved, I believe, that of which he was capable, something far above the ability of the majority of men. He has been a beneficent influence on poetry. He brought freshness of observation, a freshness which continued until the very end. He widened the horizon of English poetry. He gave new ideas and new forms to his generation and to ours. He examined the world about him and presented the results of his observations with lucidity. That in itself is much.

Yet we must not think that Hardy was working outside a tradition. Prosodically he was influenced by Shakespeare, Wordsworth, Shelley, Swinburne, Browning, and others; in ideas on poetry, by

Wordsworth's famous *Preface* more than by any other work. Basically, however, his was of a very different tradition. The ultimate influences of the French Revolution are more clearly seen in his work than in that of most of the so-called revolutionary poets. They talked about liberty, freedom, and equality. In his careful depiction of Wessex life he revealed those qualities as embodied in his rural folk. By choosing to follow his own path and to explore those rural folk he was actually taking his place in and helping to motivate a world movement which has not yet come into its full flowering, the so-called age of the common man.

The outward mark of this movement is a certain degree of abstraction of humanity with an all-embracing catholicity that will include every rank of person. The spirit which motivated Balzac to look searchingly at all strata of life about him, to present, for example, the "traveling salesman" who although outwardly different today is basically still the same as when he first limned him, is the same spirit which motivated Dickens to write his novels of the middle and lower classes in the city, and, to a lesser extent, the same that motivated Thackeray. Flaubert enlarged the scope of this tendency in *Madame Bovary* and Zola in his *Rougon-Macquart* series. Ibsen fell under the influence of this spirit in his *The Enemy of the People, Ghosts, Hedda Gabler,* and *Rosmersholm.* A deeper expression emerges from Tolstoy, Dostoievsky, and Chekhov; the finest from Whitman and Gorky. Gorky has foreshadowed in Luka from *The Lower Depths* the direction this so-called "realism" or "naturalism" must perforce take before it becomes truly great. He alone apprehended that the drama of common life must be invested with poetry. Certainly that does not mean that a sentimental glow of false values must suffuse it. Quite the contrary! When this germinating spirit blossoms one thing will become evident, as is already evident in Whitman's dithyrambic lines: the realization that common things are commonplace, not because of themselves, but because of us; because of our way of regarding them. O'Neill's Yank in *The Hairy Ape* is a good example on one level. In Hardy we occasionally glimpse the budding of this idea, but the flower never blows. It is the inability to grasp the essential quality toward which this movement must progress that constitutes his failure.

If he must dwell on the slopes of Parnassus rather than at the top, we must still remember that even so he dwells far above the average person and above many writers whose popularity is greater than his. It is difficult to say that had his horizon been narrower, his experimentation less, he would have achieved greater intensity and a higher stature as an artist. But it is to such a conclusion, I think, that one must necessarily come. He looked at too many men whose lives were spiritually barren and did not concentrate on the few whose natures merited continuous study. He tried too many poetic forms to wrest from any one its greatest potentialities. His intellectual restlessness took him far afield, but because he looked in the wrong direction he did not find that calmness of spirit, the depth of which would perforce have revealed itself in his work. He had a certain measure of calm to be sure, but he could not conscientiously invest man with enough dignity or with a great enough stature to permit him to look up to him, even beyond him to the stars, and past the stars into those dark spaces between. And it is those interstellar spaces that tease one beyond thought. He saw man too much in his workaday guise and failed to see the dreams and visions that even to the most seemingly prosaic person give a quality beyond the ordinary. He gives us what we might call the summation of folk wisdom, but that has its limitations as well as its power. He was content to be a realist, and like realists, he suffers from a limited vision that tends to turn him into a sentimentalist. And there is a large element of the sentimental in Hardy. An idealist not only sees all that the realist sees, but his vision is great enough for him to see beyond mere terrestrial manifestations to something greater, as Dante and Milton were able to do. Too often he was content with man as he shows himself to the world and not as he shows himself to himself when he knows he is unobserved; when he struggles with his frustrations and refuses to let them keep him from new and greater experiences of life. Although Hardy never mistakes facts for knowledge, he sometimes mistakes knowledge for wisdom.

APPENDICES

A: The Origin of Species

ALTHOUGH THE PROOFS of *The Origin of Species* had been read only by Lyell and Hooker, numerous advance copies were sent to leading scientists. On November 22, two days before publication, Huxley wrote to Darwin announcing his essential agreement and allegiance. He not only saw more clearly than any of Darwin's friends, or even than Darwin himself, the uproar and terrific excitement that the *Origin* would produce as soon as it became generally known, but took it upon himself to be the leader in Darwin's campaign. Rarely have rumor and the author's friends given a book such excellent advance publicity. Instead of waiting years for his ideas to filter to the masses from the scientists, his work struck the public with the force of lightning. On the day of publication the entire edition of 1,500 copies was sold. Fortunately for Darwin, Huxley was among the first to catch the ear of the general public with a review in the respectable and influential London *Times,* which was simple and sober, yet remarkably persuasive. He warned against a blind acceptance of Darwin's theories, yet emphasized their fruitful possibilities. He wrote a longer review for the *Westminster* (April, 1860). In the same month a brutal attack by Professor Owen appeared in the *Edinburgh Review.* Darwin felt that Owen had very unfairly misrepresented and altered what he said.

Huxley and Owen represented the extremes of opinion, with those of Owen overwhelmingly prevailing during the early years of the conflict, even among scientists. Not only did scientists debate Darwin's ideas, however, but men ill-qualified by training reviewed his work—the famous Bishop Wilberforce, for example, with whom Huxley held his celebrated debate. We need not review here the details of that famous Saturday meeting of Section D of the Zoological Section of the British Association, at Oxford. To Wilberforce's insolent question regarding his ancestors, Huxley made his now familiar answer: "I asserted—and I repeat—that a man has no reason to be ashamed of having an ape for a grandfather. If there were an ancestor whom I should feel shame in recalling it would rather be a man—a man of restless and versatile intellect—who, not content with an equivocal success in his own sphere of activity, plunges into scientific questions with which he has no real acquaintance, only to obscure them by aimless rhetoric, and distract the attention of his hearers from the real point at issue by eloquent digressions and skilled appeals to religious prejudice."

The effect was tremendous. One woman fainted. Another jumped up in her chair. The applause increased to an ovation. This spectacular scene assured a wide public interest in the theory of evolution.

B: The Revised Version of the Bible

IN MATTERS about which he was well informed, Bishop Wilberforce could be constructive. It was he, for example, who on February 10, 1870, moved the resolution in the Upper House of Convocation for a revision of the *Authorized Version of the New Testament,* a motion enlarged by Bishop Thirlwall also to include the *Old Testament.* The problems encountered do not concern us. The anticipation was naturally great and the reception mixed. (The revision of the *Old Testament,* commenced on June 30, 1870, and ended on June 20, 1884, was completed in 85 sessions occupying 792 days. The revision of the *New Testament,* begun on June 22, 1870, taking less time, was published in 1881.) The revision of the *New Testament* was criticized on two grounds: first, that the choice of Greek text taken as a basis for the revision; and second, that the changes made in the translation marred the style of the authorized version. The choice of text for the revision of the *Old Testament* was less hotly discussed, but not so the verbal changes. Some felt that the changes were too extreme; others that they were not extreme enough, that the translation remained archaic. H. W. Horwill, for example, in *The Contemporary Review* (May, 1896) contended that "no words or construction should be used in the translation which are not as familiar to nineteenth century Englishmen as were those of the original to the first readers of the actual text. . . . The meaning should everywhere be sufficiently clear without the assistance of commentaries, for the poor and uneducated, to whom the Bible was sent as much as to others, cannot afford to buy such aids nor have they the knack of using them."

For several years newspapers and magazines, both religious and secular, devoted innumerable pages to the discussion of the revision, and, as one writer remarked, "no possible consideration has been overlooked save that which is fundamental." Hardy must not only have been interested in the discussion, but he must have read the revised version carefully. This reading must not only have inspired several poems on biblical subjects, but must also have influenced his thinking on the inspiration behind the Bible.

C: A Footnote on Music

HARDY'S INTEREST in music is everywhere evident in his work and yet it is one of the least capturable of themes as a separate entity in the present study. The rhythm of a hymn tune, of a popular song, or of an old ballad inspires, as we have already seen, a poem in that particular meter. A fragment of an old song awakens memories that will alter the course of life and love; the sight of a musical instrument will stir old passions; a visual object will evoke an image drawn from music. This footnote can only suggest, therefore, two other phases of that story: its possible exemplification of his poetic aesthetic and its use as subject matter.

The development of his musical taste parallels that for pictorial art. He shows an acquaintance with the popular favorites of the day—*Il Trovatore* and *The Bohemian Girl*—but little grasp of musical form. He rather inclines to read into the musical forms such human emotions as terror, mystery, love, and hate. He uses music as a means to the emotions of life rather than as an end in itself. This is clear from his remark about the third movement of Tschaikowsky's *Symphony No. 6, in B Minor,* which to him "was the only music he knew that was able to make him feel as if he were in a battle." The music of Wagner was "*weather* and *ghost* music —whistling of wind and storm, the strumming of a gale on iron railings, the creaking of doors; low screams of entreaty through key-holes, amid which trumpet voices are heard." When he watched the smiling members of the ballet "linked in one-pulsed chain," he could not forget that each had a world of her own; that the "chain" represented a cross-section of woman in all her phases.[1]

As a subject for poetry his use of music is chiefly sentimental. We have seen, for example, the manner in which a musical instrument or an old melody revives past memories, destroys or furthers love, or illuminates woman. Here, as elsewhere he reveals the sentimentality of the realist who from the limitations of his vision must necessarily be a sentimentalist, a seeming paradox. Twice at least music motivates poems in the *ubi sunt* vein. In one, "Reminiscences of a Dancing Man," Hardy recalls the famous London places of amusement—Almack's, Cremorne Gardens, the Argyle, famous for their dances. In the second, "Haunting Fingers," several musical instruments come to life like the dolls in "The Toy Shop" and discuss the days when they were in their glory. The instruments—ranging from the viol, 'cello, harpsichord, to the melancholy shawm, the robust drum, and the lyre—evoke past scenes of every mood and manner.

Sharpness of contrast may be accentuated by music. When nature is introduced as a further agent the result is moving ("The Country Wedding"). Music lends, too, a poignant ironic touch to an otherwise ordinary occurrence. A little boy offers to play for a convict being taken to prison.

---

[1] This associative value has inspired many poems in which a town or city is valuable to him because of its connection with his wife. Even in landscape, he wrote on February 10, 1897: "I cannot help noticing countenances and tempers in objects of scenery, e.g., trees, hills, and houses." The reverse is also true. A person may be interesting to him because of his setting—a house of antiquity or a bit of natural scenery.

With unconscious irony he plays "This life so free/ Is the thing for me!" ("At the Railways Station, Upway"). Hardy once uses music as a means for a variation of the theme that, in our preoccupation with getting, we see little in nature that is really ours ("At the Aquatic Sports").

D: Hardy's Humaneness

NOWHERE do Hardy's sentiment and sentimentality so nearly fuse as in those poems dealing with his dumb friends. He loved birds and animals of every sort, manifested great interest in their welfare and protection, and had he been in the position of the ancient mariner would not be unaware that he was blessing the water snakes. Bird-catching and cruelty to dogs stirred his imagination and aroused his indignation as they generally do the sensibilities of the average Englishman, who is horrified by the treatment of animals in the Latin countries. His sentimental approach to problems involving animals throws much light on Hardy and his general philosophy of life although as poems they are of little worth.[1] In fact, the majority of the poems on this subject are of little general interest. They possess a "laureate" quality, are limited in their appeal, and do no more than scratch the surface of profound emotion. Whether it be an ode in commemoration of the centenary of the S.P.C.A., or verses to one of his own pets—a favorite cat or his beloved dog—Wessex in particular, or verses evoked by the sight of a stranger burying his pet cat, the result is the same.[2]

He achieves more than laureate quality in those poems where the animals are merely incidental to the main theme of the poems—the problems of life.[3]

When he reveals his humanitarian interest in man, the result is different, and his vision is greater, a greatness, unfortunately, which he does not always sustain in more important aspects of his thinking.[4] Elsewhere he reveals his humility and the realization that pride, however disguised, is littleness. It is the obstacle that keeps us from enriching experience. We can never know from what source a beneficent influence may come. It may be from a casual acquaintance, from a wanderer resigned to his miserable existence, from a sodden tramp who in the face of adversity can maintain his cheerful outlook, or it may be from the sudden realization that the conditions about which he is grumbling were to the earlier generations the rule rather than the exception.[5]

[1] "The Bird Catcher's Boy," "The Mound."
[2] "Compassion," "Last Words, etc.," "The Roman Gravemounds," "Dead Wessex, etc.," "A Popular Personage at Home."
[3] "The Milestone by the Rabbit Barrow," "Wagtail and Baby," "The Boy's Dream."
[4] "Then and Now," "Often When Warring."
[5] "The Casual Acquaintance," "The Wanderer," "Christmastide," "A Wet Night."

INDEX